The Ruling Class

Reports for the Fondazione Rodolfo Debenedetti

Education and Training in Europe
Edited by Giorgio Brunello, Pietro Garibaldi, and Etienne Wasmer

The ICT Revolution: Productivity Differences and the Digital Divide
Edited by Daniel Cohen, Pietro Garibaldi, and Stefano Scarpetta

Immigration Policy and the Welfare System
Edited by Tito Boeri, Gordon H. Hanson, and Barry McCormick

The Role of Unions in the Twenty-First Century
Edited by Tito Boeri, Agar Brugiavini, and Lars Calmfors

Structural Reforms Without Prejudices
Edited by Tito Boeri, Micael Castanheira, Riccardo Faini, and Vincenzo Galasso

Women at Work: An Economic Perspective
Edited by Tito Boeri, Daniela Del Boca, and Christopher Pissarides

The Ruling Class

Management and Politics in Modern Italy

Edited by
Tito Boeri, Antonio Merlo, and Andrea Prat

With

Giuliano Amato, Oriana Bandiera, Vittorio Colao,

Vincenzo Galasso, Luigi Guiso, Massimiliano Landi,

Andrea Mattozzi, Lucrezia Reichlin,

Raffaella Sadun, and Luigi Zingales

OXFORD
UNIVERSITY PRESS

OXFORD
UNIVERSITY PRESS

Great Clarendon Street, Oxford OX2 6DP

Oxford University Press is a department of the University of Oxford.
It furthers the University's objective of excellence in research, scholarship,
and education by publishing worldwide in
Oxford New York

Auckland Cape Town Dar es Salaam Hong Kong Karachi
Kuala Lumpur Madrid Melbourne Mexico City Nairobi
New Delhi Shanghai Taipei Toronto

With offices in

Argentina Austria Brazil Chile Czech Republic France Greece
Guatemala Hungary Italy Japan Poland Portugal Singapore
South Korea Switzerland Thailand Turkey Ukraine Vietnam

Oxford is a registered trade mark of Oxford University Press
in the UK and in certain other countries

Published in the United States
by Oxford University Press Inc., New York

© Fondazione Rodolfo Debenedetti 2010

The moral rights of the author have been asserted
Database right Oxford University Press (maker)

First published 2010

All rights reserved. No part of this publication may be reproduced,
stored in a retrieval system, or transmitted, in any form or by any means,
without the prior permission in writing of Oxford University Press,
or as expressly permitted by law, or under terms agreed with the appropriate
reprographics rights organization. Enquiries concerning reproduction
outside the scope of the above should be sent to the Rights Department,
Oxford University Press, at the address above

You must not circulate this book in any other binding or cover
and you must impose the same condition on any acquirer

British Library Cataloguing in Publication Data
Data available

Library of Congress Cataloging in Publication Data
Data available

Typeset by SPI Publisher Services, Pondicherry, India
Printed in Great Britain
on acid-free paper by
MPG Books Group, Bodmin and King's Lynn

ISBN 978–0–19–958828–2

1 3 5 7 9 10 8 6 4 2

Acknowledgements

The two studies that make up this volume were originally prepared for the tenth European conference of the Fondazione Rodolfo Debenedetti, which was held in Gaeta in May 2008. This book draws extensively on the discussion in Gaeta, which involved a qualified audience of academics, professional economists, representatives of unions and employers' associations, managers, and policy-makers. Needless to say, we are greatly indebted to all those who attended that conference and contributed actively to the discussion.

In particular, we wish to express our gratitude to Antonio Raimondi (Mayor of Gaeta) and Marcello Marzocca (Head of the Fiscal Police located in Gaeta) for their warm welcome not only to Gaeta, but also to one of the best locations of this charming seaside city. We are also indebted to Roger Abravanel (Director Emeritus McKinsey), Angelo Panebianco (Università di Bologna), Roberto Perotti (IGIER-Università Bocconi), and Eric Salmon (Eric Salmon & Partners) for their insightful comments in the final panel session. A special thank to ManagerItalia, and notably to President Claudio Pasini and to Enrico Pedretti, for their support in gathering the data for this volume. We are also indebted to the Office of the Presidency of the Camera dei Deputati and to Fausto Bertinotti for their assistance in obtaining information on the compensation of Italian MPs.

The tenth European conference of the Fondazione was also an opportunity for us to assess ten years of activity at our research institution. We are most grateful to Carlo De Benedetti, who allowed the Fondazione to exist and made possible this event, to which he also contributed some particularly insightful opening remarks. Carlo De Benedetti has, after all, for decades been a leading member of the Italian ruling class.

Contents

Contents

Part II. Italian Managers: Fidelity or Performance?

Andrea Prat, Oriana Bandiera, Luigi Guiso, and Raffaella Sadun

List of Figures

List of Tables

List of Contributors

Giuliano Amato, (European University Institute)

Oriana Bandiera, (London School of Economics)

Tito Boeri, (Fondazione Rodolfo Debenedetti and Bocconi University)

Vittorio Colao, (Vodafone Italia)

Vincenzo Galasso, (Università Bocconi)

Luigi Guiso, (European University Institute)

Massimiliano Landi, (Singapore Management University)

Andrea Mattozzi, (California Institute of Technology)

Antonio M. Merlo, (University of Pennsylvania)

Andrea Prat, (London School of Economics)

Lucrezia Reichlin, (University College London)

Raffaella Sadun, (London School of Economics)

Luigi Zingales, (The University of Chicago Booth School of Business)

Introduction

In the 1972 film *The Ruling Class*, Peter O'Toole lifts up a table with the strength of his beliefs. By the time he has counted up to ten, the table had challenged the law of gravity and is floating in the air. Our notion of the ruling class does not encompass miracles. It should not necessarily be as close to God as the obsessed aristocrat masterly interpreted by Peter O'Toole. In fact, we have had enough of obsessed members of the ruling class. But we would certainly like to have ruling classes lifting up our economies.

The ruling class plays a major role in our societies. It enables what would otherwise be unfeasible, by removing those constraints that stand in the way of long-term growth. Two components of the ruling class are particularly important in this context. On the one hand, the political class has the fundamental role of removing political constraints, creating coalitions that support wide-ranging reforms, and increasing the efficiency in the allocation of resources. On the other hand, the managerial class can remove resource constraints by discovering and mobilizing hidden resource endowments and promoting the human capital and technological spillovers that endogenously spur on growth.

There is a long-standing tradition of sociological studies on the ruling class. At least since the pioneering work of Max Weber (1921), the main traits, evolution, and selection of elites have been thoroughly investigated by social scientists in a variety of countries. One of the main lessons of this literature is that the ruling class is necessarily country specific, as it originates from unique combinations of cultural roots, family ties, corporate governance structures, and rules for being co-opted into the elite. Although we are often desperately looking for a global ruling class, the latter does not exist as yet.

Economists have so far devoted much less attention than sociologists to the study of ruling classes. This is a pity, as a number of economists' theoretical tools can be very powerful in understanding what drives the formation of a ruling class. In particular, the tools used in labour economics can be very useful in studying the selection of the ruling class, the labour market of politicians, the allocation of managers' time, and their incentives, remunerations, and career paths.

One of the reasons for the limited attention devoted so far by economists to the study of the ruling class is related to data availability. There is a paucity of data on the characteristics of the ruling class. We are dealing with small numbers, and available surveys do not provide adequate representation of small population groups. Although there is currently more disclosure than in the past about the incomes and the professional activities of politicians, this information is poorly organized. Researchers have to spend a lot of time and effort seeking this information. It is also quite difficult to design questionnaires capturing the various dimensions of the managerial class, notably in isolating different managerial styles.

This volume contributes to filling these gaps. It draws on contributions from two teams of leading scholars in the field and on a large data-gathering effort undertaken by the Fondazione Rodolfo Debenedetti. Part I presents the contribution of the first team, which was coordinated by Antonio Merlo (University of Pennsylvania) and included Vincenzo Galasso (IGIER-Università Bocconi), Massimiliano Landi (Singapore Management University), and Andrea Mattozzi (California Institute of Technology). The focus of this part is on the labour market of politicians. Part II is devoted to the managerial class. It presents the report of the second team, led by Andrea Prat (London School of Economics) and including Oriana Bandiera (London School of Economics), Luigi Guiso (European University Istitute), and Raffaella Sadun (London School of Economics). The two teams, in cooperation with the Fondazione Rodolfo Debenedetti, contributed to the development of new datasets.

The first part of the book draws on detailed information on personal characteristics, incomes, performance in office, and career paths (before, after, and during the parliamentary mandate) of all the politicians who were elected to the Italian Lower Chamber (*Camera*) between 1948 and 2008. This is the first time that this information has been gathered and summarized for some key indicators. It is true, as stressed by Giuliano Amato (who was twice Prime Minister of Italy and spent twenty years in the Italian Parliament) in his comments in Part I, that quantitative indicators may conceal a number of relevant qualitative features of the job of a politician. However, the dataset is built as a census of the Italian *deputati* (4,465 MPs belonging to 124 different parties), and hence the statistics that it provides, the distributions tabulated by Merlo, Galasso, Landi, and Mattozzi, are very informative. Moreover, the authors exploit the panel structure of the data (notably the fact that there are repeated observations for the same individual) to develop a rather ingenious method of capturing unobserved characteristics of the politicians.

The second part of the volume is based on a variety of sources, including cross-country surveys of managers covering a very interesting sample of European countries, ad hoc surveys carried out in cooperation with the largest union of managers in the service sector, social security records, and, last but not least, the first time-use survey ever carried out on the allocation of top executives' time. Prat, Bandiera, Guiso, and Sadun also worked skilfully in linking these different datasets to administrative records and other data sources (for example, data on the balance sheets of the firms run by the managers), thus expanding their informational content considerably.

Although this volume presents new data processed by some of the most authoritative scholars of the field, I believe that there is much more that can be learned from the information gathered in this process. I do hope that this book will offer the statistical support for a new generation of studies on the Italian ruling class. To this end, the microdata used to produce the two studies have been uploaded and made publicly available on the Fondazione Rodolfo Debenedetti website (www.frdb.org).

Unlike in previous volumes of this series, the focus in this volume is on a specific country—namely, Italy—for the reasons detailed above. In order to characterize a ruling class sufficiently, it is necessary to focus on a mix of cultural and historical traits as well as on social customs and institutional features, which are unavoidably different from country to country. Thus, pursuing a greater degree of generalization would have reduced the heuristic value of the two studies. At the same time, cross-country comparisons are made by the authors whenever they are meaningful and are sufficiently supported by available data. The first part of the book draws on comparisons of the Italian and US experiences in selecting cohorts of MPs, while the second part is developed out of cross-country surveys eliciting the educational attainments and other personal characteristics of managers.

It should also be stressed that the study of the Italian ruling class is particularly interesting, as in Italy we find a broad spread of pathologies that elsewhere concern only a limited component of the ruling class and hence may be harder to observe and characterize. To give some orders of magnitude, almost 3,000 members of the Italian ruling class, mostly politicians, but also managers of public enterprises and industry leaders, were prosecuted by judges in the mid-1990s under the so-called Tangentopoli trials, uncovering a widespread network of bribes built on the misallocation of public resources.

In Italy we also find overrepresented with respect to other countries those managerial styles that reward fidelity to the firm's owner over and above performance. One manager of Italian firms out of four is hired via informal channels—basically family and friends—and the most important reason for leaving the firm is related to the deterioration of the relationship with the owners rather than to the state of the market or the performance of the manager. Another reason for considering Italy as an interesting case study lies in the natural experiments that it provides. For instance, Italy has repeatedly changed its electoral law since the beginning of the 1990s, modifying the rules governing the selection and the accountability of politicians.

Following the tradition of the other volumes in this series, the two parts of this volume are self-contained. In these introductory remarks I shall therefore confine myself to characterizing the links between the two parts of this volume, notably the interconnections between the political and managerial components of the ruling class. The two components of the ruling class are indeed strictly interrelated; sometimes they overlap, as can be grasped from the datasets collected for this volume. And the links and overlap between the two sets have only increased over time.

One way to characterize these links is by exploring the transitions from the managerial class to the political class using the data collected by Merlo, Galasso, Landi, and Mattozzi. The MPs coming from the managerial class have broadly the same characteristics (in terms of age and educational attainments) as the other new acquisitions to the Italian Lower Chamber, except for gender. Both the political and the managerial class are male dominated, but the gender gap in the interregnum between management and politics is even stronger. We counted only one woman who had formerly been a manager in the ranks of the new entrants to the Italian *Camera* since 1975. Over the same time span, the percentage of women among the new cohorts of MPs was about 12 per cent. Managers moving to politics typically have a shorter duration in office than other MPs (on average, about one year less). At the same time, they do not leave politics altogether at the end of their mandate(s). Four MPs out of ten from the managerial class remain involved in politics after leaving the Italian Parliament. These 'stayers' have been more numerous in more recent cohorts of managers obtaining a parliamentary seat. Managers elected to Parliament are twice as likely to be involved in scandals—that is, judges have requested the removal of the parliamentary immunity for them, according to the records collected by Golden (2007)—than other MPs. They also display lower attendance rates (measured in terms of participation in electronic plenary voting sessions) and earn more than the other MPs, as they generally keep a foothold in their original business.

Another way to look at the interactions between the political and the managerial classes is to investigate the allocation of time of top CEOs by drawing on the unique dataset assembled by Prat, Bandiera, Guiso, and Sadun. This dataset suggests that more than one-third of managers meet politicians and members of public administrations at least once a week. The proportion of time devoted to meetings with politicians is unsurprisingly larger among managers of firms owned by the government and of public utilities. It should be stressed that at the end of 2008 these types of firms accounted for almost 40 per cent of the stock-market capitalization of the Borsa Italiana. Significantly, the amount of time spent with politicians or public administrations is not lower than the time allotted to banks by the top executives of all the other firms, except those operating in the financial sector.

All this suggests that the Italian political class is increasingly and directly involved in private business and that a large proportion of Italian capitalism is deeply oriented towards politics. Politics also plays a role within firms, especially family firms. In another survey, the authors study the differences between managers who work for non-family firms and (non-family) managers who work for family firms. The latter are less likely to be evaluated on the basis of performance—or even to be evaluated at all, as the majority of Italian family firms do not carry out any formal assessment of their managers. Compared to other firms, family firms are more likely to hire their managers through friends and family members, and they are more likely to promote them on the basis of their relationship with their owners rather than on their performance. As a result, the survey shows that managers who end up working for family firms have less human capital and are more risk averse (and they are less satisfied with their job).

The mixture of private business and politics can easily degenerate into a set of political appointees often lacking any accountability. This risk is magnified in the aftermath of the great recession, as the latter provides a formal justification for a stronger involvement of the state in the private sector. In the presence of rather weak regulatory authorities, a regression of the Italian corporate governance structure to the state capitalism of the First Republic cannot be ruled out.

Other risks concern the behaviour of the political class. One way of reading the behaviour of the widening ranks of managers moving into politics is that we are dealing with individuals who are actively pursuing the private interests of their firm, even more than those of their lobby, well into their public position. This interpretation points to potential conflicts of interests with respect to the mandate received by the voters and is quite worrying, as the last (2008) cohort of entrants to the Italian Lower Chamber is dominated by managers (one out of four of the new MPs came from the managerial class). More data are needed to assess the relevance of this interpretation. Unfortunately, no public disclosure is offered as yet of individual assets owned by MPs and of the specific sources of their incomes before and during their mandate. It is, however, encouraging that a bill inspired by the above findings—brought to the public debate by a journal article (see Boeri 2008)—induced a brave MP, Senator Pietro Ichino of the Democratic Party, to present a draft bill on the disclosure of the activities and investments carried out by the members of Parliament, that will hopefully be approved by the Italian Senate.

The practical relevance of this book goes, in any event, well beyond the Italian case. The risks outlined above are present, at different degrees, in many other types of capitalism, and the scope of the 'politicized management' is expanding worldwide under local responses to the global recession. We hope that this book will raise public awareness that something must be done to prevent this degeneration. Rephrasing the title of a successful book of one of the contributors to this volume (Rajan and Zingales 2003), we need to save capitalism from state capitalists.

Tito Boeri

References

Boeri. T. (2008). 'Uno, cento, mille conflitti di interesse', *La Repubblica*, 19 July.

Golden, Miriam A. (2007). 'Dataset on Parliamentary Malfeasance, Chamber of Deputies, Republic of Italy, Legislatures I–XI (1948–94)', www.golden.polisci. ucla.edu/italy posted 21 March 2007.

Rajan, R., and Zingales, L. (2003). *Saving Capitalism from Capitalists*. New York: Crown Business.

Weber, M. (1921). *Economy and Society*, trans. and ed. Guenther Roth and Claus Wittich. New York: Bedminster Press.

Part I

The Labour Market of Italian Politicians*

Antonio M. Merlo, Vincenzo Galasso, Massimiliano Landi, and Andrea Mattozzi

* Paper presented at the X European Conference of the Fondazione Rodolfo Debenedetti on 'La Selezione della Classe Dirigente', Gaeta, Italy, 24 May 2008. We would like to thank Luca Anderlini, Tito Boeri, Daniela Iorio, Petra Todd, and Ken Wolpin for their helpful comments and suggestions. We would also like to thank Giancarlo Bartoloni, Fausto Bertinotti, Vincenzo Busa, Sandro Panarello, Teo Ruffa, and Agenzia delle Entrate, Associazione Ex-Parlamentary, Servizio Prerogative e Immunità, and Ufficio di Presidenza della Camera for their help and assistance with the collection and the interpretation of the data. A special thank you to the Fondazione Rodolfo Debenedetti for its help and financial support. Landi also acknowledges the financial support from the Office of Research at Singapore Management University, the hospitality of Servizio Prerogative e Immunità della Camera during the consultation of the archive of the tax returns of the elected members of the Italian Parliament, and the hospitality of collegio Carlo Alberto, where part of the work was done. Financial support from National Science Foundation grant SES-0617901 to Mattozzi and SES-0617892 to Merlo is gratefully acknowledged. Valentina Adorno, Pietro Biroli, Elisa Farri, Guido Maretto, Paola Monti, Mara Squicciarini, Panos Stavrinides, Michela Tincani, and especially Francesca Benvenuti provided invaluable help and excellent assistance throughout the construction of the dataset.

Introduction

Like voters (*the represented*), politicians (*the representees*) are the heart and soul of representative democracy. But is not being a politician just like any other job? After we get past the rhetoric, is politics any different from other occupations? In the political sector, voters, parties, and politicians represent the counterparts of consumers, firms, and workers/managers in the market sector. In fact, the analogy is much deeper than it may appear at first sight. In the market sector, consumers determine to a large extent the success of a firm and ultimately the management's fate. However, managers are chosen by the firms, which typically have an objective that is different from those of consumers and managers. Likewise, while in all democratic systems the voters ultimately determine who is elected, it is typically the case that political parties nominate candidates for public office. Furthermore, the objectives of voters and parties with respect to the selection of candidates may differ, and are constrained by the career ambitions of individuals with political aspirations. But, then, what really makes a career in the political sector different from a career in any other economic sector?

There are at least three distinctive features that characterize the labour market in the political sector. First, politicians are typically 'under the spotlight', receiving the attention of the media and of a variety of citizens' organizations. This makes politics a 'showcase', where politicians in office can display their political skills, while it might be more difficult for individuals working in the market sector to reveal their market ability. Second, inter-party competition for potential politicians is likely to be of secondary importance, as ideological preferences are more likely to attract individuals towards specific parties at the beginning of their political careers. Third, it is often the case that political parties 'take care of their losers' by reserving party's positions to defeated incumbents. As a result, while individual careers within the political sector are inevitably linked to the opportunities available within parties, the extent to which individual endowments of 'political' and 'market' skills are correlated, or experience in the political (market) sector is also valuable in the market (political) sector, links the labour markets of the two sectors. This link affects the selection of politicians, the politicians' careers, and the relationship between parties and voters.

In his famous 1918 lecture 'Politics as a Vocation', Max Weber writes:

> Politics, just as economic pursuits, may be a man's avocation or his vocation.... There are two ways of making politics one's vocation: Either one lives 'for' politics or one lives 'off' politics.... He who lives 'for' politics makes politics his life, in an internal sense. Either he enjoys the naked possession of the power he exerts, or he nourishes his inner balance and self-feeling by the consciousness that his life has meaning in the service of a 'cause'.... He who strives to make politics a permanent source of income lives 'off' politics as a vocation. (Gerth and Mills 1946: 83–4)

This quotation highlights the importance of analysing the motivations of politicians in the context of their career decisions over the life cycle, and represents the starting point of a large literature where scholars from different disciplines within the social sciences have been tackling these issues from a variety of angles.[1]

In this study, we analyse the career profiles of Italian legislators in the post-war period. Using a unique, newly collected dataset that contains detailed information on all the politicians who were elected to the Italian Parliament between 1948 and 2008, we address a number of important issues that pertain to their career paths prior to election to Parliament, their parliamentary careers, and their post-Parliament employment. Our data span two institutional regimes: Italy's First Republic (1948–94) and the Second Republic (1994–), characterized by different electoral rules and party structures.

---

[1] The contributions by sociologists and political scientists are particularly numerous, and it is outside the scope of this study to survey this literature, which is vast even if one were to restrict attention to the case of Italy. In addition to the references we cite in the remainder of this study, there are many others we read to help us place our work in the context of the literature. In particular, we refer the interested reader to Aberbach, Putnam, and Rockman (1981), Bartolini and D'Alimonte (1996), Caciagli and Barnes (1994), Cotta and Isernia (1996), Di Palma (1977), Di Palma and Cotta (1986), Dogan (1975, 1989), Doring (1995), Eldersveld (1989), Ignazi and Ysmal (1998), La Palombara (1987), La Palombara and Weiner (1996), Morlino (1998), Norris (1997), Norris and Lovenduski (1995), Patzelt (1999), Putman (1976), Sartori (1966), Spotts and Wieser (1986), Verzichelli (1994, 1996), Vianello and Moor (2000), and Wertman (1988). The economics literature on this topic is more recent and quite small, and is surveyed by Merlo (2006).

In Chapter 1, we present a brief overview of the Italian political system. Countries differ with respect to their political institutions, which affect the way in which voters, politicians, political parties, the legislature, and the government interact, as well as the 'industrial organization' of the political sector. The overview of the institutional details of the Italian political system we provide highlights the role played by parties in the selection of politicians and the way in which changes in the electoral law may have affected the selection process as well as the parties' internal organization and the overall structure of the party system.

In Chapter 2, we provide a comprehensive view of the career profiles of Italian legislators over the entire sample period 1948–2008. In particular, we document the extent to which the characteristics of Italian legislators (such as their age, gender, education, occupation, and income prior to entering Parliament) changed over time and highlight the major differences between the First and Second Republics. To provide a term of comparison, we also contrast the profiles of Italian legislators and their evolution over the post-war period to those of the members of the United States Congress.

In Chapter 3, we use our data to address a number of questions that pertain to the selection of Italian politicians, their labour market, and their overall quality. We then draw some general conclusions that contribute to the debate about the relative efficacy and desirability of alternative policies regarding the selection and the compensation of elected representatives.

Before turning our attention to the details of our study of the careers of Italian politicians, it is legitimate to ask whether Italy represents a good case study in a broader European context or, in other words, to what extent Italian legislators are similar to their counterparts in other European

Table 1 Legislators' characteristics in selected European countries, 2005–7

Country	Year	Average age	% female	% college degree
Austria	2006	49.1	31.1	36.6
Belgium	2007	44.0	37.9	79.3
Denmark	2007	45.3	37.7	67.4
Finland	2007	46.2	42.0	66.5
France	2007	56.4	18.3	n.a.
Germany	2005	49.3	32.5	86.7
Iceland	2007	49.7	31.7	n.a.
Italy	2007	52.0	16.3	68.5
The Netherlands	2006	42.2	36.6	60.0
Sweden	2006	49.0	47.3	66.7
Switzerland	2007	51.0	28.5	n.a.
United Kingdom	2005	48.2	19.8	67.0
Average		48.5	31.6	66.5

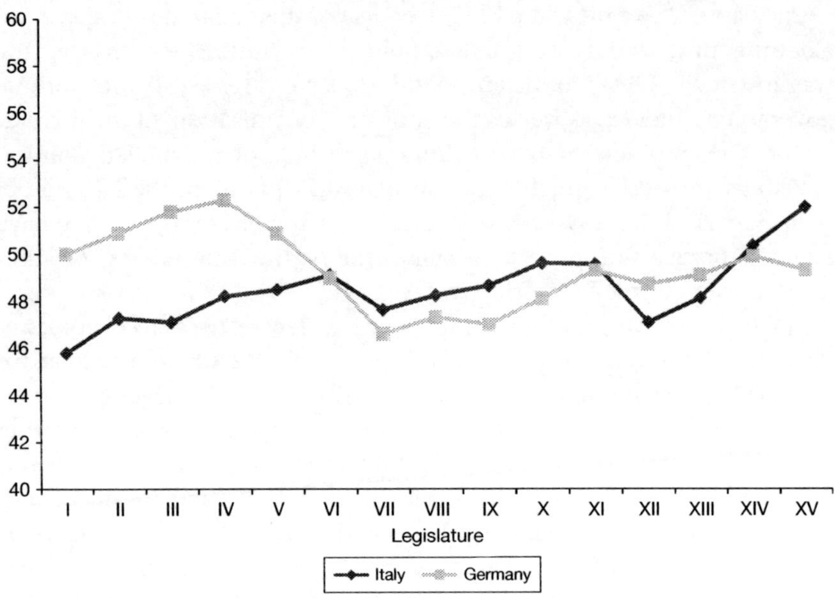

Fig. 1 Average age of legislators by legislature

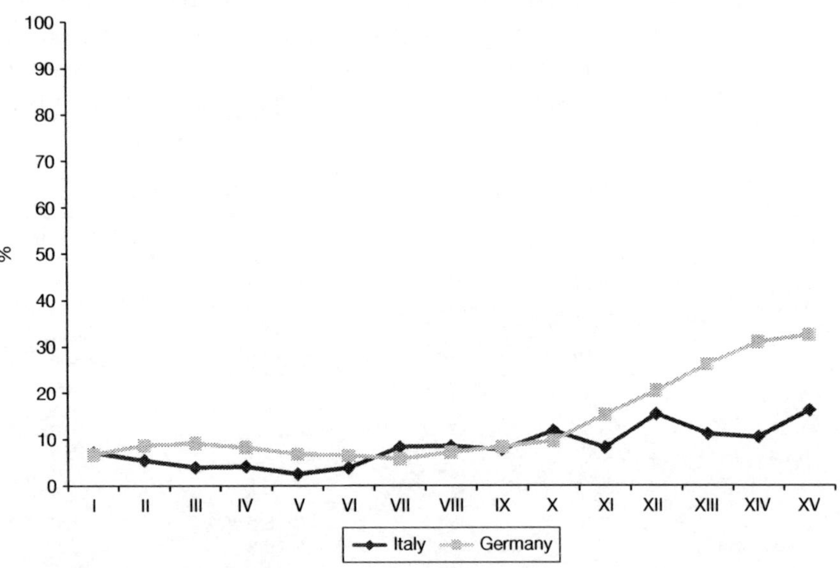

Fig. 2 Percentage of female legislators by legislature

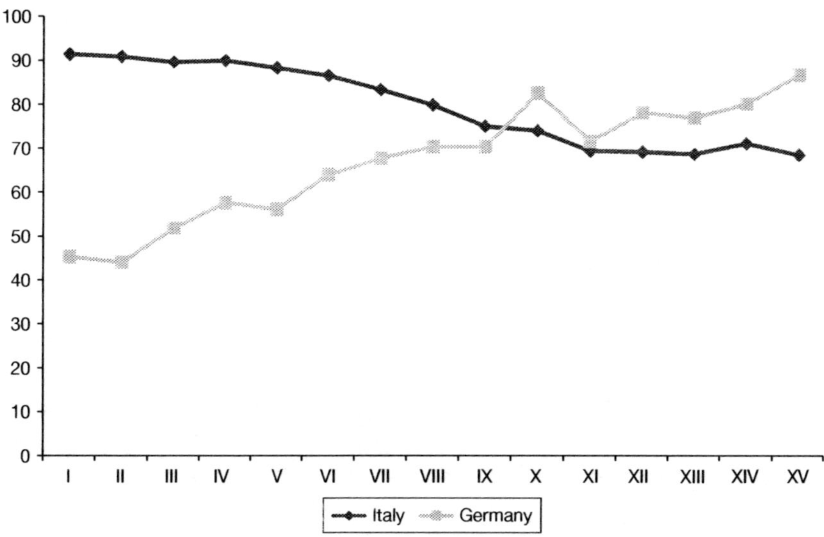

Fig. 3 Percentage of legislators with a college degree by legislature

countries with respect to their demographic characteristics. To address this issue, Table 1 reports the average age, the percentage of female legislators, and the percentage of legislators with a college degree in the most recent legislature for a number of European countries; while Figures 1, 2, and 3 depict the time series of these variables for Italy and Germany over their first fifteen legislatures. As we can see from Table 1, Italy is by no means an outlier with respect to any of these measures, although the cross-country variation in each of these dimensions of the data is quite substantial. With respect to changes over time in the composition of the legislature, Figures 1–3 show that the average age and the percentage of females in the legislature followed similar patterns in Italy and in Germany. The percentage of legislators with a college degree, on the other hand, decreased over time in Italy while it increased in Germany.

1

Institutional Background

The set of political institutions put in place by the 1948 Italian Constitution was designed to prevent the concentration of power in the hands of the majority, and required the political and institutional led power to be shared among many actors. This was achieved through the establishment of a strong bicameral parliamentary system where the balance of power between the legislative and the executive branches favoured the former, and through a proportional electoral law, which guaranteed the representation of many political forces in Parliament leading to a multiparty system and to executive power sharing within broad coalition governments. The combination of all these features makes Italy a consensus democracy.

1.1. The Italian Parliament

Italy is a parliamentary democracy with a perfect bicameral structure, where the House (*Camera dei Deputati*) and the Senate (*Senato della Repubblica*) have symmetrical legislative power. In fact, during the *iter legis*, which represents the procedure to finalize a law, the text of the law has to be approved by both chambers.[1] Approvals typically require a simple majority of votes of the members who are present at the time of deliberation (*quorum funzionale*).

---

[1] Typically, the initiative to draft a law arises within the government or is brought up by some members of the Parliament, and is then assigned to a committee for further investigation. The newly drafted text has to be approved by (simple) majority by the committee and then by the two chambers of Parliament. If either chamber modifies the text that was previously approved by the other chamber, the text has to go back to the previous chamber for a new approval.

14

The presence of a majority of the members of each chamber is, however, needed for any decision to be valid (*quorum strutturale*).[2]

The House is composed of 630 members (MPs), all chosen by the Italian electorate during general political elections.[3] The Senate, on the other hand, has 315 elected members chosen through competitive elections, but also a handful of non-elected members. Non-elected members of the Senate are past Italian Presidents (*senatori di diritto a vita*) and those citizens who have been declared senators for life (*senatori a vita*) by Italian Presidents, as the highest national recognition for exceptional achievements in science, art, or social life.

The constitutionally mandated duration of a parliamentary term or legislature is five years. Within seventy days before the end of a legislature, new elections have to take place to nominate the members of the new Parliament. Early elections may, however, take place before the regular end of the legislature. Indeed, early elections have been relatively frequent in Italy, as documented in Table 1.1, which reports the beginning and end dates of the fifteen Italian legislatures between 1948 and 2008. The authority to dissolve Parliament and to call early elections rests with the President of the Republic, who by calling an early election acknowledges and certifies that the current Parliament is unable to support the formation of a government (that is, no government can obtain a majority of the votes in each of the two chambers of Parliament).

The (active) electorate for the House is composed of all Italian citizens who have reached 18 years of age, whereas the voting age for the Senate is 25 years. Differences in age restrictions across elections are a peculiar feature of the Italian system, since everywhere else in Europe the minimum age to vote in all elections is 18 years, with the sole exception of Belgium, where voters have to be at least 21 years old. Age restrictions are also imposed on the passive electorate. To be eligible to become a member of Parliament, an Italian citizen has to be at least 25 years old for the House and at least 40 years old for the Senate. The latter is the highest age limit in Europe.[4]

---

[2] In the House, abstentions are not counted as votes—effectively reducing the number of votes required to pass a law; in the Senate, abstentions are counted as votes—thereby maintaining the number of votes required to pass a law constant.

[3] The number of representatives became fixed at 630 in the 1963 election. In the previous three legislatures, it depended on the size of the population in each electoral district. The number of representatives who were elected to the House prior to 1963 was 574 in 1948, 590 in 1953, and 623 in 1958.

[4] The only other European country that imposes such a limit is the Czech Republic. In Belgium, candidates have to be older than 21 years of age, in France 23, and in Greece 25.

Table 1.1 Italy's legislatures, 1948–2008

Legislature	Date begins	Date ends
I	8 May 1948	24 June 1953
II	25 June 1953	11 June 1958
III	12 June 1958	15 May 1963
IV	16 May 1963	4 June 1968
V	5 June 1968	24 May 1972
VI	25 May 1972	4 July 1976
VII	5 July 1976	19 June 1979
VIII	20 June 1979	11 July 1983
IX	12 July 1983	1 July 1987
X	2 July 1987	22 Apr. 1992
XI	23 Apr. 1992	14 Apr. 1994
XII	15 Apr. 1994	8 May 1996
XIII	9 May 1996	29 May 2001
XIV	30 May 2001	27 Apr. 2006
XV	28 Apr. 2006	28 Apr. 2008

The members of the Italian Parliament enjoy a special status. Regardless of the party list or of the geographic location of the district in which they have been elected, the members of Parliament have the legal duty of representing the interests of the entire nation. For instance, their electoral-affiliation party has no formal control over their political or voting behaviour while they are in Parliament. Moreover, MPs cannot be arrested or prosecuted without a previous permission having been granted by the chamber of Parliament to which they belong, except in few special instances.

The relative importance of the legislative power (Parliament) vis-à-vis the executive power (the government) is captured by two important institutional features that regulate the interaction between these two functions. First, the head of the government (the Prime Minister) is not directly elected by the citizens, but is instead selected by Parliament. Typically, the name of the Prime Minister (and the composition of his Cabinet) emerges from consultations among the major parties. However, to assume power, the government must be approved by a majority in each chamber of Parliament (the investiture vote). Second, the Prime Minister is responsible to Parliament. Thus, in order to remain in power, the government must retain the support of a parliamentary majority, and either chamber of Parliament can remove the Prime Minister from office at any time with a legislative vote of no confidence.

Political parties play an important role within the organization and the daily working of the Italian Parliament. Each chamber of Parliament has a President and an Office of the President, which represent all the parties and have mainly administrative duties, as well as some (permanent) committees. In addition, the parties also have some institutional organizations within Parliament: the parliamentary groups (where typically each group represents a different party, although the mapping between parties and groups has become increasingly complicated over the years), and the heads of these groups (*Capigruppo*), who jointly form a body called *Conferenza dei Capigruppo*, which has an important agenda-setting role, since it determines the calendar of Parliament and the issues to be discussed during each parliamentary session.

1.2. The electoral law

The 1948 Italian Constitution instituted an electoral law with proportional representation for both chambers of Parliament. In the House, the proportionality applied at the national level in the election of all the representatives. The entire electorate was divided into large electoral districts. In each district, several MPs were elected. In the Senate, on the other hand, the proportionality applied at the regional level. Each of the twenty Italian regions elected a share of the 315 senators, according to its population, with a minimum of seven senators per region, except for small regions, such as Valle d'Aosta (one senator), and Molise (two senators).

The proportional rule that had regulated the Italian electoral system since the Second World War, however, came under strain at the end of the 1980s. This was partially because of the increasing instability of the governments, which was often blamed on the increase in the number of parties, and on the growing relevance of small parties in the coalition governments. As we can see from Table 1.2, which lists all Italian governments from 1948 to 2008, during the 1980s Italy experienced twelve governments, that lasted on average less than a year.[5]

These short lasting executives were typically coalition governments, and in four instances the Prime Minister did not belong to the largest party, which at that time was the Christian Democratic Party or *Democrazia Cristiana* (*DC*). A move from a proportional to a majoritarian electoral rule was thus presented as an effective way of reducing the power of the small parties and thereby increasing the stability of the executive.

---

[5] One cabinet, led by Amintore Fanfani, lasted only eleven days.

Table 1.2 Italy's governments, 1948–2008

Government	Date begins	Date ends	Coalition	Legislature	Republic
De Gasperi V	23 May 1948	14 Jan. 1950	DC, PLI, PSDI, PRI	I	I
De Gasperi VI	27 Jan. 1950	19 Jan. 1951	DC, PSDI, PRI	I	I
De Gasperi VII	26 July 1951	7 July 1953	DC, PRI	I	I
De Gasperi VIII	16 July 1953	2 Aug. 1953	DC	II	I
Pella	17 Aug. 1953	12 Jan. 1954	DC, Independent	II	I
Fanfani I	18 Jan. 1954	8 Feb. 1954	DC	II	I
Scelba	10 Feb. 1954	2 July 1955	DC, PSDI, PLI	II	I
Segni	6 July 1955	15 May 1957	DC, PSDI, PLI	II	I
Zoli	19 May 1957	1 July 1958	DC	II	I
Fanfani II	1 July 1958	15 Feb. 1959	DC, PSDI	III	I
Segni II	15 Feb. 1959	23 Mar. 1960	DC	III	I
Tambroni	25 Mar. 1960	26 July 1960	DC	III	I
Fanfani III	26 July 1960	21 Feb. 1962	DC	III	I
Fanfani IV	21 Feb. 1962	21 June 1963	DC, PSDI, PRI	III	I
Leone I	21 June 1963	4 Dec. 1963	DC	IV	I
Moro I	4 Dec. 1963	22 July 1964	DC, PSI, PSDI, PRI	IV	I
Moro II	22 July 1964	23 Feb. 1966	DC, PSI, PSDI, PRI	IV	I
Moro III	23 Feb. 1966	24 June 1968	DC, PSI, PSDI, PRI	IV	I
Leone II	24 June 1968	12 Dec. 1968	DC	V	I
Rumor I	12 Dec. 1968	5 Aug. 1969	DC, PSI, PRI	V	I
Rumor II	5 Aug. 1969	27 Mar. 1970	DC	V	I
Rumor III	27 Mar. 1970	6 Aug. 1970	DC, PSU, PSI, PRI	V	I
Colombo	6 Aug. 1970	17 Feb. 1972	DC, PSI, PSDI, PRI	V	I
Andreotti I	17 Feb. 1972	26 June 1972	DC	V	I
Andreotti II	26 July 1972	7 July 1973	DC, PLI, PSDI	VI	I
Rumor IV	7 July 1973	14 Mar. 1974	DC, PSI, PSDI, PRI	VI	I
Rumor V	14 Mar. 1974	23 Nov. 1974	DC, PSI, PSDI	VI	I
Moro IV	23 Nov. 1974	12 Feb. 1976	DC, PRI	VI	I
Moro V	12 Feb. 1976	29 July 1976	DC	VI	I
Andreotti III	29 July 1976	11 Mar. 1978	DC	VII	I
Andreotti IV	11 Mar. 1978	20 Mar. 1979	DC	VII	I
Andreotti V	20 Mar. 1979	4 Aug. 1979	DC, PRI, PSDI	VII	I

Cossiga I	4 Aug. 1979	4 Apr. 1980	DC, PSDI, PLI	VIII	I
Cossiga II	4 Apr. 1980	18 Oct. 1980	DC, PSI, PRI	VIII	I
Forlani	18 Oct. 1980	28 June 1981	DC, PSI, PRI, PSDI	VIII	I
Spadolini I	28 June 1981	23 Aug. 1982	DC, PSI, PSDI, PRI, PLI	VIII	I
Spadolini II	23 Aug. 1982	1 Dec. 1982	DC, PSI, PSDI, PRI, PLI	VIII	I
Fanfani V	1 Dec. 1982	4 Aug. 1983	DC, PSI, PSDI, PLI	VIII	I
Craxi I	4 Aug. 1983	1 Aug. 1986	DC, PSI, PSDI, PLI, PRI	IX	I
Craxi II	1 Aug. 1986	17 Apr. 1987	DC, PSI, PSDI, PLI, PRI	IX	I
Fanfani VI	17 Apr. 1987	28 July 1987	DC, Ind.	IX	I
Goria	28 July 1987	13 Apr. 1988	DC, PSI, PSDI, PLI, PRI	X	I
De Mita	13 Apr. 1988	22 July 1989	DC, PSI, PSDI, PLI, PRI	X	I
Andreotti VI	22 July 1989	12 Apr. 1991	DC, PSI, PSDI, PLI, PRI	X	I
Andreotti VII	12 Apr. 1991	24 Apr. 1992	DC, PSI, PSDI, PLI	X	I
Amato I	28 June 1992	28 Apr. 1993	DC, PSI, PSDI, PLI	XI	I
Ciampi	28 Apr. 1993	10 May 1994	DC, PSI, PSDI, PLI, Ind.	XI	I
Berlusconi I	10 May 1994	17 Jan. 1995	Centre-right	XII	II
Dini	17 Jan. 1995	17 May 1996	Technical	XII	II
Prodi I	17 May 1996	21 Oct. 1998	Centre-left	XIII	II
D'alema I	21 Oct. 1998	18 Dec. 1999	Centre-left	XIII	II
D'alema II	22 Dec. 1999	25 Apr. 2000	Centre-left	XIII	II
Amato II	25 Apr. 2000	11 June 2001	Centre-left	XIII	II
Berlusconi II	11 June 2001	23 Apr. 2005	Centre-right	XIV	II
Berlusconi III	23 Apr. 2005	17 May 2006	Centre-right	XIV	II
Prodi II	17 May 2006	28 Apr. 2008	Centre-right	XV	II

In 1990, a popular referendum was proposed by several politicians with two objectives: eliminate the proportional electoral rule for the Senate, and the option of expressing preferences for multiple candidates on each ballot for the House. While the Italian Constitutional Court ruled against the admissibility of the former referendum, the latter was held in 1991. Almost 95 per cent of the thirty million Italians who voted (65 per cent of the electorate) agreed on abandoning the much criticized multiple vote of preference for House elections. Two years later, the legitimacy of the referendum to eliminate the proportional electoral rule for the Senate was approved by the Italian Constitutional Court and, on 18 and 19 April 1993, 77 per cent of the Italian electorate voted in the referendum and determined by a large majority (82.7 per cent) the end of the proportional electoral rule for the Senate.

Soon after the 1993 referendum, a major modification of the Italian electoral system was implemented for both chambers of Parliament by the so-called *Legge Mattarella* of 1994 (named after the Christian Democrat legislator Sergio Mattarella, who sponsored it). In the House, Italy moved from a pure proportional system to a mixed system, where 75 per cent of the representatives were elected with a majoritarian system and the remaining 25 per cent according to the proportional system.[6] Italy was divided into 475 uninominal House districts. In each district, one representative was elected by simple plurality according to a pure first-past-the-post election. The remaining representatives were then selected with a proportional rule among the candidates of those parties that were able to reach a threshold of at least 4 per cent of the votes, with a mechanism favouring the losing parties in the uninominal districts. The 1994 law also modified the electoral rule for the Senate. In the new mixed system, 232 senators were elected according to a simple plurality rule in the 232 uninominal Senate electoral districts into which Italy was partitioned. The remaining eighty-three representatives of the Senate, previously allocated in fixed numbers among the twenty Italian regions, were then selected according to a proportional system. In each region, the representatives elected in the

---

[6] The choice of attributing 25% of the seats according to the proportional rule was highly criticized by the proposers of the 1993 referendum, who claimed that the 1994 law contradicted the spirit of the referendum of abandoning the proportional system. Two additional referenda in April 1999 and May 2000 tried to eliminate the 25% proportional quota. However, neither referendum reached the required quorum of 50% of the votes (the turnout in the 1999 referendum was 49.6% of the population of eligible voters, thereby falling short of the threshold by less than 210,000 votes).

proportional system were selected using the votes received by the losing candidates in the uninominal districts of the region.[7]

Three legislatures later, on the eve of the 2006 national elections, the Italian electoral system was again modified to move back to a proportional system, although with some notable differences with respect to the original proportional system, which had been in use between 1948 and 1994. Representatives to the House are now elected according to a proportional rule with a double threshold. If a party does not belong to a coalition, in order to gain a seat in the House, it has to reach the threshold of 4 per cent of the total votes. If, instead, the party is linked to other parties in a coalition, the threshold (for each party in the coalition) becomes 2 per cent. Special rules apply to allow the first two parties that do not reach these thresholds to gain a seat in the Parliament. In the House, the strict proportionality rule is also modified to allow for a premium (in terms of additional seats in Parliament) to be assigned to the party (or coalition) that obtains the relative majority. Accordingly, the party with the relative majority is guaranteed at least 340 seats out of the 630 seats available.

An analogous change was implemented in the electoral law for the Senate. The proportional representation was introduced to assign the seats at the regional level with a premium (in terms of additional seats) for the party with the relative majority, again at the regional level. Single parties were allowed to form coalitions to reach the majority premium. The coalition enjoying the relative majority within the region is awarded a number of representatives in the Senate equal to 55 per cent of the representatives in the region, unless the received votes would provide the coalition with even more seats. The minimum (regional) threshold to obtain a seat is equal to 20 per cent of the votes in the region for a coalition and to 8 per cent for a single party (or for a party in a coalition that fails to reach 20 per cent of the votes).[8] Within each coalition, votes are shared among the parties that have received at least 3 per cent of the votes.

A controversial feature of this electoral system is that voters are allowed to cast a ballot only for the party, and not for individual candidates. Clearly, this system (which is typically referred to as 'closed-list proportional representation') enhances the power of the political parties and strengthens their influence over the selection of legislators. In fact, since voters cannot choose among the various candidates within a party list, the elected

---

[7] The votes received by the winning candidates in the uninominal districts were not counted.

[8] The effective thresholds are indeed higher, because of the small number of seats per region.

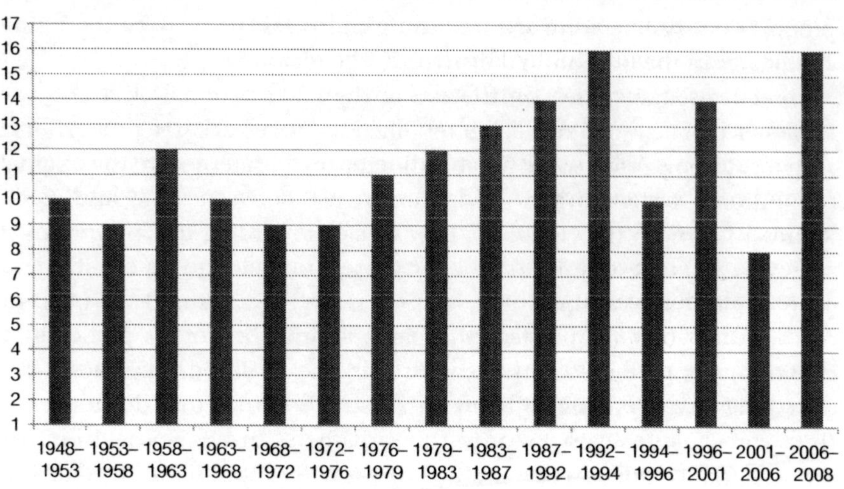

Fig. 1.1 Number of parties represented in Parliament

representatives are effectively selected by the parties, which decide how to rank the candidates in their list. We address the issue of the selection of elected representatives and the role of parties in the selection process in more detail below.

It is interesting to note that the introduction of the mixed-majoritarian proportional system in 1994 had initially proved effective in reducing the number of parties represented in Parliament with respect to its 1992 level (Figure 1.1). Yet, this effect appeared to be quite short lived and unstable, as the number of parties increased in the 1996 election before dropping again after the 2001 election. After the 2006 election, following the return to a proportional system, the number of parties that obtained parliamentary representation increased again. The duration of the Italian governments also changed somewhat after the changes in the electoral law. Since the 1994 election, Italy has experienced an increase in the average duration of a government of about one year with respect to the average government duration over the period 1948–94.

1.3. A tale of two Republics

In addition to the first major change in Italy's electoral law that we described above, 1994 also marked the end of an era in Italian politics, and the beginning of a new phase. It is now common to refer to the period that goes from the beginning of the first Legislature to the end of the 11th Legislature as Italy's First Republic (May 1948–April 1994), and the period inaugurated with the election of the 12th Legislature in April 1994 as Italy's Second Republic.

The process that eventually lead to the demise of the old system started in February 1992, when judge Antonio Di Pietro had Mario Chiesa, a member of the Socialist Party or *Partito Socialista Italiano* (*PSI*), arrested on a corruption charge. The event marked the beginning of a massive judicial investigation into political corruption, which soon became known as 'Operation Clean Hands' (*Mani Pulite*) (see, e.g., Colajanni 1996). In the ten years that followed, the pool of Milan-based judges that worked on the case prosecuted more than 3,000 people, many of whom were politicians, but who also included industry leaders and public managers. According to the official judicial records, 1,254 individuals were convicted, while 910 were found not guilty. This investigation uncovered a large corruption network (which is commonly referred to as 'Bribeville' or 'Tangentopoli'), which controlled several critical aspects at the junction between the economic and the political system. The demise of this network had profound consequences for the Italian political system, and led to a dramatic change in the structure and organization of its political parties. Therefore, we discuss the role of the political parties in the recruitment of politicians during the First and the Second Republic separately.

1.3.1. The political parties of the First Republic

The political class of Italy's First Republic was considerably different from the political class of the pre-war period. In fact, while the latter was composed mainly of landowners and nobility (the *notables*), the post-war political scene has been increasingly dominated by modern party professionals. The transformation process was very gradual, and some scholars suggest that elements indicating an ongoing change in this direction were already present at the beginning of the twentieth century, with an increasing proportion of blue-collar workers and, in particular, public-sector employees being elected to Parliament. This trend affected virtually all political parties.

The early renewal process of the Italian political class, however, came to a grinding halt during the Fascist dictatorship. What is particularly relevant for our purposes is that this non-democratic regime had long-lasting consequences on the post-war recruitment of politicians, affecting in particular the fate of the smaller political parties. In fact, only two parties, namely the *DC* and the Communist Party or *Partito Comunista Italiano* (*PCI*), managed to preserve their organization structure during the dictatorship. Indeed, the *DC* was able to maintain a relatively strong and functioning organization because it was traditionally built on the large network of Catholic organizations that, as a consequence of the 1929 Lateran Pacts, were protected from the regime's repression. More generally, parties with a cohesive organization structure were relatively more successful in overcoming the dictatorship period, as in the case of the *PCI*, which managed to survive in a covert way while many of its members were in exile. As a result, following the breakdown of the Fascist regime, the *DC* and the *PCI* were the only two large political parties still capable of carrying out the function of political recruitment, and therefore of being able to replace the old guard in the early post-war years. This was not the case for smaller parties, as, for example, the *PSI*, which instead had to rely on its old political class and was therefore delayed in its attempt to adjust to the new political scenario (see, e.g., Henig and Pinder 1969; Best and Cotta 2000).

In the 1948 election, which was the first free political election after the Constituent Assembly had drafted the Italian Constitution between 1946 and 1948, the *DC* experienced a landslide victory, and led the first executive of the First Republic with a coalition government that also included the Liberals or the *Partito Liberale Italiano* (*PLI*), the Republicans or the *Partito Repubblicano Italiano* (*PRI*), and the Social Democrats or the *Partito Social Democratico Italiano* (*PSDI*). From the first election until the 1992 election, which was the last election of the First Republic under the proportional electoral rule, the *DC* always won the elections, becoming the party of relative (and sometimes absolute) majority (Figure 1.2). In fact, *DC* representatives were present in all forty-seven governments of the First Republic, and headed the executive in all but six instances (see Table 1.2).[9]

The *DC* represented an Italian anomaly, as it ruled the country uncontested for almost fifty years, yet giving raise to unstable governments. As we can see from Tables 1.1 and 1.2, from 1948 to 1994 the average duration of a government was around one year, and half of the elections took place before the natural end of the legislature. The other Italian anomaly was the existence of an 'uncontested' opposition party: the *PCI*. Although it has never been part of a governing coalition, the *PCI* represented the second

---

[9] The Republican Giovanni Spadolini from 1981 to 1982, the Socialists Bettino Craxi from 1983 to 1987 and Giuliano Amato from 1992 to 1993, and a former Governor of the Bank of Italy, Carlo Azelio Ciampi, from 1993 to 1994 were the only non-*DC* politicians who led a government during the First Republic.

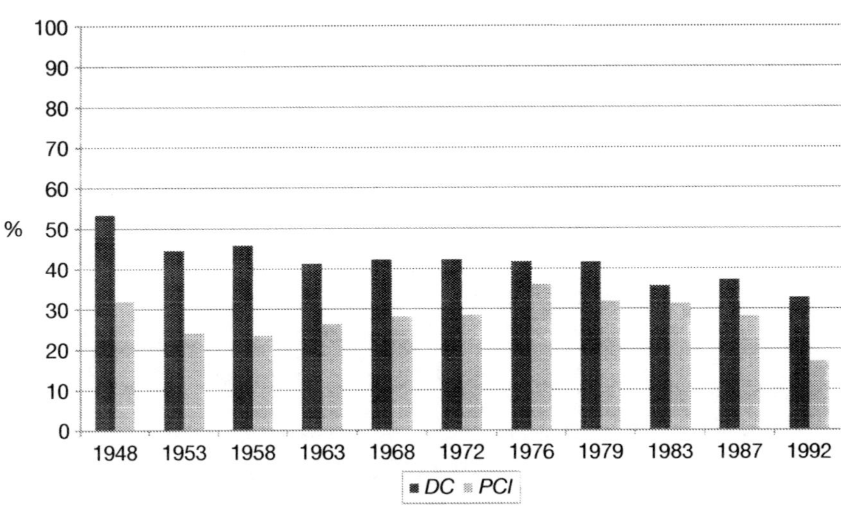

Fig. 1.2 Share of seats in the House of *DC* and *PCI*

largest party in the country, controlling as much as 36 per cent of the seats in the House in 1976 (see Figure 1.2).

The typical organizational structure of the parties of the First Republic was composed of three distinct levels: national, provincial (or federal), and local. The national structure of each party (for example, the National Council for the *DC*, or the Central Committee for the *PCI* and the *PSI*) was elected by the party congress and appointed the party's directorate and secretariat, which controlled the party and ran its operation. The party leader was the head of the national secretariat. The provincial committee (for example, the federal committee for the *PCI* and the *PSI*) was elected by the provincial congress and also had an executive and a provincial secretariat. By and large, the selection of candidates for public office took place at the provincial level, although it then needed to be approved by the national leadership. The local level was the basic territorial unit of a party, which coordinated the party's activities in each village or city.

Although most features of the recruitment process of politicians differed across the political parties of the First Republic, there were also some important common traits. For example, albeit with some distinctions, the selection process was mostly under the control of the parties' secretaries (that is, the parties' leaders). In addition, the selection process was clearly influenced by the electoral law, which provided for open lists for each party and the possibility for the voters of casting both a vote for the party list and at the same time a (preference) vote for one or more candidates on the party list. Furthermore, almost all the parties of the First Republic (with the notable exception of the *PCI*) relied heavily on the public sector for the supply of new politicians. Not only were political parties increasingly drawing their recruits from this sector, but parties with a long government tradition like the *DC* were also appointing their members to key positions in publicly owned firms and in various public economic agencies (the *sottogoverno*), creating a complex two-way flow between the public and the political sectors (see, e.g., Galli and Prandi 1970).

If we turn to the main differences in the career paths of politicians within the various parties of the First Republic, it is again useful to begin by comparing the two main parties: the *DC* and the *PCI*. In the *DC*, there was a very small distinction between MPs and the party's national leadership. In fact, election to Parliament was almost regarded as a necessary condition to be considered a viable candidate for a leadership position within the party. This was not the case for the *PCI*, where the overlap between national leadership and MPs was fairly minimal (see, e.g., Henig and Pinder 1969; Morlino 2001). In fact, in the *PCI*, holding a parliamentary seat carried a much lower weight within the party than holding a post in the party's *nomenklatura*, and switching candidatures (that is, constantly rotating different party members on the electoral lists) was common practice.

Holding a post within the party organization at the provincial (or federal) level, on the other hand, was an important stepping stone for a successful political career within the party for both the *DC* and the *PCI* (see, e.g., Galli and Prandi 1970). At the same time, however, professional (career) politicians were relatively less prevalent in the *DC* than in the *PCI* (where the party structure played an absolutely critical role in the recruitment process as well as in every other function performed by the party), although a previous experience in local public offices was a common trait of most *DC* and *PCI* leaders alike. The two parties also differed with respect to the background of their politicians and their training. In particular, while a significant number of *DC* leaders started their political career by holding a post in youth sections of a powerful Catholic organization called Catholic Action or *Azione Cattolica*, a large proportion of the *PCI* national leaders held a post in the General Confederation of

Italian Workers (*CGIL*), one of the largest trade unions in Italy. With respect to the socio-economic background of its politicians, Galli and Prandi (1970: 148–9) point out that, while 'a political career in the DC was clearly not a vehicle for social mobility for workers and peasants, but almost exclusively for the middle status groups...only in the Communist Party were national positions open to party members who had manual occupations'. In this respect, it is interesting to note that, while the *PCI* required its elected MPs to contribute to the party's finances by donating a large percentage (40 per cent) of their parliamentary wage, the *DC* did not.

Among the other parties of the First Republic, the *PSI* was also a mass party very much like the *DC* and the *PCI*. Indeed, the *PSI* organizational structure was originally similar to the one of the *PCI*, with a marked pyramidal configuration. However, as several scholars pointed out, it is important to note that a differentiation along the standard ideological dimension might be very misleading, since, in fact, there are more similarities between the *DC* and the *PSI* than between the *PSI* and the *PCI*, in particular regarding their recruitment process.

The parliamentary history of the *PSI* can be divided in two different periods. The first phase goes approximately until the early 1950s, corresponding to the period when the similarities with the *PCI* were more apparent. The second period begins when the *PSI* became a government party with the first Moro Cabinet in 1963. The *PSI* maintained the role of a (minority) government party, aside from some relatively short interludes, until the end of the First Republic.

A first important characteristic that differentiated the *PSI* from the *PCI* was the particularly weak 'Party on the Ground' structure (Katz and Mair 1994).[10] The limited grass-roots participation together with the power of the provincial federations provided a fertile ground for the emergence of strong intra-party factions, which were a distinct trait of the *PSI*, thus making it more similar to the *DC* than to the ideologically more homogeneous *PCI*.[11] The limited involvement of the rank-and-file members in the internal decision process is also proved by the fact that the delegates to federal or national congresses were typically appointed from the party leadership.

---

[10] For example, the militants-to-members ratio was in the order of 1:50 for the *PSI* as compared to 1:23 for the *DC* and 1:18 for the *PCI*, respectively (see, e.g., Henig and Pinder 1969; Morlino 2001).

[11] The power of internal factions in the *PSI* was formally acknowledged in its statute in 1959 with the adoption of a proportional voting rule for all internal elections. See Morlino (2001).

In order to be considered as a potential electoral candidate in the national elections, a politician needed a training period in the *PSI* that was typically shorter than the one 'imposed' by the *PCI* and longer than the one of *DC*.[12] In the 1960s, with an increasing concentration of power at the top, socialization within the party became less important, and the selection process was completely under the control of the party leadership. Furthermore, the remarkable overlap between the roles of MPs and *PSI* party officials, in conjunction with the limited grass-roots participation, led some scholars to define the *PSI* as a propaganda/electoral machine. *PSI* became increasingly populated by professional politicians and local bosses who used the party solely as a means to win a parliamentary seat. The change that occurred with Craxi's leadership (1976–93) did not generate a reversal in the trend.

The other relevant political parties of the First Republic were the *PSDI*, the *PLI*, the *PRI*, and the Social Movement or *Movimento Sociale Italiano* (*MSI*). The first three political parties were quite similar in terms of their organizational structure. They were all opinion parties characterized by a relatively limited number of members. Moreover, they shared a strong tradition of being government parties (in particular the *PSDI*).[13] The only party that was instead much closer to a mass party was the *MSI* (the political party heir of the Fascist tradition), which was characterized by a strong central apparatus and leadership. Furthermore, a majority of the *MSI* electoral candidates had party experience and had also been members of its youth organization (the *Fronte della Gioventù* or *FdG*).

1.3.2. The political parties of the Second Republic

Big changes had begun to occur in Italian politics ever since the fall of the Berlin Wall. In particular, the events in East Germany contributed to an acceleration of a transformation that had already been ongoing in the *PCI* since the mid-1970s: a gradual shift towards reformist positions closer to those of the European Left and towards overcoming the *conventio ad excludendum* (the informal agreement among government parties to exclude the *PCI* from any ruling coalition). In February 1991, during its annual Congress, the majority of the delegates of the *PCI*, which at the time held

---

[12] This is reflected in the percentage of newly elected politicians in the *PSI* who were affiliated with the party before the age of 25, which is typically in between the values for the *DC* and *PCI* until the 1950s. See Best and Cotta (2000).

[13] In 1963 the *PSDI* merged with the *PSI* forming a unified party, the *Partito Socialista Unificato* (*PSU*). The alliance was abandoned in 1969 after a modest electoral performance.

177 seats in the House, chose to turn the *PCI* into a social democratic party. The name (and symbol) was changed to the Democratic Party of the Left or *Partito Democratico della Sinistra* (*PDS*). Some delegates, namely the radical left wing of the PCI, chose not to participate in the new political entity and to preserve the Communist identity by founding the Party of the Communist Rebirth or *Rifondazione Comunista* (*RC*), taking with them about 10 per cent of *PCI* members. In the 1992 election, the *PDS* won 16 per cent of the votes and 107 seats in the House, while the *RC* won 5.6 per cent of the votes and 35 seats.

During the April 1992 election, while the corruption scandal was quickly spreading to the entire political system, for the first time in its history the *DC* obtained less than 30 per cent of the seats in each chamber of Parliament. Meanwhile, the Northern League or *Lega Nord* (*LN*), a local party based in the north of Italy, received almost three and a half million votes, which translated into 55 seats in the House. The coalition government, which included the *DC*, *PSI*, *PSDI*, and *PLI*, and was led by the Socialist Giuliano Amato, lasted for only one year, and in September of 1992 had to face one of the deepest financial crises of post-Second World War Italian history. Following the large support in favour of the abrogation of the existing proportional electoral law in the referendum of April 1993, Amato resigned. Parliament was unable to produce a new government, and Carlo Azeglio Ciampi, a former Governor of the Bank of Italy, was appointed to lead a 'technical' transition government, which was backed by the *DC*, *PSI*, *PSDI*, and *PLI*. However, as a consequence of the mounting charges of corruption towards their members and a disastrous performance in the local elections, where their electoral vote share was halved, each of the four parties in the 1992 government coalition was about to disappear, while the *LN* was becoming the strongest political force in northern Italy.

The 1994 elections represented a major turning point for Italian politics. New parties had emerged, replacing most of the old parties of the First Republic, and the electoral competition was to take place with the new mixed electoral system. Three large and very heterogeneous coalitions ran for election. A centre coalition, named Pact for Italy or *Patto per l'Italia*, included the Popular Party or *Partito Popolare Italiano* (*PPI*) which was part of the former *DC*, and parts of the former *PSDI*, *PRI*, *PLI*, and *PSI*, among others. A left-wing coalition, named the Party of Progress or *Progressisti*, included the *PDS*, part of the former *PSI*, the *RC*, the Green Party, and the Social Christians (who were also part of the former *DC*), among others. A right-wing coalition ran under the two different names of Party of Freedoms or *Polo delle Libertà* in the north and Party of Good

Government or *Polo del Buon Governo* in the centre and south of Italy. The right-wing coalition was led by Silvio Berlusconi, a media tycoon participating for the first time in an election with his party, *Forza Italia* (*FI*), and also included the *LN*, the National Alliance or *Alleanza Nazionale* (*AN*), which was the former *MSI*, and the Christian Democratic Party of the Centre or *Centro Cristiano Democratico* (*CCD*), among others. The right-wing coalition won the election with 42.8 per cent of the votes, and, thanks to the new rules in place with the mixed-majoritarian system, received 57 per cent of the seats in the House. The left-wing coalition obtained 33.8 per cent of the House seats, while the centre coalition received a mere 7.3 per cent. The composition of the new Parliament demonstrated the magnitude of the change, with the largest turnover rate since 1948.

Unlike what happened during the First Republic, where the *DC* dominated the political scene by winning all the elections, in each election since 1994 the ruling party (or more precisely the ruling coalition) has always been defeated. Hence, at least until 2010, the Second Republic has been characterized by two leading coalitions, one stably located in the centre-left of the political spectrum and the other in the centre-right (in spite of the frequent changes in their names), alternating in office. In fact, after the political crisis in the centre-right coalition initiated by the *LN*, which brought down the first Berlusconi government, and the experience of a one-year-long 'technical' government led by Lamberto Dini (who had been a minister in the previous Berlusconi government), the 1996 election led to a change in the balance of power, with the centre-left coalition then named the Olive Tree or *L'Ulivo* (*ULIVO*) led by Romano Prodi obtaining a parliamentary majority and hence the control of the executive. After the election in 2001, it was again the turn of the centre-right coalition to rule the country, until the 2006 election (which was the first election of the Second Republic after the reintroduction of proportional representation), which led to a new change in the leadership in favour of the centre-left coalition. The most recent election of April 2008 was no exception, as the centre-right coalition regained power.

The institutional changes that occurred with the transition from the First to the Second Republic, together with the aftermath of the large-scale corruption that had wiped out a large part of the previous political elite have had profound effects on the political parties of the Second Republic and the recruitment of new politicians. The entry of a new political class coming from the business sector largely modified the political selection process. Moreover, the changes in the electoral law altered the existing procedure of bargaining over electoral lists and parties' positions. As a result, the 12th Legislature witnessed the entry into politics of a large contingent of young middle-class representatives from the *LN*, and upper-class managers and entrepreneurs from *FI*. The public sector, which throughout the First Republic was the major source of new blood in politics, had been replaced in its role by the private sector. An immediate consequence of this phenomenon was a marked reversal in the direction taken by the recruitment process that characterized the First Republic, with a significant drop in the proportion of professional career politicians sitting in Parliament.

Most of the parties of the Second Republic have a similar organizational structure, albeit with some notable differences. *FI* was founded in 1993 by Silvio Berlusconi as a fresh political movement that was distinguished from the previous political parties by a less structured, in fact minimal, internal organization. Berlusconi imported a managerial model prevalent in the private sector into politics: the new organizational scheme was based on a few hierarchical levels, and members were mostly recruited among the managers and employees of Berlusconi's companies. For example, *FI* is the only party whose President is also the party leader. The President is appointed by a small Presidential Committee and, after 1997, by the National Congress, which is the assembly of the party members. The Presidential Committee is the main deliberative body within the party and is composed of a majority of members directly appointed by the President and a minority appointed by the National Congress. In this respect, a primary characteristic of the movement that led to the creation of *FI* was the absence of professional politicians: the candidates for the 1994 elections were recruited with the intent of forming a critical mass of 'yes-men' who would legitimate Berlusconi as the unquestioned political leader of this group. *FI* was born as a movement centred on a charismatic leadership, almost completely lacking a 'Party on the Ground' organization and much closer to an electoral committee than to a traditional political party (Paolucci 2007).[14]

In terms of the occupational and social background of the *FI* MPs, the vast majority came from free professions, self-employment, and the private sector. Using Weber's dichotomy, politics seemed more to be an *avocation*

---

[14] According to Morlino (2001: 129), 'in Forza Italia, members are components of local electoral committees or promoters of a "product", centered around the leader and founder of the party, with no role to play outside election campaigns'. Some scholars refer to *FI* as 'the party of the elected (representatives)'.

for the MPs of *FI* than a *vocation*. One of the few characteristics that *FI* has in common with other more traditional parties is the high degree of overlap between party leaders and MPs. Indeed, in the whole period 1994–2001, only about one-third of the Presidential Committee members were not members of Parliament.

The selection process in *FI* is markedly pyramidal and the predominant feeling among elected officials is that their parliamentary careers are almost totally in the hands of Berlusconi, who also controlled entry in the national electoral lists (Poli 2001). However, while there is little doubt about *FI* being the party with the lowest level of political professionalization, scholars agree that, after a first phase when *FI* exemplified the model of a *light* party under the founder/leader control, elements of a structural change can be detected since the late 1990s. In fact, the early termination of the Berlusconi government in 1994, the defeat in the 1996 elections, and the prospect of remaining in opposition increased the need for a more stable party structure and an inflow of experienced professional politicians, which was partly achieved with 'lateral moves' from other parties (for example, the former *DC* and *PSI*).[15] Furthermore, there were more recent examples of successful political careers within the party (as opposed to the traditional practice of horizontal cooptation) with the candidacy of several local coordinators in the 2001 elections. With respect to the party's finances, it is worth mentioning that, since 2003, *FI* has required its MPs to give back to the party an amount of approximately 1,000 Euros per month out of their parliamentary wage.[16]

A second important political force of the Second Republic is represented by the parties that were formed from the ashes of the former *PCI*. As we have already mentioned, the *PCI* changed its name to *PDS* in 1991, and then to Democrats of the Left or *Democratici di Sinistra* (*DS*) in 1998. After the 1991 split of the *RC*, a new splinter occurred in 1998, when the majority of the *RC* decided to withdraw their support from the centre-left coalition, and a minority of the party, which instead continued to support the Prodi government, founded the Party of the Italian Communists or *Partito dei Comunisti Italiani* (*PdCI*) taking with them about a quarter of the *RC* members.

Although the monolithic structure of the mass party was only a vague memory, the *PDS* managed to preserve a grass-roots organization similar to

---

[15] As Mannheimer (1994), among others, suggests, *FI* originates as a party machine conceived to win elections, and it is, therefore, structurally unprepared to take a defeat.

[16] See Paolucci (2007) and also an interview with MP Ferrigno that can be found at www.mclink.it/com/inform/art/07n18617.htm.

the *PCI* for at least the first half of the 1990s. However, after 1998 the *DS* party structure resembled that of a *modern cadre party* (Koole 1996), characterized by a strong leadership with a substantive presence of professional politicians and a low members-to-voters ratio. At the same time, it maintained a structure with vertical ties, which is typical of a mass party.

Regarding candidate selection, there is evidence of a clear transformation from the absolute centrality of the party structure in the recruitment process (that characterized the *PCI* experience) to a more open and less hierarchical system fostering a larger participation of rank-and-file members and supporters in the decision process. For example, the 2001 *DS* statute refers to open primaries, closed primaries, and cooptation as possible selection methods, with a very limited use of the latter as compared to methods of nomination from below. Furthermore, from the second half of the 1990s, political career paths that had started in local public offices gained the same dignity as the traditional *cursus honorum* within the party. The most recent statute also requires an equal representation of men and women in the electoral lists.

In the transition from the *PDS* to *DS*, there was an increase in the overlap between the MP's role and the party leadership: from a proportion of 45 per cent MPs in the 1991 National Secretary to more than 50 per cent in 2001, and from about one-fifth of the 1991 National Direction to one-third in 2001 (De Rosa 2007). At the same time, the presence of the party inside the government became substantial, with more than 50 per cent of the Cabinet posts held by *PDS–DS* MPs between 1996 and 2000 (Prodi I, D'Alema I and II, Amato II). The obvious overall effect was a marked drop in the political weight of party officials.

The *RC* moved away from the *PCI* tradition of 'democratic centralism', by reducing the National Political Committee's role in the candidates' selection process. Moreover, in order to foster political turnover, in the *RC* outgoing MPs cannot run again after a second term (with the exception of the National Secretary of the party). The *RC* statute also prescribes that the majority of the National Secretary must be composed of non-elected party officials, and in fact the percentage of MPs in the National Secretary was around 11 per cent in 2005.

With respect to MPs' contributions to the party, the *DS* statute provides for a contribution of 40 per cent of the parliamentary wage. Moreover, MPs are required to give back to the party 15 per cent of their severance pay. As for the *RC*, MPs' contributions to the party decreased from 60 per cent of the parliamentary wage in 1991 to 20 per cent in 2003–4 (Bertolino 2004).

A third major political force of the Second Republic is the *AN*, which was born during the 17th *MSI* national congress in January 1995. The need for a new right-wing political entity that was fully integrated within the democratic system of political forces (*arco constituzionale*) was already clear at the end of the 1980s, when the *MSI* was experiencing a decline in its electoral support. The transformation became almost a necessity with the change of the electoral law in the 1990s, which would have severely penalized the relatively small and isolated parties. The idea was to soften the more radical position of the *MSI* in order to create a new political movement that was able to attract the right-wing component of the former *DC* and, more importantly, a political entity that could be part of a government coalition. The timing of the transition was strategic, since it shortly followed the remarkable and somewhat unexpected success of the *MSI* in the 1993 local elections. The success of the transformation was evidenced by the participation of the *AN* in the first Berlusconi government and by the creation of a splinter party, the *MSI–FT*, which maintained the Fascist legacy.

The transition from the *MSI* to the *AN* can be described as a change from a mass party to a modern movement party (Morlino 2001). Indeed, there are several elements of continuity with the tradition of mass parties: a top-down recruitment mechanism (while the National Direction is responsible for approving the lists proposed by the Provincial Executive, the President of the party is in fact the ultimate decision-maker); an experience within the party or as a local administrator as an important stepping stone for a successful political career; and some overlap between public and central office positions (more than one-third of the members of the National Secretary's Office were MPs).

Another important phenomenon of the Second Republic is the emergence of regional parties advocating a variety of local issues from fiscal federalism to secession. This phenomenon actually began in Veneto and Piedmont (two regions that were under the *DC* control until 1987) in the early 1980s, and then spread over to Lombardy. The *LN* party was born as a federation of several autonomist groups and regional parties (for example, *Lega Lombarda* and *Liga Veneta*) in 1991. In 1994 the *LN* became the second largest parliamentary party after the *PDS*. Under the first Berlusconi government the *LN* secured five Ministers (including the internal affairs Cabinet) and the Speaker of the House. However, more than half of the elected MPs left the party in the first months of 1995, joining the ranks of *FI*. In 1996 the *LN* withdrew its support of the second Berlusconi government and ran alone in the 1996 political elections, securing 10 per cent of the votes at the national level (a remarkable result for a party with a regional base).

The *LN* is characterized by a markedly hierarchical structure, a strong leader, and the centrality of the party apparatus. Some scholars consider the *LN* as a hybrid party somewhat in between an updated version of the mass party and a *modern cadre party* without a professional leadership (Morlino 2001). Political recruitment follows a top-down approach, and it is almost completely under the control of the Federal Council. The MPs typically have some experience as grass-roots activists in regional parties, and they also hold posts in central offices (7–30 per cent of MPs among top party officials from 1995 to 2010, and a maximum of 55 per cent in 1994).

In addition to the major political parties mentioned above, a number of post-*DC* parties were formed during the Second Republic after the crisis of the *DC* in 1992–4. The 1994 mixed-majoritarian electoral rule favoured the formation of large coalitions of parties on opposite sides of the political spectrum, and reduced the political weight of the centre, thus making the political unity of the Catholics a feature of the past. With the exception of the *PPI*, which was born in 1994 in the desperate attempt to revamp the *DC* legacy, the other newly formed Catholic parties (*CCD, CDU, UDEUR, DL*) are essentially 'elite parties', with an evanescent organizational structure more similar to electoral committees supporting single political figures (Morlino 2001). The elected politicians typically come from a career in the public sector and hold positions both in Parliament and in the party leadership. Since 1994, the partisan composition of all the ruling coalitions has contained at least one of these Catholic parties.

1.4. The role of trade unions

Trade unions have historically been an important player in the Italian political arena. With a coverage rate well above 80 per cent of the Italian workforce, unions have been responsible for negotiating most of the labour contracts in both the private and the public sector throughout the post-war period. Furthermore, they have enjoyed a strong support among workers. Union density (measured by the rate of union membership among Italian workers) has varied between 50 per cent in the late 1970s and 30 per cent at the beginning of the twenty-first century, following a decreasing trend that is common to most industrialized countries.

The strong ties between the trade unions and the political system can also be seen in the political careers that several of the most representative leaders of trade-union organizations undertook after leaving their positions within these organizations. Perhaps the first secretary general of a trade union to gain a seat in Parliament was Giuseppe Di Vittorio. He was elected secretary of the *CGIL* in 1945 and became a member of the Italian Parliament in its Constituent Assembly in 1946 with the *PCI*. Notably, he never resigned from his post in the *CGIL*. From their post of secretary general of the *CGIL*, all subsequent trade unionists after Di Vittorio (namely, Agostino Novella, Luciano Lama, Antonio Pizzinato, and Bruno Trentin) were also elected to Parliament with the *PCI*; while Sergio Cofferati, who led the *CGIL* from 1994 to 2002, was elected Mayor of Bologna with the centre-left coalition of the *ULIVO* in 2004 (Table 1.3).

The recruitment of politicians from among top trade unionists also occurred from the Catholic union *CISL*. Of the seven general secretaries who ended their mandate between 1950 and 2006, three became members of Parliament with the *DC*, and three with the centre-left coalitions of the Second Republic. In addition, Pierre Carniti has been a member of the European Parliament in two legislatures between 1989 and 1999, with the *PSI* in his former mandate and with the *PDS* in the latter one.

The third largest Italian trade union, *UIL*, which was founded by the *PRI* and the *PSDI*, also had strong ties with the political system, although its

Table 1.3 Political careers of Italy's trade-union leaders, 1948–

Name	Union	Secretary general	MP	Party
Giulio Pastore	*CISL*	1950–8	Yes	*DC*
Bruno Storti	*CISL*	1958–77	Yes	*DC*
Luigi Macario	*CISL*	1977–9	Yes	*DC*
Pierre Carniti	*CISL*	1979–85	No	
Franco Marini	*CISL*	1985–91	Yes	*ULIVO*
Sergio D'Antoni	*CISL*	1991–2000	Yes	*ULIVO*
Savino Pezzotta	*CISL*	2000–6	Yes	*UNIONE*
Raffaele Bonanni	*CISL*	2006–	No	
Giuseppe Di Vittorio	*CGIL*	1944–57	Yes	*PCI*
Agostino Novella	*CGIL*	1957–70	Yes	*PCI*
Luciano Lama	*CGIL*	1970–86	Yes	*PCI*
Antonio Pizzinato	*CGIL*	1986–8	Yes	*PDS*
Bruno Trentin	*CGIL*	1988–94	Yes	*PCI*
Sergio Cofferati	*CGIL*	1994–2002	No	*ULIVO*
Guglielmo Epifani	*CGIL*	2002–	No	
Italo Viglianesi	*UIL*	1953–69	Yes	*PSU*
Lino Ravecca	*UIL*	1969–71	No	
Ruggero Ravenna	*UIL*	1969–71	No	
Raffaele Vanni	*UIL*	1969–76	No	
Giorgio Benvenuto	*UIL*	1976–92	Yes	*DS*
Pietro Larizza	*UIL*	1992–2000	Yes	*DS*
Luigi Angeletti	*UIL*	2000–	No	

leaders were slightly less successful in their political aspirations to be elected to Parliament. Among the six general secretaries who have led the union since 1952, only three—Italo Viglianesi, Pietro Larizza, and Giorgio Benvenuto—eventually become members of Parliament. Viglianesi was elected to the Senate and later became a Minister, Benvenuto, who was secretary of the *PSI* in 1993, was elected to the House in the *DS* lists, while Larizza became senator for the *DS* in 2007.

2

Stylized Facts

This study uses a newly collected, unique, longitudinal dataset, which contains detailed information on all individuals who have been elected to the *Camera dei Deputati* of the Italian Parliament (the House), since the inception of the Italian Republic in 1948. The data span sixty years (1948–2008), fifteen legislatures, and the two Republics (Italy's First Republic, from 1948 to 1994, and the Second Republic, which began with the election of the 12th Legislature in 1994).

In addition to comprehensive information on individuals' demographic characteristics (such as their age, gender, and education), their last occupation prior to entering Parliament, and their electoral history and record of service in Parliament (including, possibly, election to the Senate, committee membership, and government positions), our dataset also contains partial information on legislators' attendance at parliamentary voting sessions (for Legislatures VIII–XV), their annual income from their tax returns (from 1981 to 2006), their involvement in scandals (from 1948 to 1994), and their occupation after leaving Parliament (for a representative subsample of individuals). Details on the collection of the data and the sources we used are contained in the Appendix.

In this chapter, we use these data to establish a number of interesting stylized facts pertaining to the careers of Italian politicians. Whenever possible, we also draw a comparison with the USA.

2.1. Career profiles

Our data document several important aspects of the career profiles of 4,465 Italian legislators, from the time they enter the House to when either they leave Parliament or the sample ends (387 individuals in our sample were re-elected to the 16th Legislature in April 2008).

The overwhelming majority of politicians (82.9%) spend their entire parliamentary career in the House. A small percentage (4.1%) goes from the Senate to the House. The remaining 13% moves from the House to the Senate during the course of their legislative tenure (with 1.1% eventually returning to the House). Most politicians (89.4%) have uninterrupted parliamentary careers, while 9.9% of them leave and re-enter once (multiple re-entries are extremely rare).

The average duration of a (complete) parliamentary career is 10.6 years or 2.5 legislatures, with a standard deviation of 7.6 years or 1.8 legislatures (the median duration is 9 years or 2 legislatures). Over a third of all politicians (36.2%) remain in Parliament for only one term, and only 11% have parliamentary careers that last longer than twenty years. Male legislators (who represent 90.2% of the sample) tend to have longer parliamentary tenure (10.8 years or 2.5 legislatures on average) than female legislators (whose parliamentary careers last 8.5 years or 2.1 legislatures on average).

The percentage of legislators who die in office is 4.8%, and 0.1% become President of the Italian Republic and/or Senator for life. Of the remaining legislators with complete parliamentary careers, 58.7% leave office without seeking re-election (while the other 41.3% fail to be re-elected). The proportion of politicians seeking re-election has declined steadily over time, from 91.4% at the end of the 1st Legislature (in 1953), and 85% in 1972, to a record low of 50.8% at the end of Italy's First Republic in 1994. During the Second Republic, this figure has oscillated between 66% and 78%. Re-election rates, on the other hand, have increased during the First Republic from 71.3% in 1953, to 86% in 1987, before declining to 60.5% in 1994. During the Second Republic, re-election rates have increased from 70.5% in 1996 to 77.1% in 2006, before dropping to 65% in the 2008 election. These patterns are illustrated in Figure 2.1.

The overall parliamentary turnover rate (measured by the percentage of new entrants) over the period 1953–2008 is equal to 40%.[1] In the 2nd Legislature (1953–8), it was equal to 37.6%, and it reached its minimum level of 26.3% in the 8th Legislature (1979–83). In the 12th Legislature (1994–6), which marked the beginning of Italy's Second Republic, the turnover rate spiked at 69.5%, and has been roughly constant at around 45–50% ever since (see Figure 2.1).

---

[1] Since 1948 was the beginning of the First Republic, the proportion of new entrants in the 1st Legislature was 100%.

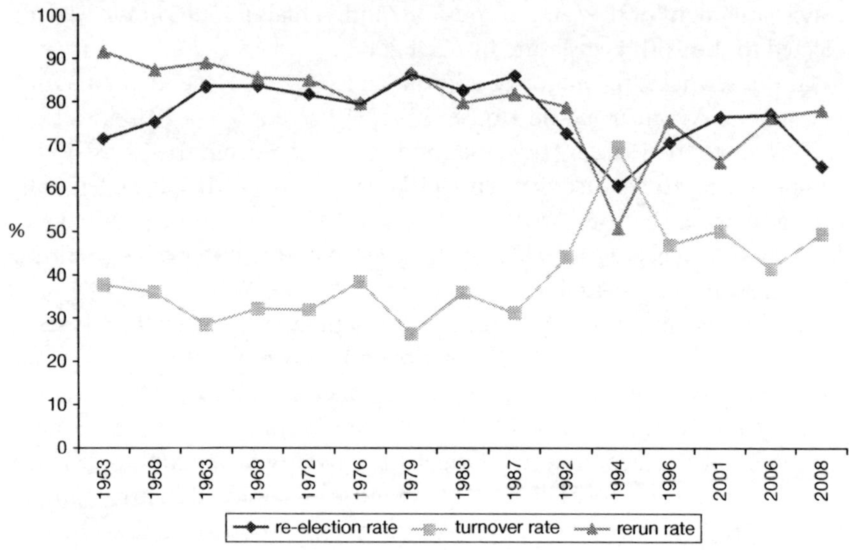

Fig. 2.1 Turnover in the Italian Parliament

To provide a term of comparison, Figure 2.2 illustrates the proportion of legislators seeking re-election at the end of a term, their re-election rates, and the overall turnover rate in the US House of Representatives during the period 1951–94 (US Congress 81–103).[2] Note that the duration of a House term in the USA is fixed and equal to two years. As we can see from comparing Figure 2.2 to Figure 2.1, both the proportion of legislators who seek re-election at the end of a term and their re-election rates are systematically lower in Italy than in the USA. As a result, turnover rates are significantly higher. Interestingly, however, the duration of (complete) congressional careers of US legislators is comparable to that of Italian legislators, and is equal to 10.4 years on average, with a standard deviation of 7.7 years and a median duration of 8 years. The percentage of US legislators who have congressional careers that last longer than twenty years (10%) is nearly the same as in Italy (11%). Differences across genders are also similar in the two countries, with male US legislators having longer congressional careers (10.5 years on average) than female US legislators (whose parliamentary careers last 7.9 years on average). However, in the

---

[2] The US data we use here are from the study of Diermeier, Keane, and Merlo (2004, 2005). Their dataset contains detailed information on all individuals who served in the US Congress between 1947 and 1994.

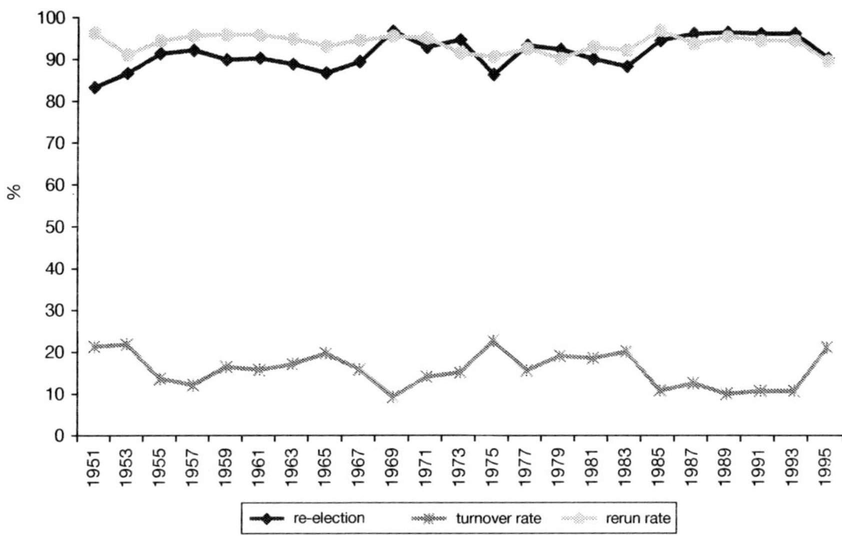

Fig. 2.2 Turnover in the US Congress

USA, the percentage of House members who remain in Congress for only one term (20%) is lower than the corresponding figure for Italy (36.2%).

Another interesting question we can address with our data is whether the characteristics of the Italian politicians who are elected to Parliament have changed over time. To assess the extent to which such change may have occurred, we focus on the composition of the cohorts of new House entrants in each of the fifteen legislatures from 1948 to 2006. Figure 2.3 plots the patterns in the average age at first entry, the percentage of new legislators who are women, and the percentage with a college degree ('Laurea') that we can observe from the data.

As we can see from this figure, the composition of the cohorts of new House entrants has changed greatly over the years along each of these three dimensions. The average age at entry, which was equal to 45.8 years at the beginning of the 1st Legislature, declined to 42.7 in the 7th Legislature (1976), and then started to rise monotonically to reach 50 in the 15th Legislature (2006). The percentage of women in the cohorts of new entrants has almost tripled between 1948 and 2006, from 7.2% to 20.8%. The smallest percentage, 1.7%, was in the cohort that first entered the House during the 5th Legislature (1968–72). The average level of education in the cohorts of new entrants has also changed dramatically over time. The percentage of new entrants with a college degree, which was equal to 91.4% at the beginning of the 1st Legislature, has been declining monotonically

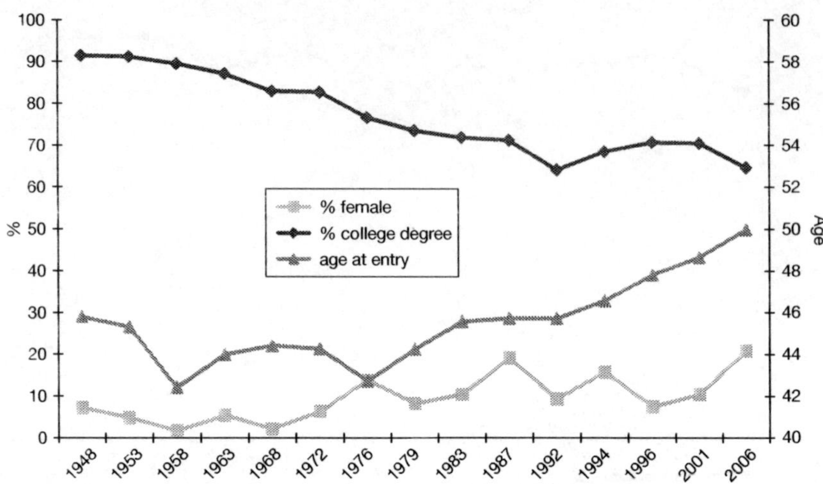

Fig. 2.3 Characteristics of Italian legislators by entry cohort

over time, and was equal to only 64.6% in the cohort that entered the House for the first time in 2006. Focusing on the differences between the cohorts of politicians who first entered Parliament during the First Republic (1948–92) and the Second Republic (1994–2006), we document that the average age at entry has increased from 44.7 to 48.1, the proportion of women has also increased from 8% to 13.9%, while the percentage of politicians with a college degree has declined from 80.5% to 68.5%. It is also interesting to point out that, while the average age at entry of both men and women has increased from the First to the Second Republic (from 45 to 48.3 years for men and from 41.1 to 46.5 years for women), and the percentage of legislators with a college degree is lower in the Second Republic than it was in the First Republic (when the percentages were 80.1% for men and 75.1% for women) for either gender, during the Second Republic a larger percentage of female legislators has a college degree (70.1%) than their male counterparts (68.2%).

To assess whether the trends we observe for Italy are indicative of a more general phenomenon, in Figure 2.4 we plot the patterns in the average age at first entry, the percentage of female new legislators, and the percentage of entering legislators with a college degree ('Bachelor') in the US data. With the exception of the proportion of women in the cohorts of new entrants to Congress, which displays a similar, increasing pattern as the one we observe for Italy, the trends we observe in the other two variables for the USA are quite different. In fact, the percentage of individuals first elected to the US

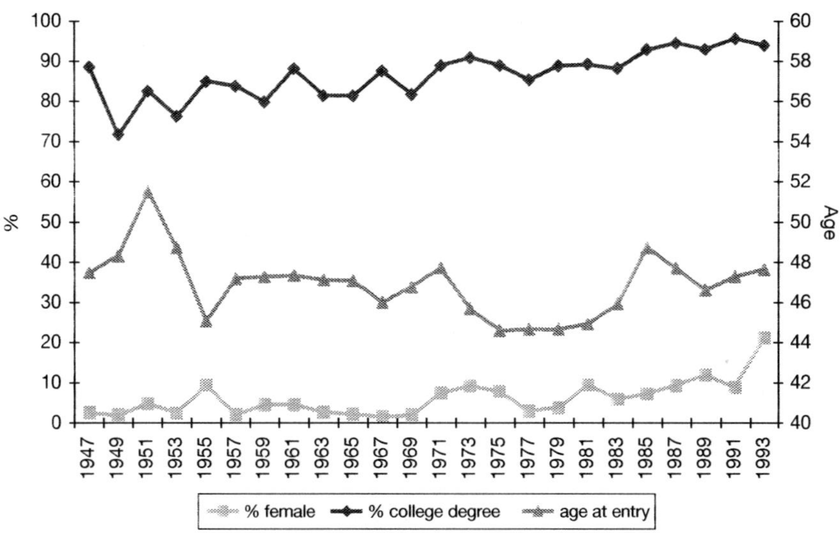

Fig. 2.4 Characteristics of US legislators by entry cohort

Congress who have a college degree steadily increases over time (from 88.5% in 1947 to 93.9% in 1993), while the average age at first entry remains fairly stable at around 47.5 years.

Turning attention to how the professional background of Italian legislators has evolved over time, we classify the last occupation held by an individual prior to entering Parliament into twelve broad categories, which correspond to their sector of employment and/or type of occupation. The categories we consider are: agriculture (e.g., farmers), education (e.g., teachers and professors), health care (e.g., doctors), industry workers (e.g., blue-collar and white-collar workers), industry managers (e.g., middle-management and executives), legal (e.g., lawyers and judges), lobbying (e.g., trade-union officials), media (e.g., journalists), military (e.g., professional soldiers), political (e.g., party officials), public (e.g., employees of public firms), and self-employment (e.g., consultants and small entrepreneurs). We also add an additional category to account for individuals who, prior to entering Parliament, were out of the labour force. Table 2.1 summarizes the distribution of occupations held by individuals prior to entering Parliament for each of the fifteen cohorts of new entrants, as well as for the overall sample, the samples of men and women, and the samples of politicians who entered Parliament during the First and the Second Republic.

Table 2.1 Distribution of pre-Parliament occupations of Italian legislators by entry cohort, 1948–2006 (%)

Cohort	Sector of employment												
	AGR	EDU	HTH	INDW	INDM	LEG	LOB	MED	MIL	POL	PUB	SE	OLF
1948	3.41	19.08	4.26	6.30	6.13	33.90	4.94	8.69	1.87	1.70	2.39	6.81	0.51
1953	4.60	13.39	3.35	6.28	7.11	29.71	10.46	8.79	1.26	3.35	5.86	5.44	0.42
1958	1.32	21.59	3.52	9.25	7.49	20.70	11.45	11.45	0.44	3.08	4.41	4.85	0.44
1963	3.03	19.91	6.49	10.82	5.19	20.78	10.82	9.52	0.87	3.03	3.03	6.49	0.00
1968	2.59	18.10	4.74	11.21	6.90	21.98	7.33	7.33	0.43	4.74	7.33	7.33	0.00
1972	0.00	12.92	4.78	14.83	8.13	21.53	6.70	11.48	0.96	4.31	7.18	7.18	0.00
1976	1.50	24.44	4.51	15.41	7.52	13.53	3.76	9.02	1.13	8.27	4.14	6.02	0.75
1979	1.60	20.32	4.28	14.97	9.09	14.44	3.21	11.76	0.00	6.95	5.88	7.49	0.00
1983	1.51	19.25	6.04	11.32	6.42	12.83	4.91	10.57	0.38	9.43	8.30	9.06	0.00
1987	0.43	28.57	5.63	6.06	5.63	12.12	2.60	11.69	0.87	10.39	8.66	5.63	1.73
1992	0.70	19.72	5.28	7.39	14.08	11.62	3.87	8.45	0.35	8.10	9.51	10.56	0.35
1994	2.41	21.05	8.55	4.82	18.64	15.35	1.75	7.46	0.22	4.82	7.02	7.02	0.88
1996	0.32	20.45	7.47	6.17	18.51	17.21	1.95	5.19	0.97	5.84	4.22	8.77	2.92
2001	0.34	15.36	8.53	5.46	20.82	15.02	0.68	7.51	0.68	7.85	5.80	9.22	2.73
2006	0.33	16.56	6.62	4.97	18.21	10.60	2.98	8.94	0.00	15.23	5.96	8.28	1.32
Sample													
All	1.74	19.41	5.74	8.36	11.12	18.95	4.79	8.92	0.76	6.21	5.74	7.39	0.86
Men	1.85	17.49	5.90	8.03	11.62	20.42	5.03	8.8	0.85	5.69	5.87	7.69	0.77
Women	0.72	37.32	4.31	11.48	6.46	5.26	2.63	10.05	0.00	11.00	4.55	4.55	1.67
1st Rep	2.06	19.74	4.77	9.77	7.51	20.93	6.15	9.67	0.91	5.38	5.68	7.03	0.41
2nd Rep	1.03	18.69	7.87	5.30	18.98	14.64	1.84	7.28	0.44	8.02	5.89	8.17	1.84

Note: AGR = agriculture, EDU = education, HTH = health care, INDW = industry workers, INDM = industry managers, LEG = legal, LOB = lobbying, MED = media, MIL = military, POL = political, PUB = public, SE = self-employment, OLF = out of the labour force.

Several interesting patterns emerge from the table. The percentage of new entrants coming from the legal sector has declined steadily, from 33.9% in the 1st Legislature to 10.6% in the cohort entering the 15th Legislature. While always relatively small, the proportion of new entrants coming from the agriculture sector has also declined. On the contrary, the percentage of newly elected legislators with prior work experience in the industrial sector (regardless of the type of job) has increased from 12.4% in the 1st Legislature to 26.3% in the 14th Legislature (2001–6). At the same time, the composition of the group of new entrants coming from the industrial sector has also changed over time, as the percentage of workers decreased from 6.3% to 4.9% while that of managers increased from 6.1% to 18.2% between Legislatures I and XV. The percentage of new entrants with a background in the political sector and that of new entrants with a background in the public sector have also grown from 1.7% and 2.4% in the 1st Legislature to 15.2% and 5.9% in the 15th Legislature, respectively, although their patterns have been non-monotonic. Another variable that displays an interesting non-monotonic pattern is the percentage of entering legislators coming from trade unions (the lobbying sector), which more than doubled (from about 5% to 11%) over the course of the first four legislatures, but then dropped in the early 1970s and has been fluctuating around 3% since then. On the other hand, the relative prevalence of other occupations within each cohort of new legislators (as, for example, the proportion of people working in the media, the education, and the health-care sector, as well as the self-employed), has remained fairly stable over time.

Overall, looking at the extent to which the composition of Parliament has changed between the First and the Second Republics with respect to the professional background of its members, we observe the following percentage changes (averaged over all the cohorts of new entrants in each of the two Republics): agriculture −1, education −1.1, health care +3.1, industrial workers −4.5, industrial managers +11.5, legal −6.3, lobbying −4.3, media −2.4, military −0.5, political +2.6, public +0.2, self-employment +1.1, and out of the labour force +1.4 percentage points. It is also interesting to note that 37.3% of all female legislators come from the education sector (compared to only 17.5% of all male legislators), only 5.3% from the legal sector (the corresponding figure for men is 20.4%), and, although the overall percentages of female and male legislators coming from the industrial sector are comparable (19.7% for men and 17.9% for women), relatively more female legislators hold lower-level (blue-collar and white-collar) jobs prior to entering Parliament (11.5%) than male legislators (8%), while the opposite is true with respect to managerial occupations

(6.5% for women and 11.6% for men). These patterns of differences in the occupational background of male and female legislators are similar in the First and Second Republics.

Some peculiar features of the Italian labour market, in particular the presence of a very large public sector and professional party officials who hold regular, paid full-time jobs within various political organizations, make it hard to compare the professional background of Italian and US legislators. Nevertheless, Table 2.2 reports the percentages of individuals who worked in the legal and the business sector prior to entering the US Congress for each of the twenty-four cohorts of new entrants over the period 1947–94.

As we can see from this table, in spite of the large differences in the levels, the US data also display a sharply declining trend in the proportion of legislators coming from the legal sector, which is similar to the one we observe in the Italian data. On the other hand, the percentage of newly elected legislators with prior work experience in the business sector is quite different in Italy and the USA, both in levels and with respect to its trend

Table 2.2 Distribution of occupations of US legislators by entry cohort, 1947–2003 (%)

	Sector of employment			
Cohort	Business	Education	Legal	Other
1947	17.95	6.41	62.82	12.82
1949	20.20	7.07	51.52	21.21
1951	19.05	4.76	53.97	22.22
1953	20.24	3.57	51.19	25.00
1955	13.21	9.43	54.72	22.64
1957	12.24	4.08	55.10	28.57
1959	21.35	4.49	48.31	25.84
1961	20.90	5.97	52.24	20.90
1963	17.33	2.67	53.33	26.67
1965	19.78	7.69	46.15	26.37
1967	14.06	7.81	42.19	35.94
1969	12.24	12.24	44.90	30.61
1971	18.52	12.96	42.59	25.93
1973	19.74	11.84	42.11	26.32
1975	24.44	13.33	41.11	21.11
1977	27.94	7.35	44.12	20.59
1979	25.00	12.50	31.25	31.25
1981	33.78	8.11	36.49	21.62
1983	5.95	1.19	16.67	76.19
1985	14.29	9.52	30.95	45.24
1987	7.41	7.41	33.33	51.85
1989	19.05	19.05	30.95	30.95
1991	22.22	11.11	28.89	37.78
1993	16.67	14.04	39.47	29.82

over time. In fact, in the USA this figure has remained fairly stable over the years, ranging between 15% and 20%.

In addition to the last occupation held prior to being elected to the Italian Parliament, which we observe for 4,317 individuals out of the 4,465 legislators elected to the House between 1947 and 2007, for a representative sample of 860 individuals (768 men and 92 women) our dataset also contains information on their occupation after leaving Parliament. The average age at departure in the sample is equal to 56 years, which is the same as the average age at departure in the population of legislators with complete parliamentary histories. The percentage of people in the sample who retire at the end of their parliamentary career is 5.6%, while 2.7% end up in jail. Using the same classification as before, the distribution of post-Parliament occupations for the remaining individuals in the samples is summarized in Table 2.3, for the overall sample as well as for the samples of men and women. When compared with the distributions of pre-Parliament occupations contained in Table 2.1, the figures reported in Table 2.3 suggest a dramatic shift away from most private-sector occupations and into the political sector, both in the overall sample and for each gender.

To explore this issue further, Table 2.4 reports the pre-Parliament to post-Parliament occupation transition matrix for the sample of individuals for whom we observe both occupations.[3] There are three quantitatively most striking phenomena that emerge from this table.

First, most legislators (57.4%) do not return to the occupation they had before entering Parliament at the end of their parliamentary tenure. Second, the category of people who are least likely to return to their previous

Table 2.3 Distribution of occupations of a sample of former Italian legislators at exit (%)

Sample	Sector of employment											
	AGR	EDU	HTH	INDW	INDM	LEG	LOB	MED	MIL	POL	PUB	SE
All	1.01	11.53	3.04	0.89	11.28	8.49	2.03	8.11	0.25	44.23	5.83	3.30
Men	1.00	11.25	3.28	1.00	11.25	9.54	1.85	8.26	0.28	43.16	5.84	3.28
Women	1.15	13.79	1.15	0.00	11.49	0.00	3.45	6.90	0.00	52.87	5.75	3.45

Note: AGR = agriculture, EDU = education, HTH = health care, INDW = industry workers, INDM = industry managers, LEG = legal, LOB = lobbying, MED = media, MIL = military, POL = political, PUB = public, SE = self-employment.

[3] Since the agriculture sector and the military account for less than 1% of the observations, we drop them from Table 2.4. Also, the number of observations for former female legislators is too small to produce separate transition matrices for each gender that would have statistical meaning.

Table 2.4 Pre- to post-Parliament occupation transition matrix of Italian legislators (%)

Post Pre	EDU	HTH	INDW	INDM	LEG	LOB	MED	POL	PUB	SE
EDU	43.26	0.00	0.00	5.08	0.56	1.69	5.06	34.27	8.47	1.13
HTH	7.55	43.40	0.00	0.00	0.00	0.00	1.89	45.28	0.00	1.89
INDW	2.13	0.00	4.26	17.02	0.00	10.64	2.13	61.70	0.00	2.13
INDM	0.00	0.00	1.25	46.25	0.00	2.50	2.50	37.50	2.50	5.00
LEG	5.26	0.00	0.00	7.02	53.51	0.00	0.88	28.07	4.39	0.88
LOB	0.00	0.00	0.00	12.50	0.00	20.83	0.00	62.50	4.17	0.00
MED	2.25	0.00	0.00	5.62	0.00	0.00	46.07	43.82	1.12	1.12
POL	0.00	0.00	3.23	6.45	0.00	0.00	8.06	74.19	4.84	3.23
PUB	0.00	0.00	0.00	7.84	1.96	0.00	3.92	54.9	27.45	3.92
SE	1.89	0.00	1.89	13.21	3.77	0.00	1.89	49.06	5.66	22.64

Note: EDU = education, HTH = health care, INDW = industry workers, INDM = industry managers, LEG = legal, LOB = lobbying, MED = media, POL = political, PUB = public, SE = self-employment, OLF = out of the labour force.

occupation after leaving Parliament (4.3%) is that of workers in the industry sector. In fact, 17% of them do return to the industry sector, but in managerial occupations. Third, politics appears to be an absorbing state. A large proportion of individuals who were working in other sectors prior to entering Parliament end up taking another political job after leaving Parliament. This percentage varies from 28.1% for individuals whose pre-Parliament occupation was in the legal sector, to 37.5% for people with managerial occupations in the industry sector, to 49.1% for people coming from self-employment, to 54.9% for people coming from the public sector, to 61.2% for people with a background as regular employees in the industrial sector. At the same time, 74.2% of the individuals who prior to entering Parliament were already in the political sector continue their post-Parliament career in that sector, and only 21% switch to the private sector (with the remaining 4.8% taking a job in the public sector). Of all the former members of Parliament who remain in politics, 21.5% are elected or appointed to a public office at the local (that is, city or province) level, 14.3% at the regional level, and 10.6% at the national level. The remaining 53.6% take a position within a party organization.

Interestingly, although as we pointed out before, the Italian and US data on occupations are not directly comparable, in the USA we observe the exact opposite phenomenon. Namely, a much larger percentage of former members of Congress who do not retire after leaving have post-congressional careers in the private sector (59.8%) rather than taking another political job (40.2%). The percentage of US legislators who retire after leaving Congress is also higher (13%) than the corresponding figure for their Italian counterparts, although their average age at exit is the same (56 years).

2.2. Incomes

In Italy, the (before-tax) real annual parliamentary wage (*indennità parla-mentare*) in 2005 euros increased from 10,712 euros in 1948 to 137,691 euros in 2006 (an overall growth of 1,185.4%), at an average annual growth rate of 9.9% (Figure 2.5). In the USA, the (before-tax) real annual congressional wage in 2005 dollars increased from $101,297 in 1948 to $160,038 in 2006 (an overall growth of 58%), at an average annual growth rate of 1.5% (Figure 2.6). Over the same period of time, Italy's real per-capita GDP grew 449.5%, at an average annual growth rate of 3.2%, and the US real per-capita GDP grew 241.7%, at an average annual growth rate of 2.1%.

As we can see from Figures 2.5 and 2.6, both countries experienced a period of sharp, sustained growth in the real wage of its legislators in the 1960s, followed by a significant drop during the 1970s (mainly because of the high inflation during that decade). However, while in the USA the real congressional wage has remained essentially constant since 1980, the real parliamentary wage in Italy has been growing at an average annual rate of 3.9% since 1980.[4]

To facilitate further comparisons between the two countries, in Figure 2.7 we plot the difference between the real annual wage of Italian and US

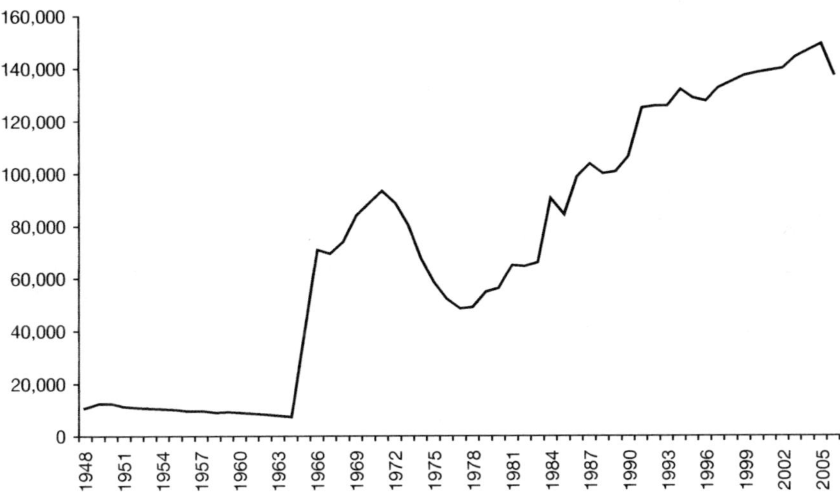

Fig. 2.5 Real annual parliamentary wage in Italy (2005 euros)

[4] Note that in both countries, the parliamentary or congressional wage is determined by the legislature itself, which every year votes on its own compensation.

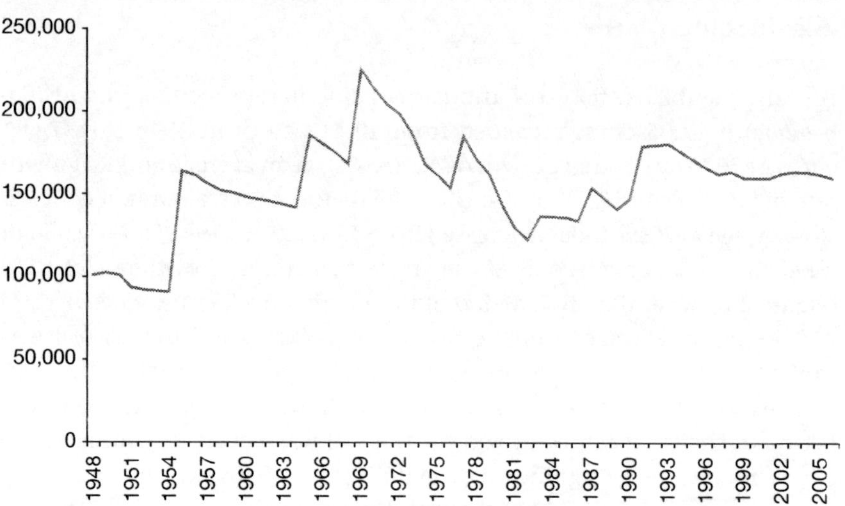

Fig. 2.6 Real annual congressional wage in the USA (2005 $US)

legislators in 2005 euros (calculated after converting 2005 dollars into 2005 euros using the 2005 average real exchange rate of 0.7 euros per dollar). As we can see from this figure, during the First Republic Italian legislators were underpaid relative to their US counterparts until the late 1980s, although the gap was closing down throughout the 1980s. Since 1994, however— that is, since the beginning of the Second Republic—we observe the

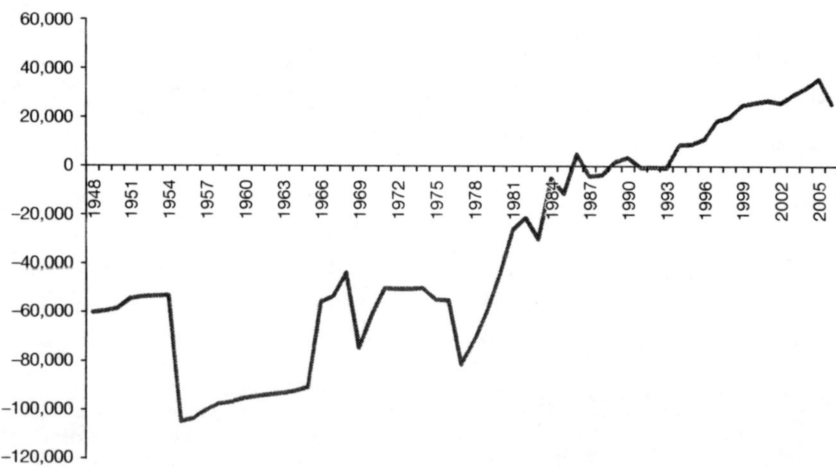

Fig. 2.7 Difference in real annual wage of Italian and US legislators (2005 euros)

opposite phenomenon. The real annual wage of the members of the Italian Parliament exceeds that of the members of the US Congress, and the gap increased during the late 1990s and early 2000s.

There are several important considerations that are relevant for the interpretation of the evidence presented in Figures 2.5–2.7. While 1948 marks the dawn of the Italian Republic and the election of its first Parliament, by that time the US political system was already a well-established democracy with a stable institutional structure. In particular, while politics was for all practical purposes an employment sector in the USA, and being a member of Congress was a full-time job, the same was not true in Italy. Most importantly, unlike US legislators, Italian legislators were allowed to keep their regular jobs outside Parliament (except for employment in other public or private institutions controlled by the government, either directly or indirectly, or other full-time salaried occupations),[5] in part so as not to cause any economic harm to them because of the relatively low wage they were receiving as elected members of Parliament. After 1965, however, the economic treatment of Italian legislators started to improve dramatically, not only relative to their US counterparts, but also relative to other private-sector occupations in Italy, thus making the case for allowing legislators to earn additional income from activities outside Parliament practically moot. In fact, as we can see from Figure 2.8, by 1985 the annual real parliamentary wage of an Italian legislator (84,229 euros) was 4.2 times larger than the average real annual earnings of an Italian private-sector worker (20,268 euros).[6]

In 2004, at 146,533 euros, it was 6.5 times the average real annual earnings of a private-sector worker (22,712 euros).[7] Nevertheless, Italian legislators can still supplement their parliamentary wage with additional income from extra-parliamentary activities (which is not allowed in the USA, except for a relatively small allowance).[8]

---

[5] Exclusion restrictions for employment of members of Parliament are regulated by the Italian Law number 60 of 13 Feb. 1953.

[6] The data on annual earnings in the private sector by type of occupation come from the administrative payroll records of INPS, the Italian Social Security Administration. These data are available only for the period 1985–2004. Average annual earnings are calculated for the samples of full-time workers in each occupation.

[7] All real incomes are in 2005 euros.

[8] In addition, Italian legislators also receive a number of allowances (e.g., *per-diem* reimbursements for each day they are in Parliament and lump-sum monthly payments for expenses related to their interaction with the voters, among others). Since these allowances are not considered part of their income, we do not include them in our analysis. See, however, Rizzo and Stella (2007).

Fig. 2.8 Average annual real earnings, 1985–2004 (euros)

Since 1982, the Italian law has required all elected officials to disclose their annual tax returns, which we collected as part of our data.[9] Since tax returns refer to incomes earned in the previous calendar year, our dataset contains information on the total (reported) income of all House legislators between 1981 and 2006. In addition, for 2,009 individuals who were first elected to the House on or after 1983, we observed their income in the year before they enter Parliament. We are, therefore, in a unique position to address a number of questions that pertain to the extra-parliamentary income of legislators, both prior to and during their tenure in Parliament.[10]

Figures 2.9 and 2.10 summarize the distribution of the real annual incomes (in 2005 euros) prior to entering Parliament for each cohort of new entrants in Legislatures IX–XV, both in levels (Figure 2.9) and as a percentage of the parliamentary wage (Figure 2.10).

To offer a term of comparison, Figure 2.11 summarizes the evolution of the distribution of the real annual earnings of all Italian salaried workers in the private sector (which includes blue-collar workers, white-collar workers,

[9] Italian Law number 441 of 5 July 1982.

[10] For a small sample of 108 individuals who entered the Italian Parliament after 1983, left, and then re-entered before 2006, we also observed their income after their first spell in Parliament.

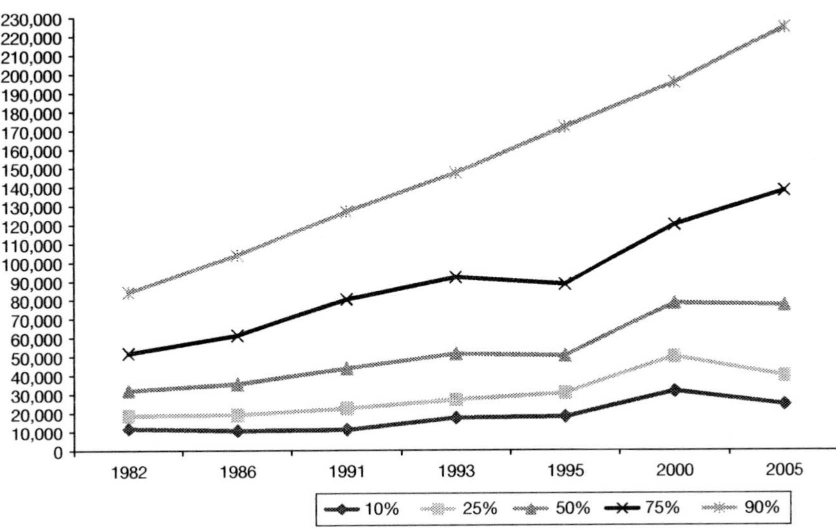

Fig. 2.9 Income distribution before entry (2005 euros)

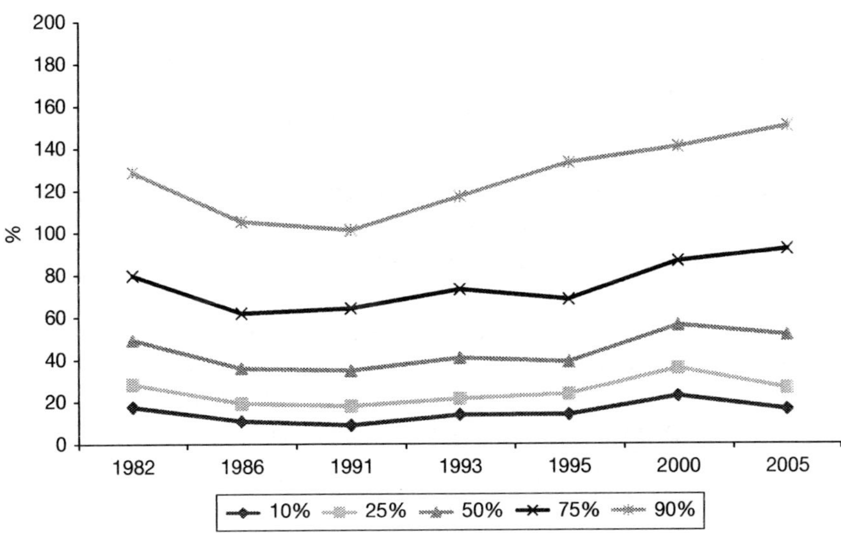

Fig. 2.10 Income distribution before entry as a percentage of the parliamentary wage

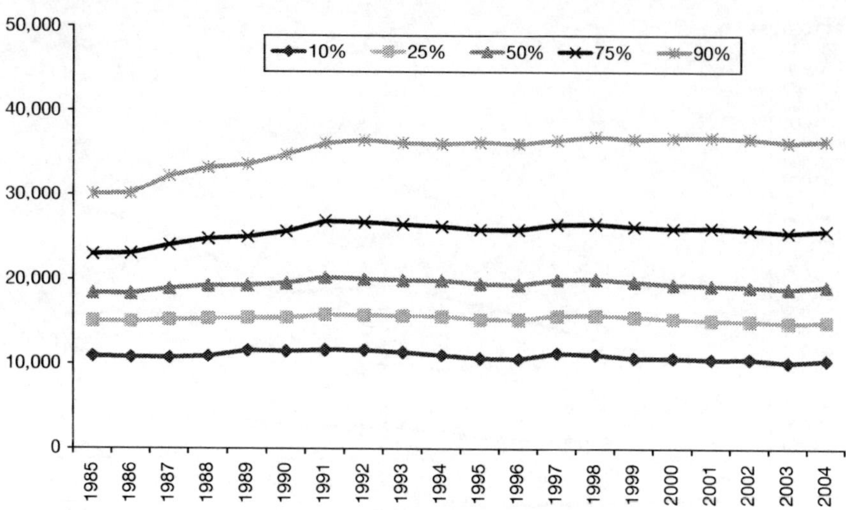

Fig. 2.11 Income distribution of private-sector workers (2005 euros)

and managers), between 1985 and 2004 (also in 2005 euros). Several interesting observations emerge from these figures. First, income inequality among the individuals who are elected to Parliament (as measured either by the distance between the 75th and the 25th percentile or the ratio of the 90th to the 10th percentile) has increased steadily over time (see Figure 2.9).

This phenomenon is due to the combination of growth in the median and the upper quantiles of the income distribution of newly elected legislators (especially in the 90th percentile) and the relative stagnation of the lower quantiles of the distribution. Given that the earnings distribution of workers in the private sector has remained fairly stable over time (see Figure 2.11), this suggests that a majority of the newly elected legislators in more recent cohorts is drawn from a different segment of the population with respect to their income. This phenomenon has been particularly evident since the beginning of the Second Republic in 1994. In fact, prior to 1994, between 10% and 25% of the newly elected members of Parliament had annual incomes that were less than or equal to the median income of individuals employed in the private sector. Since 1994, on the other hand, over 75% of newly elected members of Parliament have had pre-Parliament incomes that are higher than the annual incomes of 90% of the population of private-sector workers. A second interesting observation that emerges from Figure 2.10 is that, for all entering cohorts for which we have income data, between 75% and 90% of the newly elected legislators have a pre-Parliament annual income that is lower than the parliamentary wage.

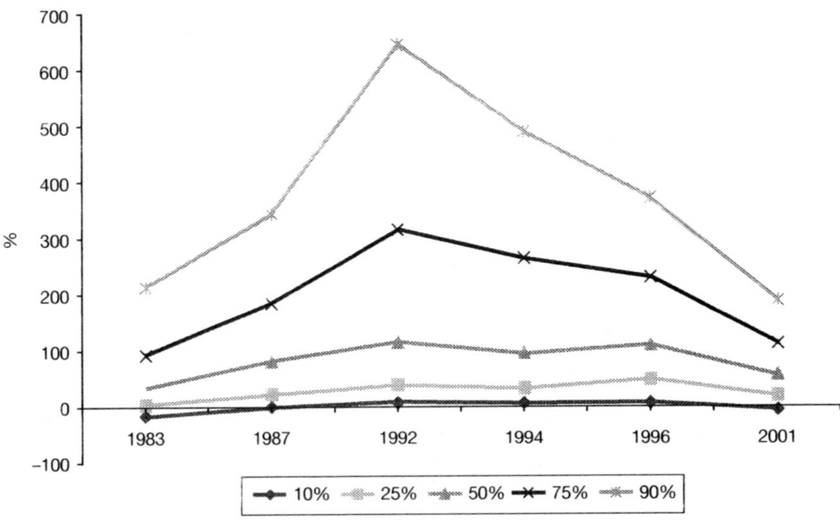

Fig. 2.12 Distribution of real income growth rates on entry

This implies that, even if they were to stop engaging in any income-earning activity outside Parliament and simply earn the parliamentary wage after being elected, entering Parliament would entail a substantial pecuniary gain for a large majority of legislators. As we have pointed out before, however, legislators can also earn additional income from extra-parliamentary activities.

To explore this issue further, Figure 2.12 summarizes the distribution of income growth rates upon entering Parliament, and Figure 2.13 plots the percentage of new entrants whose total real annual income decreased upon entry, for each cohort of new entrants in Legislatures IX–XIV.[11]

As we can see from these figures, entering Parliament is a lucrative activity for the vast majority of politicians. The annual real income of over a quarter of all legislators more than doubles upon entering Parliament, and only about 10% of all legislators experience a drop in their real annual income after being elected. Overall, the median increase in their real annual income following election to the House is 77.8%. The median increase was equal to 32.8% in 1983, increased to 109.2% in 1996, and declined to 56.2% in 2001.

---

[11] Calculation of the growth rate requires observations on the annual income of a politician in the two consecutive years before and after entering Parliament. Individuals who do not report any income prior to entering Parliament and individuals who were elected in 2006 (for whom we observe only their 2005 income) are excluded from these calculations.

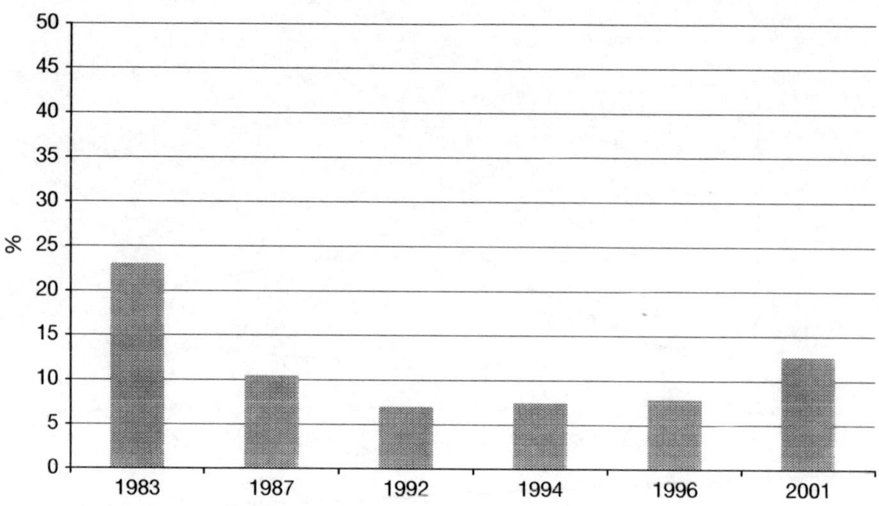

Fig. 2.13 Percentage of legislators with real income losses on entry

Figures 2.14 and 2.15 summarize the distribution of the real annual income of legislators in excess of their parliamentary wage (in 2005 euros) for each year between 1981 and 2005 and for all legislators who are in Parliament the entire year, both in levels (Figure 2.14) and as a percentage of their total annual income (Figure 2.15). For each year, Figure 2.16 plots the percentage of legislators who report incomes in excess of their parliamentary wage.

The most striking feature that emerges from Figures 2.14 and 2.15 is a clear 'regime shift' between the First and the Second Republics.[12] The distribution of real annual additional income reported by legislators is fairly stable and homogeneous until the end of the First Republic, both in levels and as a percentage of total income. After 1994, on the other hand, there is a sharp increase in the additional income reported by over a quarter of the

[12] It is important to point out that this regime shift is not an artefact of the change in the law pertaining to the reporting of taxable income by Italian legislators that occurred in 1995. Prior to 1995, legislators had to include in their tax return only 82% of their annual parliamentary wage net of the standard deductions (*contribute previdenziali*). Since 1995, on the other hand, they have to report their total parliamentary wage, either net or gross depending on the tax form they file, which is determined by whether or not they have additional income (typically related to self-employment or entrepreneurial activities, *attività d'impresa*) to report. We are extremely grateful to Vincenzo Busa of the *Agenzia delle Entrate* (the Italian IRS) for clarifying these critical aspects of the Italian fiscal law, which we used in order to measure legislators' annual income in excess of their parliamentary wage from the amounts reported in their tax returns.

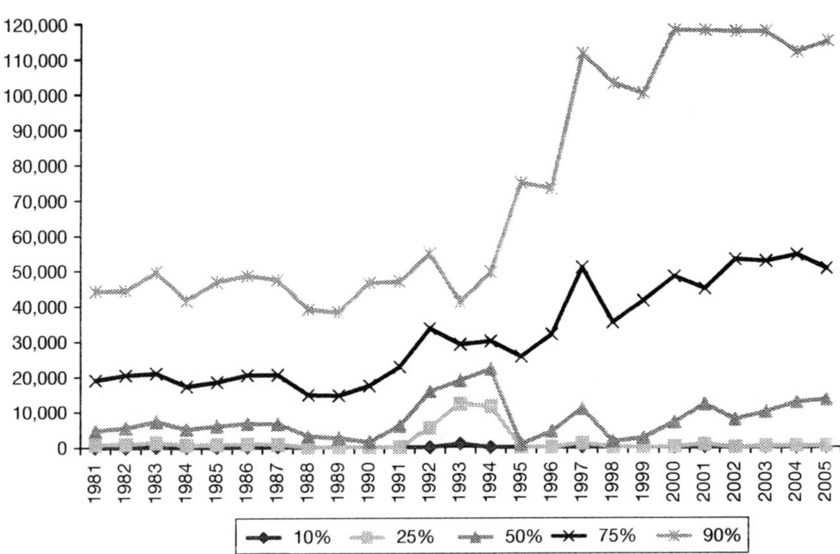

Fig. 2.14 Distribution of additional income (2005 euros)

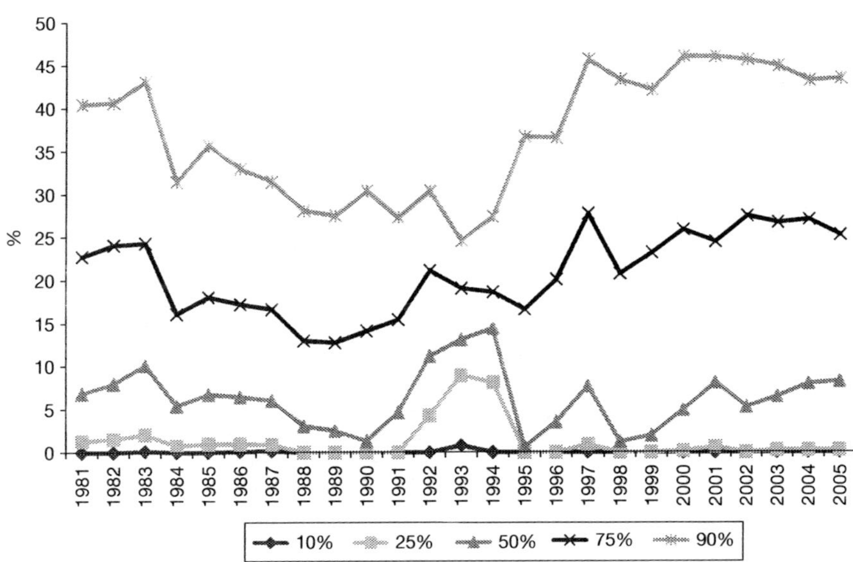

Fig. 2.15 Distribution of additional income as a percentage of total (2005 euros)

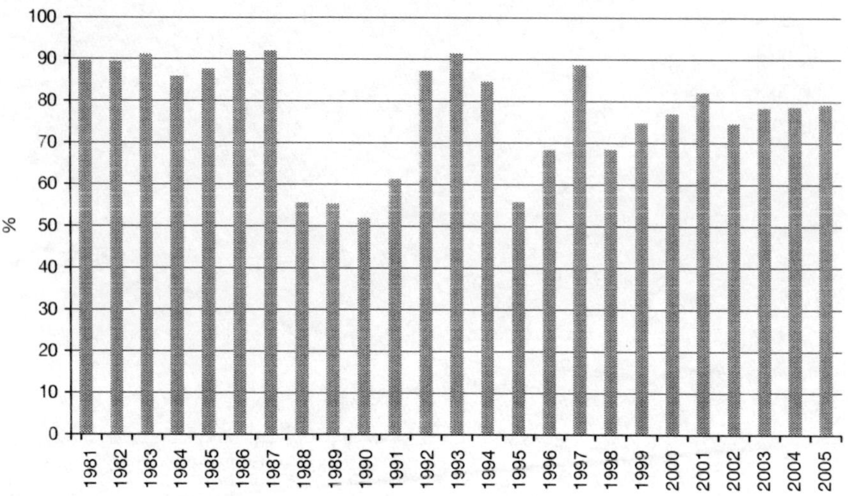

Fig. 2.16 Percentage of legislators reporting additional income

population of legislators. Although the increase is most noticeable in levels, it is also evident in the percentage of total annual income coming from sources other than the parliamentary wage. At the same time, the proportion of legislators reporting additional incomes over and above their parliamentary wage has remained fairly stable over time and, if anything, has decreased. The overall result is a dramatic increase in income inequality among legislators.

To provide once again a term of comparison, Figure 2.17 summarizes the distribution of the real annual earnings of Italian managers in the private sector between 1985 and 2004 (in 2005 euros).

When we compare this figure with Figure 2.14, we see that, until 1994, almost all legislators earned an additional annual income that was lower than the annual earnings of 75% of the managers. Since the late 1990s, on the other hand, between 10% and 25% of the legislators have had annual income in addition to their parliamentary wage that exceeds the total annual earnings of 50% of the managers.

We began this chapter by documenting the dramatic increase in the real parliamentary wage of Italian legislators over time. We conclude it by documenting another stark phenomenon about the growth in their real total income. Figure 2.18 plots the average real total annual income of elected members of the Italian Parliament between 1985 and 2004, together with their parliamentary wage and the average real annual earnings of Italian managers over the same period of time.

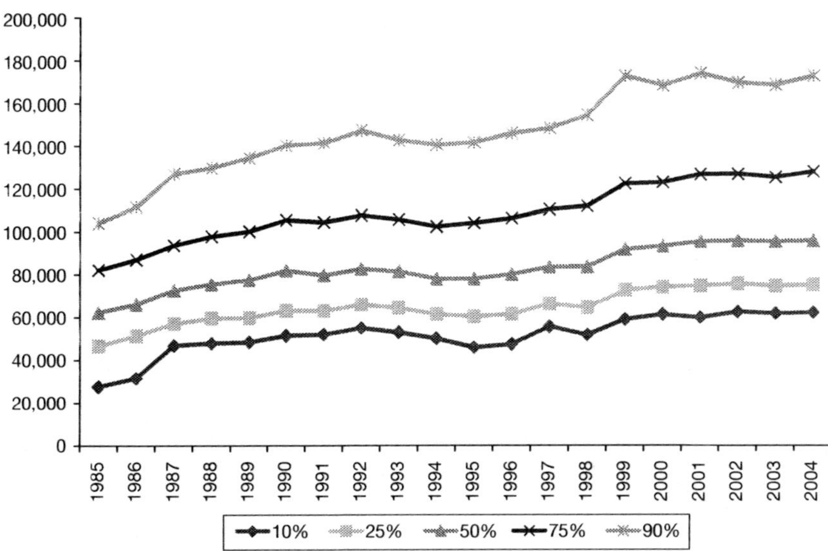

Fig. 2.17 Income distribution of managers (2005 euros)

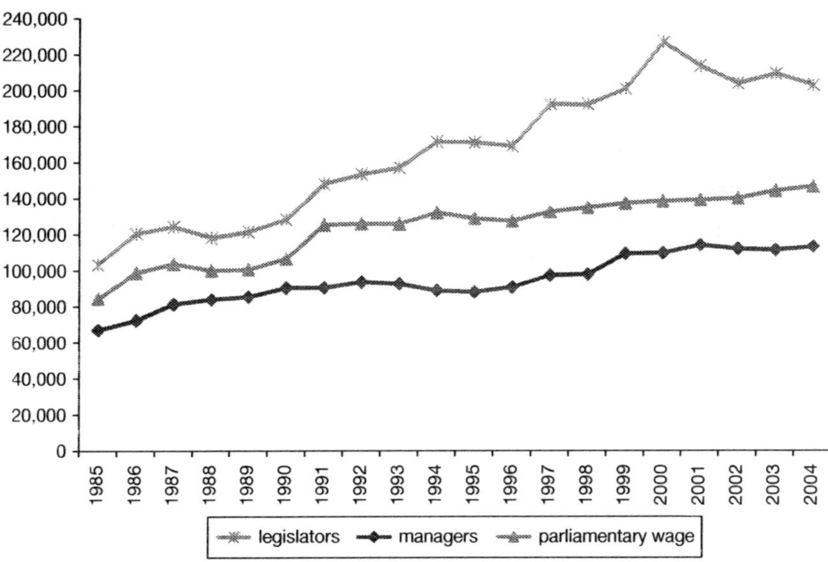

Fig. 2.18 Average annual real income of legislators (2005 euros)

Average real annual earning of managers in the private sector increased 69.2% between 1985 and 2004 at an average annual growth rate of 2.9%. During the same period, the average real total annual income of legislators grew 96.7% at an average annual growth rate of 3.8%. In 2004, an Italian legislator earned an annual parliamentary wage of 146,533 euros, plus another 56,335 euros on average from additional sources, for a total annual real income that was 1.8 times larger than the average annual real earnings of an Italian manager (113,087 euros).

2.3. Outcomes

In Sections 2.1 and 2.2, we have documented several aspects related to a number of characteristics of Italian legislators (including their income) and how they have evolved over time. In this section, we turn our attention to assessing their performance while in office. While this is an admittedly difficult task, since it is not at all clear how to measure the 'productivity' of a politician, our dataset contains two variables that can at least shed some light on their behaviour while in Parliament: their involvement in scandals and their attendance at roll-call voting sessions. Unfortunately, neither one of these measures is available for the entire time period we cover in our study, although for different reasons. To measure the involvement of a politician in a scandal, we use the data collected by Golden (2007), which record all the requests put forward by the Italian judiciary to remove parliamentary immunity from a legislator in order to bring a prosecution. These data are available only for the period 1948–94 (that is, only during the First Republic), since a constitutional amendment in November 1993 eliminated the possibility of such requests from the judiciary. To measure the extent to which politicians attend legislative sessions, we use the official record of participation in electronic voting sessions, which was introduced at the beginning of the 8th Legislature.[13] Hence, our dataset contains information on legislators' attendance at roll-call voting sessions for Legislatures VIII–XV (that is, during the period 1979–2008).[14]

---

[13] Records are released at the end of each legislature for the entire duration of the parliamentary term (i.e., only the overall attendance rates during a legislature are available for each elected representative, not their annual records).

[14] In a recent paper, in addition to the attendance at voting sessions in Legislatures XIII and XIV, Gagliarducci, Nannicini, and Naticchioni (2008) also analyse data on the number of major bills sponsored by each MP in these two legislatures as another possible measure of the productivity of Italian MPs.

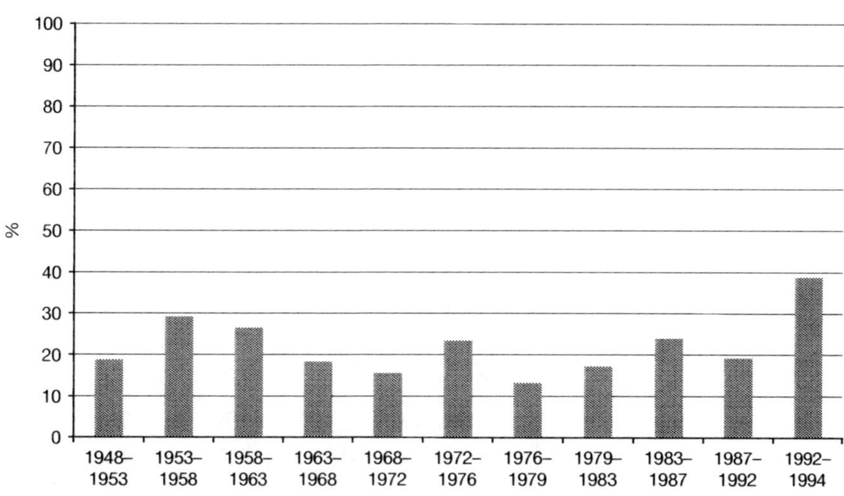

Fig. 2.19 Scandal rates in the Italian Parliament by legislature

Figure 2.19 plots the percentage of legislators involved in scandals during each of the eleven legislatures of Italy's First Republic. The overall rate is 22.1% and is higher among male legislators (22.6%) than female legislators (14.5%). This rate was fairly stable throughout the First Republic except for a sharp increase during the 11th Legislature (38.7%) because of the coordinated effort by the Italian judiciary we described in Chapter 1 ('Clean Hands') that led to the removal of a large number of legislators from office, many of whom were then prosecuted and in some cases went to jail. It is also interesting to point out that in the early legislatures (I–IV) most of the requests for indictment of MPs were for war crimes or crimes against the Republic.

Figure 2.20 plots the average attendance rates of legislators in each of the Legislatures VIII–XV. In Figure 2.21, we report the average overall attendance rates during Legislatures VIII–XV for each cohort of legislators in office during this period of time (where a cohort is defined by the legislature of first entry).

As we can see from these figures, legislators' attendance rates (measured by the percentage of roll-call votes each politician participates in during a legislature) decreased during the First Republic (from an average of 68% in the 8th Legislature to 60% in the 11th Legislature), and increased during the Second Republic (from an average of 62% in the 12th Legislature to 81% in the 15th Legislature). Interestingly, attendance rates decrease with seniority (or increase with the cohort of entry), with politicians elected

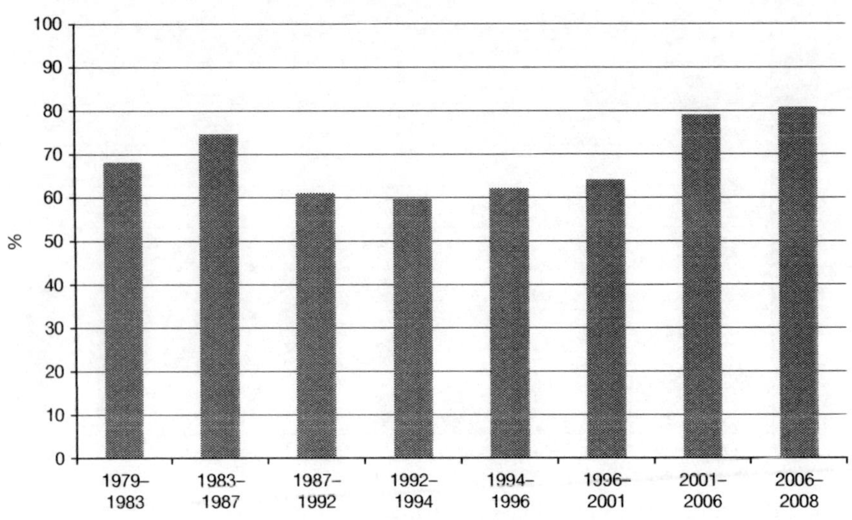

Fig. 2.20 Attendance rates in the Italian Parliament by legislature

relatively more recently participating more than legislators from earlier vintages. On average, legislators who first entered the House prior to the 12th Legislature (that is, were first elected during the First Republic) have lower attendance rates during their entire parliamentary tenure (65%) than legislators who first entered the House on or after the 12th Legislature

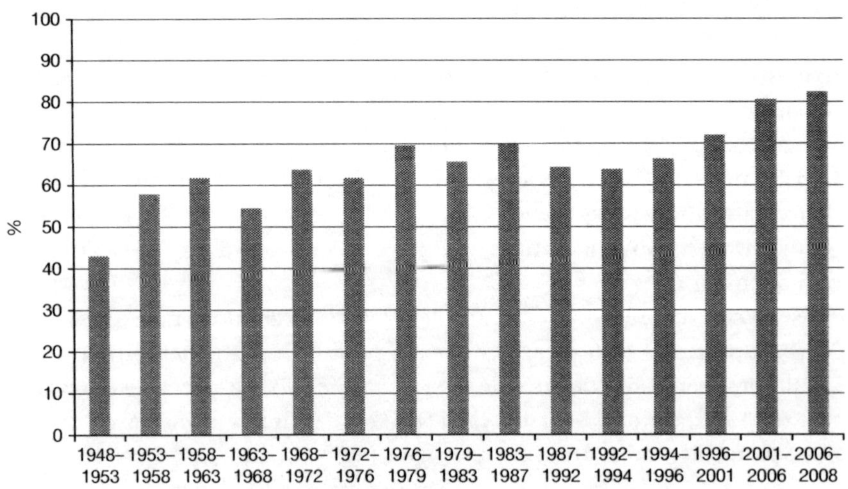

Fig. 2.21 Attendance rates in the Italian Parliament by cohort

(whose average attendance rate is equal to 73%). Mean attendance rates are also higher among female legislators (74%) than male legislators (68%).

2.4. Parties

Up to this point, our analysis has focused on individual legislators. As we discussed at length in Chapter 1, however, political parties play a critical role in the selection of legislators and their political careers. In this section, we therefore change the unit of analysis from the individual to the party, and revisit some of the issues we investigated above. In particular, for each of the two periods corresponding to the First and the Second Republics, we indentify seven parties (or groups of parties) that account for the vast majority of all legislators during that period. The seven parties of the First Republic are: *Democrazia Cristiana (DC)*, *Movimento Sociale Italiano (MSI)*, *Partito Comunista Italiano (PCI)*, *Partito Liberale Italiano (PLI)*, *Partito Repubblicano Italiano (PRI)*, *Partito Socialista Italiano (PSI)*, and *Partito Social-Democratico Italiano (PSDI)*. The seven parties (or groups of parties) of the Second Republic are: *Alleanza Nazionale (AN)*, *Centro Cristiano Democratico-Cristiani Democratici Uniti-Unione dei Democratici Cristiani (CCD)*, *Forza Italia (FI)*, *Lega Nord (LN)*, *Partito Democratico della Sinistra (PDS)*, *Rifondazione Comunista (RC)*, and *Ulivo-Margherita-Democratici di Sinistra (ULIVO)*.[15]

We begin by documenting differences and similarities among parties with respect to the demographic characteristics of their legislators. For each party, Figure 2.22 plots the average age at entry of its legislators, and Figure 2.23 the percentages of female legislators and of legislators with a college degree. Among the parties of the First Republic, *PCI* stands out as the party with the youngest legislators (with a 43.6 average age at entry), the largest proportion of female legislators (15%), and the smallest percentage of legislators who have a college degree (64.8%). Among the parties of the Second Republic, *LN* has legislators with the smallest average age at entry (41.6 years), *PDS* and *RC* the largest proportions of female legislators (30.2% and 27.9%, respectively), and *RC*, *LN*, and *PDS* the smallest percentages of legislators with a college degree (58.3%, 61%, and 62.5%, respectively).

The finding that the *PCI*, *PDS*, and *RC* have the largest proportions of female MPs can be explained by the fact that, in the first half of the First Republic, about a quarter of the *PCI* members were female, and most left-wing parties of the Second Republic have statutory norms that are meant to

---

[15] Note that the labels *CCD* and *ULIVO* that we use here each contain several parties.

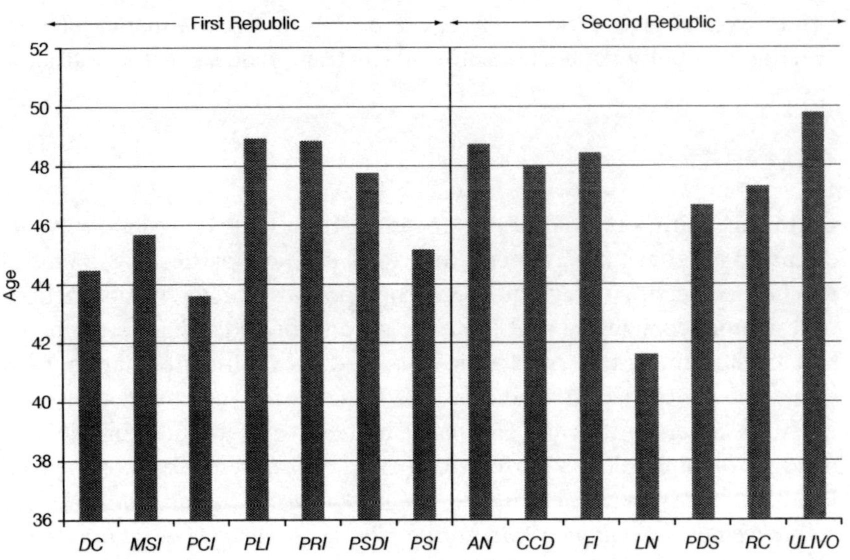

Fig. 2.22 Average age at entry

ensure equal representation across genders. However, the same logic does not apply to the *DC*, which is the party with the highest proportion of female party members among all the parties of the First Republic, but has less than 5% of MPs who are women. Given that female candidates were

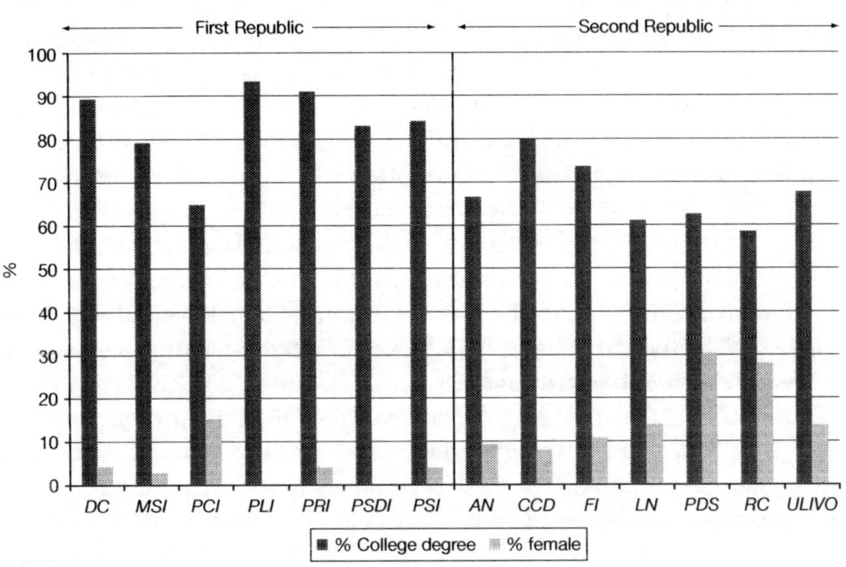

Fig. 2.23 Percentage female and percentage with a college degree

typically included in the party lists, we conclude that female *DC* voters were not voting for female candidates.[16] What is also apparent is that this gender bias displays a remarkable degree of persistence, since the post-*DC* parties of the Second Republic (*CCD*) have the smallest proportion of female legislators among all the parties of the Second Republic.

If we now turn our attention to the sector of occupation and income before entering Parliament of a party's legislators, Table 2.5 summarizes the distribution of occupations held by individuals prior to entering Parliament for each party, Figure 2.24 depicts the proportions of legislators whose last occupation prior to entering Parliament was in the industry sector, the legal sector, or the political sector for each party, and Figure 2.25 plots their average real annual income (in 2005 euros) in the year before entry. The most noticeable features that emerge from Figure 2.24 are the preponderance of lawyers among the *MSI* legislators, of individuals with a background in the industry sector among the *FI* and *LN* legislators, and of individuals coming from the political sector among the *PDS* legislators. Interestingly, the 1994 election results suggest that most voters did not consider the fact that the candidates of *FI* and *LN* had little prior political experience as a downside. In fact, as a result of the generalized discontent and disaffection towards traditional political parties that followed the 'Clean Hands' investigation, and partly in response to the personalization of politics introduced by the new majoritarian electoral system, not having being part of the old political system may have increased the appeal of the candidates of *FI* and *LN* for a large numbers of voters.

Note that, while the distribution of pre-Parliament occupations of Italian legislators is not very different across the parties of the First Republic,[17] in the Second Republic there is evidence of clustering along the (left–right) ideological dimension. For example, the education and political sectors account for nearly half of all the legislators of left-wing parties (that is, *PDS*, *RC*, and *ULIVO*), while the majority of legislators of right-wing parties (that is, *CCD*, *FI*, and *AN*) either had managerial occupations in the industry sector or were lawyers before entering Parliament (with the exception of *LN*). On the other hand, an element of continuity between the First and Second Republics is represented by the proportion of teachers and professors among legislators, which has always been above 10% across all parties

---

[16] This might be explained by the political role played by the Church parishes (the *DC* equivalent of the *PCI* cells) in coordinating the behavior of Christian Democrats voters.

[17] Besides the aforementioned overrepresentation of lawyers in *MSI*, the only other exceptions are the relatively large proportions of industry workers in *PCI* and of self-employed in *PLI*.

Table 2.5 Distribution of pre-Parliament occupations of Italian legislators by party (%)

Party	Sector of employment												
	AGR	EDU	HTH	INDW	INDM	LEG	LOB	MED	MIL	POL	PUB	SE	OLF
First Republic													
DC	3.36	22.91	5.08	4.12	10.35	26.27	4.70	4.79	0.48	1.05	9.40	7.00	0.48
MSI	0.77	10.00	4.62	2.31	4.62	44.62	3.85	17.69	3.08	2.31	0.77	5.38	0.00
PCI	1.51	19.61	3.48	22.97	1.62	9.05	10.09	11.02	0.46	11.48	2.32	6.03	0.35
PLI	1.22	12.20	2.44	15.85	12.20	7.32	0.00	8.54	0.00	0.00	2.44	32.93	4.88
PRI	1.43	21.43	11.43	1.43	12.86	22.86	0.00	11.43	1.43	1.43	4.29	10.00	0.00
PSDI	0.00	11.27	9.86	0.00	7.04	22.54	8.45	11.27	2.82	0.00	12.68	14.08	0.00
PSI	0.88	18.71	2.05	7.02	6.43	25.73	7.02	11.70	1.46	5.85	5.85	6.73	0.58
Second Republic													
AN	1.12	15.17	8.99	5.62	18.54	21.91	0.00	11.80	1.69	1.12	6.18	7.87	0.00
CCD	0.00	18.92	9.46	4.05	17.57	22.97	0.00	2.70	0.00	4.05	8.11	10.81	1.35
FI	2.26	9.68	10.65	1.94	30.97	19.03	0.32	8.06	0.65	3.23	2.90	8.71	1.61
LN	2.07	11.40	8.29	7.77	29.53	8.81	1.04	3.63	0.00	1.55	3.63	21.24	1.04
PDS	1.04	23.96	2.08	11.46	9.38	7.29	7.29	3.13	0.00	27.08	6.25	1.04	0.00
RC	0.00	28.57	4.76	13.10	2.38	3.57	1.19	14.29	0.00	15.48	8.33	4.76	3.57
ULIVO	0.00	23.96	6.21	6.51	13.61	10.36	3.85	6.21	0.30	13.02	7.40	5.92	2.66

Note: AGR = agriculture, EDU = education, HTH = health care, INDW = industry workers, INDM = industry managers, LEG = legal, LOB = lobbying, MED = media, MIL = military, POL = political, PUB = public, SE = self-employment, OLF = out of the labour force.

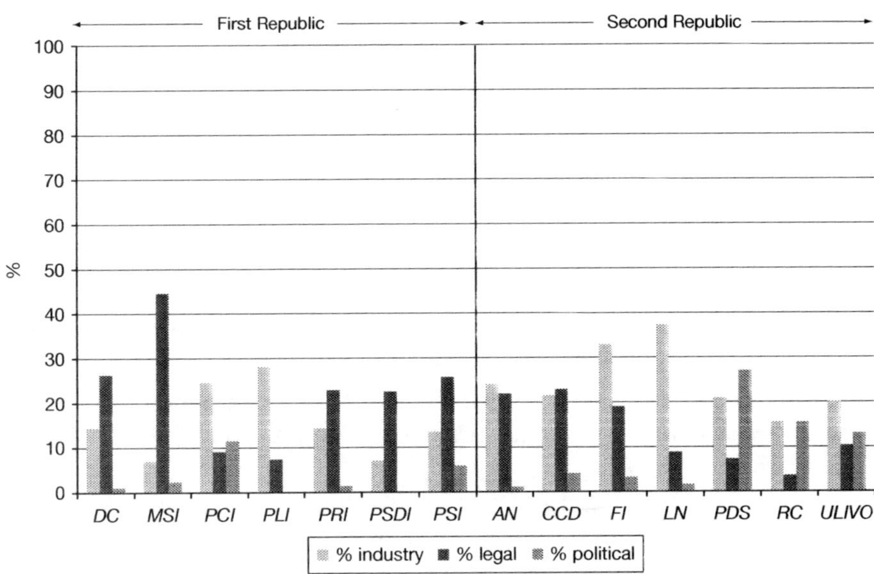

Fig. 2.24 Distribution of occupations

(with the exception of *FI*). Finally, while the similarities in the occupational background between *DC* and the post-Christian Democratic parties are apparent, it is somewhat surprising that the distribution of pre-Parliament occupations of *AN* legislators resembles more the one of *DC* legislators than of *MSI* legislators.

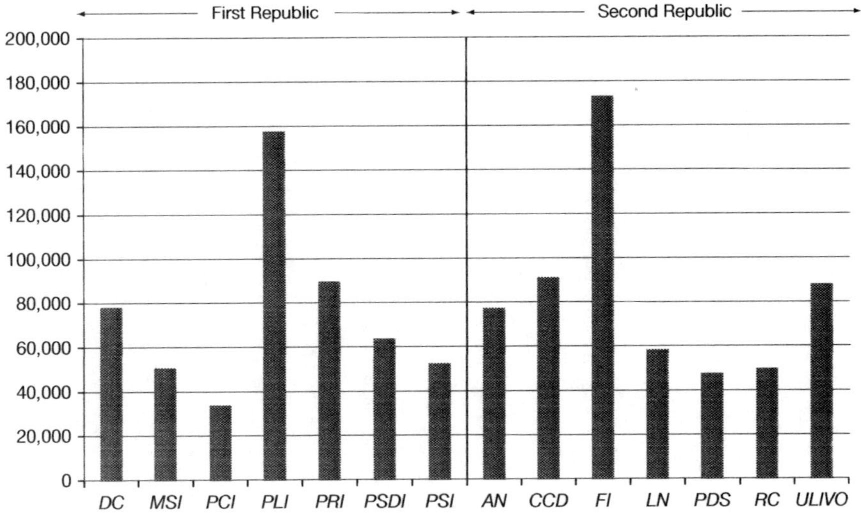

Fig. 2.25 Average real annual income before entry (2005 euros)

Another interesting aspect of the data that emerges from these figures is that, in spite of the fact that the proportion of MPs of *LN* coming from the business sector is even higher of that of the MPs of *FI*, while the legislators of *FI* have the highest average real annual income before entry among all the parties of the Second Republic (173,189 euros), the legislators of *LN* rank near the bottom in this dimension (58,243 euros). This finding can be explained by the fact that, while *LN* has been most successful in recruiting relatively young people from the working class, including small entrepreneurs, *FI* has been successfully tapping into the pool of upper-class managers and executives. Among the parties of the First Republic, the legislators of *PLI* and those of *PCI* have the highest (155,759 euros) and the lowest (33,886 euros) average real annual income before entry, respectively, which can also be explained by the different professional backgrounds of their MPs illustrated in Table 2.5.

Figure 2.26 plots the median of the distribution of real income growth rates upon entry within each party; Figure 2.27 the percentage of legislators of each party who experience an income loss upon entering Parliament; Figure 2.28 the average real annual income from additional sources while in Parliament (that is, in excess of the parliamentary wage); and Figure 2.29 the proportion of each party's legislators who report incomes in excess of their parliamentary wage. Overall, the patterns that emerge from these figures are very much in line with what we observed in the

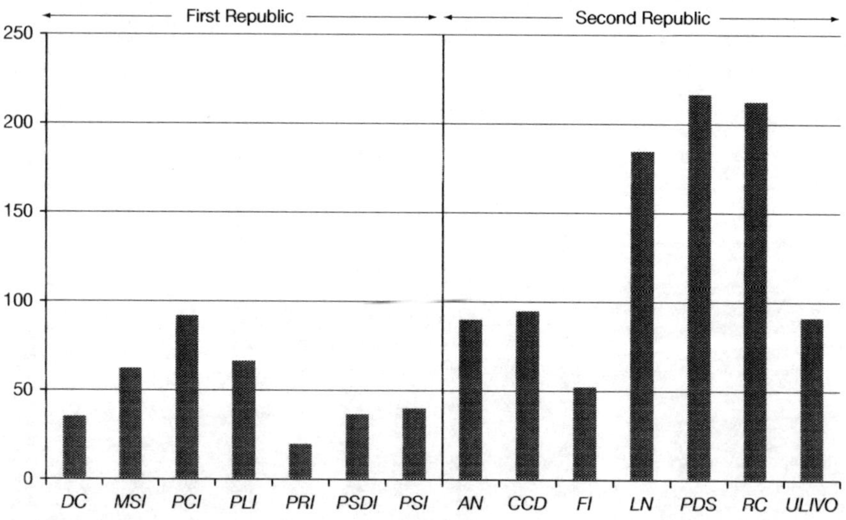

Fig. 2.26 Median real income growth rate on entry

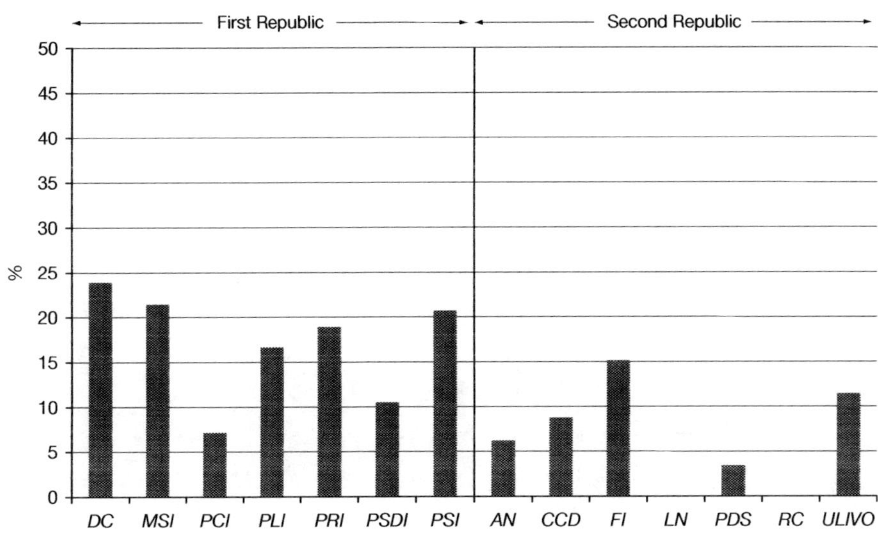

Fig. 2.27 Percentage of legislators with real income losses on entry

previous graphs, and it is quite evident that being elected to Parliament entails large pecuniary gains, especially for the legislators of *LN*, *PDS*, and *RC*.

As we pointed out in Chapter 1, grouping parties together based on their ideological proximity might be quite misleading, since, for example, there seem to be more similarities in terms of organizational structure and recruitment processes between the *DC* and the *PSI* than between the latter and the *PCI*. However, when we look at the average annual income before entry in the First Republic, it is interesting to note that this dimension of the data tends to increase as we move from left to right along the ideological spectrum (Figure 2.25).[18] The only exception is represented by the *MSI*, which always had a somewhat isolated position with respect to the rest of the party system anyway. A similar ranking of parties emerges if we look at the average real annual income in excess of the parliamentary wage (Figure 2.28) or at the proportion of each party's legislators who report incomes in excess of their parliamentary wage (Figure 2.29). On the contrary, there is some evidence of an inverse U-shaped pattern in the average annual

[18] In particular, the average annual income before entry in the First Republic is relatively low for left-wing parties such as *PCI*, *PSI*, and *PSDI*, intermediate for centre parties such as *PRI* and *DC*, and relatively high for a right-leaning party like *PLI*.

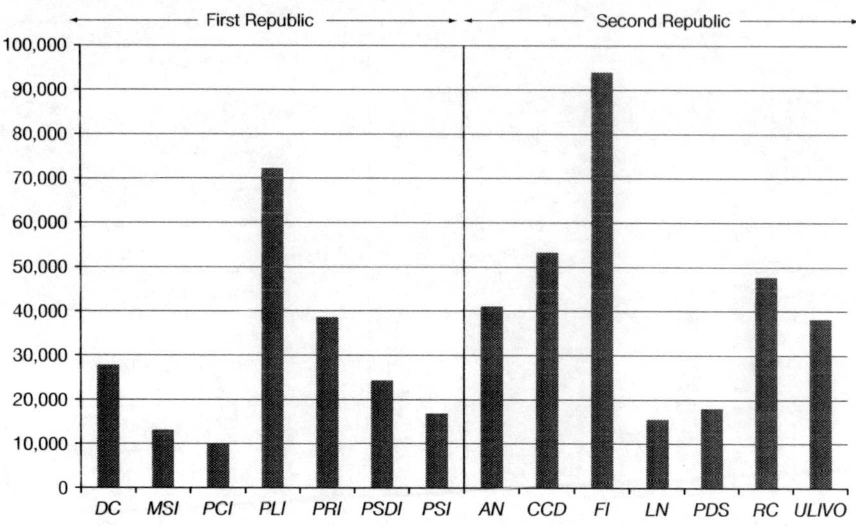

Fig. 2.28 Average real annual additional income after entry (2005 euros)

income before entry in the Second Republic, with the relatively centrist *FI*, *CCD*, and *ULIVO* having the highest values.[19]

The last issues we analyse with our data pertain to the differences among parties in the behaviour of their legislators after they are elected to Parliament. For each party, Figure 2.30 plots the average rate at which legislators seek re-election at the end of each term and their re-election rate (conditional on running), and Figure 2.31 their average attendance rate at roll-call voting sessions.

The *PCI* and the *ULIVO* are clear outliers in the First and the Second Republics, respectively. Their legislators are relatively less likely to seek re-election than legislators of other parties, but at the same time have relatively high re-election rates when they do. Also, once elected, their participation rates are the highest. Clearly, the discipline imposed by the party, which essentially determines who runs for office and coordinates the behaviour of its elected representatives, goes a long way towards explaining

---

[19] Most of the existing political science literature studying Italian political recruitment typically focuses on the analysis of the socio-occupational characteristics of MPs in order to detect similarities or differences across parties in the recruitment process. Though for the most part useful, sometimes this approach can also be misleading. For example, *MSI* and *PSI* are both traditional mass parties. Indeed, they are remarkably similar in all dimensions, including all income characteristics of their legislators. However, as Figure 2.24 shows, almost half of the legislators of MSI are lawyers as compared to relatively more similar proportions of industry, legal, and political-sector occupations in the case of the legislators of *PSI*.

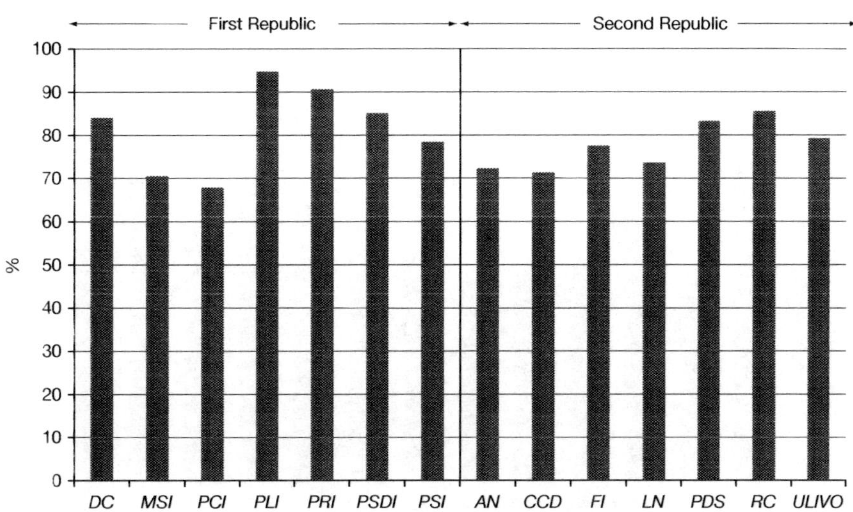

Fig. 2.29 Percentage of legislators reporting additional income

this apparent anomaly. In addition, it is worth recalling that, as we pointed out in Chapter 1, the practice of switching candidatures or rotating party members in Parliament was quite common in the *PCI*. Furthermore, in order to foster political turnover among its members, *RC* systematically forced its MPs to leave Parliament and not to seek re-election after a second

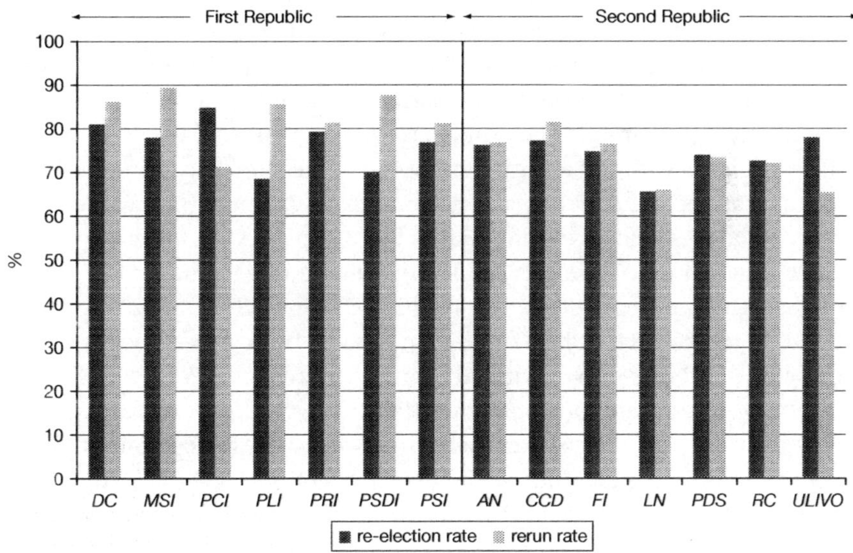

Fig. 2.30 Turnover rates

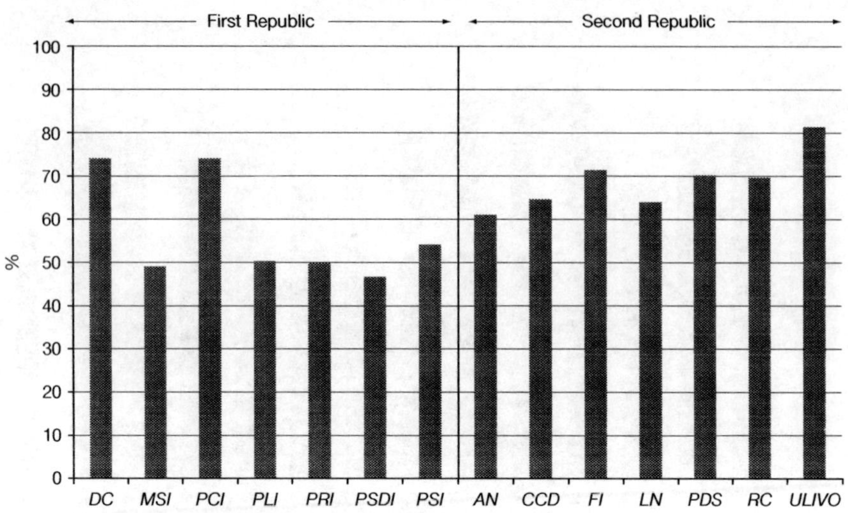

Fig. 2.31 Attendance rates

term. Another interesting case is that of the legislators of *LN*, who seek re-election at a relatively low rate, but are also relatively unlikely to get re-elected when they do. Indeed, *FI* and *LN* are the parties with the lowest re-election and rerun rates among the parties of the centre-right coalition. This apparent anomaly could be the result of the fact that more than half of the *LN* legislators left the party in the first months of 1995, joining the ranks of *FI*, and in 1996 the *LN* withdrew its support of the second Berlusconi government and ran alone. Furthermore, the large success of these parties in the 1994 election was partly the result of a strong national popularity effect, and it is possible that some incumbents would have had little chance of winning in a more competitive election. Regarding turnover rates in the Second Republic, it is also interesting to note that, while rerun rates always exceed re-election rates for the parties of the centre-right coalition (that is, *CCD*, *FI*, *LN*, and *AN*), the opposite is true for the parties of the centre-left coalition (that is, *RC*, *PDS*, and *ULIVO*). On the other hand, in the First Republic a similar pattern can be observed if we consider the partition between government parties (that is, *DC*, *PLI*, *PRI*, *PSI*, and *PSDI*) and the main opposition party (*PCI*).

The third aspect of legislators' behaviour we analyse here pertains to their involvement in scandals. As we discussed in Section 2.3 above, our dataset includes the records collected by Golden (2007) of all the instances where a formal request to strip a legislator of his or her parliamentary immunity to allow prosecution was made by the Italian judiciary during the First

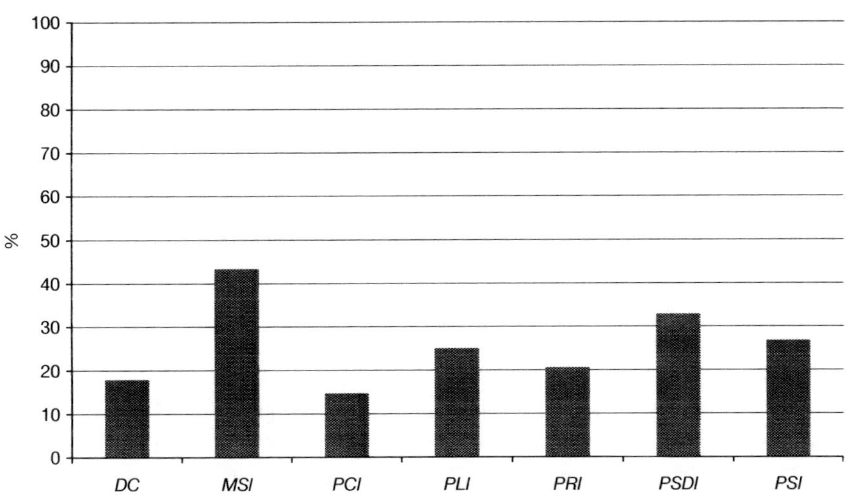

Fig. 2.32 Scandal rates

Republic. Figure 2.32 plots the average percentage of legislators who were the object of such requests during Legislatures V–XI for each of the seven major parties of the First Republic.[20] In addition, our analysis of the post-parliamentary careers of a sample of 860 former legislators revealed that 19 of them who were first elected to Parliament during the First Republic went to jail, 11 of whom belonged to *DC*, 4 to *PSI*, 2 to *PSDI*, and 1 each to *MSI* and *PRI* (see also Gomez and Travaglio 2006). Although a comparison with the parties of the Second Republic is not possible, it is interesting to note that, among those of the First Republic, some of the parties that fare relatively better with respect to other dimensions of the data fare relatively worse with respect to the proportion of their legislators who were involved in scandals. For example, there is a strong negative correlation (equal to – 0.81) between the ranking of the parties of the First Republic based on the attendance rates of their legislators, and the ranking based on their scandal rates.

---

[20] As we pointed out before, most of the indictments of MPs in Legislatures I–IV refer either to war crimes (for people who fought in the Second World War), or to crimes against the Italian Republic (for people who disputed the legitimacy of the new republican form of constitution), as opposed to scandals.

3

Analysis and Conclusions

In this chapter, we use our data to tackle several questions that pertain to the selection of Italian politicians, their labour market, and their overall quality. In order to accomplish this goal we restrict attention to the post-1981 sample for which we observe their annual income and their attendance rates at parliamentary voting sessions. We then draw some general conclusions that contribute to the debate about the relative efficacy and desirability of alternative policies regarding the selection and the compensation of elected representatives.

3.1. Private returns to legislative experience and the quality of politicians

The first question we pose is whether the earnings of politicians prior to entering Parliament can reveal some useful information about the type of individuals who are elected to represent the Italian citizens (since members of the executive are typically selected from among the legislators, this analysis extends beyond Parliament and is also relevant for the government). To address this question, we specify and estimate a simple equation, where the log of annual real income (expressed in 2005 euros) in the year before entering the Parliament is regressed on: a vector of demographic characteristics (that is, age, age squared, education level, and gender); a set of year dummies corresponding to the start of each legislature since 1981, LexVIII–LexXV, capturing possible trends and other year effects; a set of dummy variables corresponding to the twelve categories that we used in the previous chapter to classify the pre-Parliament occupations of legislators (we denote them by AGR = agriculture, EDU = education, HTH = health care, INDW = industry workers, INDM = industry managers, LEG = legal, LOB = lobbying, MED = media, MIL = military, POL = political, PUB

= public, SE = self-employment); and a set of dummy variables denoting the party affiliation upon entering Parliament, which were also introduced in Chapter 1 (these are *AN, CCD, DC, FI, LN, MSI, PCI, PDS, PLI, PRI, PSDI, PSI, RC, ULIVO*, plus a residual category OTHER for all other minor parties).[1] The omitted dummies in the regression are LexVIII, PUB, and OTHER, so that the benchmark group is the legislators affiliated with a minor party who entered Parliament during the 8th Legislature coming from employment in the public sector. Because of the possible presence of outliers, we performed a robust regression (Huber) as well as a quantile (median) regression. The results are reported at Table 3.1.

Before interpreting our findings, we should note that the results are remarkably stable across the two estimations performed, and appear to be quite robust.[2] The first set of findings refers to the (cross-section) relationship between the demographic characteristics of the sample of individuals who are elected to the Italian Parliament and their real annual earnings in the year before they are first elected. Note that, holding everything else constant, the pre-Parliament income of female legislators is between 20.5 per cent and 21.8 per cent lower (depending on whether we look at the robust or the median regression) than that of male legislators, and a college degree increases the pre-Parliament income of legislators by between 30.8 per cent and 32.2 per cent. Also, the average (and median) pre-Parliament earnings of the legislators coming from the public sector are comparable to those of the legislators coming from the legal and the media sector as well as from managerial occupations in the industry sector, and are significantly higher than those of legislators coming from other sectors. Most importantly, even after controlling for demographic characteristics, sector of employment, and differences across time period, many of the coefficients associated with party dummies are statistically different from zero. They are positive for (in order of the size of the estimated coefficient) *PLI, PRI, DC, FI,* and *PSI,* and negative for *LN* and *RC*; for all other parties, the coefficients are not statistically different from zero. This finding clearly indicates the presence of unobserved heterogeneity with respect to the (income-earning) ability of legislators, and may be interpreted as a measure of the relative

---

[1] Recall that, according to our classification, *CCD* includes Centro Cristiano Democratico, Cristiani Democratici Uniti, and Unione dei Democratici Cristiani, and *ULIVO* includes l'Ulivo, La Margherita, and Democratici di Sinistra.

[2] In addition to the results reported here, we performed a number of robustness checks using a variety of specifications and alternative estimation techniques (including simple OLS), all of which produced point estimates that are within the confidence intervals of the estimated parameters in Table 3.1.

Table 3.1 Cross-section regressions of log pre-Parliament real annual earnings

N = 1,910	Robust regression		Median regression	
Variable	Coefficient	Std error	Coefficient	Std error
Intercept	7.2810**	0.4771	7.9123**	0.5453
Age	0.0653**	0.0139	0.0469**	0.0170
Age^2	−0.0004**	0.0001	−0.0002	0.0002
Female	−0.2053**	0.0470	−0.2184**	0.0583
College degree	0.3083**	0.0393	0.3222**	0.0487
AGR	−0.6587**	0.1672	−0.7099**	0.1998
EDU	−0.2714**	0.0684	−0.3258**	0.0854
HTH	−0.3213**	0.0830	−0.3749**	0.1031
INDW	−0.3513**	0.0895	−0.3289**	0.1105
INDM	0.0822	0.0721	0.0404	0.0898
LEG	−0.0011	0.0714	−0.0258	0.0890
LOB	−0.4051**	0.1144	−0.4281	0.1410
MED	0.0498	0.0813	0.0686**	0.1012
MIL	−0.0641	0.2349	−0.2213	0.2808
POL	−0.4623**	0.0836	−0.4912**	0.1039
SE	−0.1507*	0.0796	−0.1780*	0.0989
LexIX	0.8068**	0.3408	0.6733*	0.3701
LexX	0.9515**	0.3415	0.7793**	0.3708
LexXI	1.1746**	0.3431	1.0108**	0.3744
LexXII	1.28158**	0.3474	1.1400**	0.3802
LexXIII	1.2580**	0.3495	1.0598**	0.3831
LexXIV	1.55196**	0.3504	1.4014**	0.3846
LexXV	1.6953**	0.3494	1.5136**	0.3830
AN	−0.0169	0.0718	−0.0858	0.0893
CCD	−0.0496	0.0948	−0.1403	0.1178
DC	0.3546**	0.0858	0.3306**	0.1066
FI	0.3029**	0.0630	0.2489**	0.0784
LN	−0.2158**	0.0694	−0.2263**	0.0860
MSI	−0.0305	0.1484	−0.0735	0.1771
PCI	−0.0614	0.0955	−0.1011	0.1185
PDS	−0.1353	0.0892	−0.1064	0.1097
PLI	0.4029**	0.2059	0.7278**	0.2378
PRI	0.5082**	0.1336	0.45619**	0.1649
PSDI	−0.0212	0.1698	0.0624	0.2048
PSI	0.2307**	0.1025	0.2436**	0.1275
RC	−0.3592**	0.0909	−0.3988**	0.1129
ULIVO	−0.0245	0.0656	−0.0401	0.0815

Note: **denotes significance at the 5% level;
*at the 10% level.

success of different parties to recruit higher-quality politicians. On the other hand, another possible (although more cynical) interpretation is that being affiliated with specific parties generates different employment opportunities, and the simple cross-section regressions we performed cannot determine which interpretation (if either) is correct. We return to these issues in more detail below.

The second issue we consider here is to measure the private returns to an individual from a career in politics. In particular, using our data we can quantify the returns to experience in the Italian Parliament, or, in other words, the extent to which each year spent in Parliament increases a legislator's income from sources outside Parliament. To achieve this goal, we specify and estimate a panel regression model where the log of the annual real income of legislators (in 2005 euros) from all sources other than the parliamentary wage (henceforth, extra income) is regressed on: the legislators' age and age squared; their parliamentary experience (measured by their number of years in Parliament) and experience squared; the fraction of the year they are in Parliament (which is equal to zero the year before they are elected for the first time, and a number between zero and one the year they are first elected and their last year in Parliament, since the beginning of a new legislature never coincides with the beginning of a calendar year, and one otherwise); and a set of time (year, legislature, and cohort specific) dummy variables that capture possible trends in real income and all other effects systematically related to events occurring over time (as, for example, changes in the real parliamentary wage). In addition, the error term in the panel regression contains two components: an idiosyncratic term capturing random (iid) shocks, and an individual specific component or fixed effect. The role of the fixed effects is to control for all (observed and unobserved) characteristics of each individual legislator. In addition, to the extent that earning (and reporting) extra income is the consequence of a choice each individual makes, the fixed effects also control for the 'selection effects' such choices may introduce in the data. The results are reported in Table 3.2.

Table 3.2 Panel regression of log real annual extra earnings (N = 13,250)

Variable	Coefficient	Std error
Intercept	11.1887**	3.6095
Age	0.0337	0.1002
Age^2	0.0001	0.0002
Experience	0.0462**	0.0224
Experience^2	−0.0019**	0.0003
Fraction of the year in Parliament	−1.8820**	0.1050

Note: The estimates of the 2,760 fixed-effect coefficients and the coefficients of the 57 time dummies that were included in the regression are not reported here to economize on space.
** denotes significance at the 5% level; * at the 10% level.

As we can see from Table 3.2, holding everything else constant, the amount of extra annual income a legislator earns decreases with the fraction of the year the legislator is in Parliament, but does not vary with his or her age. Most importantly, it significantly increases with experience. Using our estimates, we calculate that the first year in Parliament increases the extra wage of a legislator by 4.2 per cent. The marginal effect of an additional year in Parliament then declines slowly with the number of years in Parliament and reaches zero after twelve years of experience. Diermeier, Keane, and Merlo (2005) performed a similar exercise for the USA and estimated the returns to congressional experience in post-congressional wages. They estimated an annual rate of return in all post-congressional occupations of 2.6 per cent for the first year in Congress, and found that the marginal effect of an additional year in Congress decreases quite rapidly with experience. Figure 3.1 plots the estimated marginal returns as a function of the number of years of legislative experience for both countries. It is interesting to note that, in addition to being higher, the returns on legislative experience in Italy are earned by a politician during his or her parliamentary tenure, while US legislators can realize such returns only after they leave Congress.

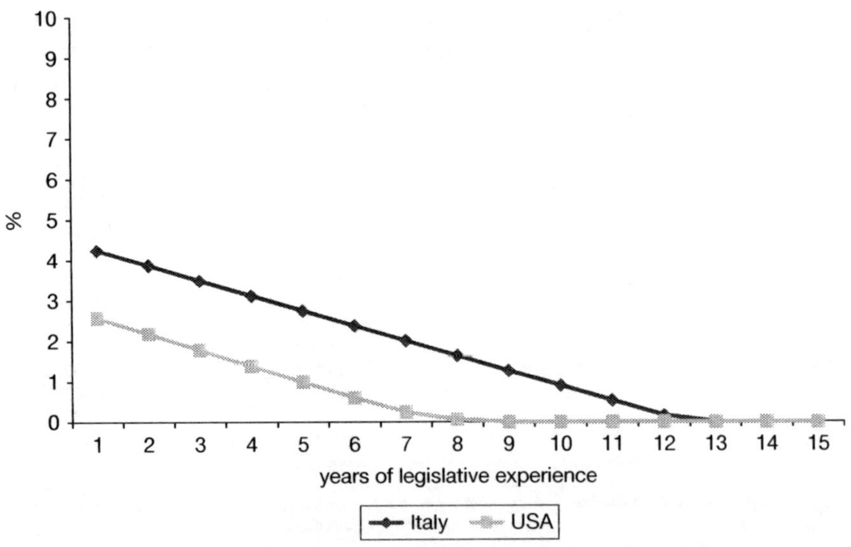

Fig. 3.1 Annual rate of return of legislative experience

In our dataset, there is a small sample of 108 individuals who enter the Parliament for the first time after 1981, leave Parliament, and then re-enter prior to 2006. This implies that for these individuals we observe their annual income while they are not in Parliament both before and after their first spell of parliamentary tenure. While this sample is hardly representative of the entire population of Italian legislators, we can nevertheless use these observations to supplement our previous analysis and gain some insights about the overall returns to parliamentary experience. A simple calculation based on the difference between the two annual incomes (both expressed in 2005 euros) for each of the individuals in this sample yields an average (median) return per year of experience in Parliament of 4,276 euros (3,251 euros), corresponding to a 23.1 per cent (10.2 per cent) increase over their annual income before their first entry.

We are now in a position to revisit the issue relating to the quality of politicians and to potential differences across parties in their ability to recruit legislators of different quality. Furthermore, we also want to assess the extent to which the quality of politicians has changed over time, especially between the First and Second Republics. An important aspect of the quality of politicians is their skill endowment, which includes both observable characteristics (for example, education), as well as characteristics that are intrinsically hard to measure directly (for example, general ability). In addition to the estimates reported in Table 3.2, the panel regression we performed to estimate the returns to political experience in Parliament also generated estimates of the individual fixed effects, one for each of the 2,760 legislators in our sample for whom we have data on their annual income. Recall that an individual's fixed effect summarizes all of his or her characteristics that are fixed over time and that are relevant for his or her income-earning ability. In other words, it represents a summary of an individual's overall endowments (both observable and unobservable). To the extent that the individuals' skills in the labour market are positively correlated with their ability as politicians (see, e.g., Mattozzi and Merlo 2008), decomposing the fixed effects into their two components (that is, the part that can be explained by measurable characteristics and the residual) can shed some light on the overall skill endowments of Italian politicians.

To accomplish this goal, we regress these fixed effects on individual-specific observable characteristics (namely, education, gender, and sector of employment prior to election to Parliament), and then summarize the distribution of the residuals we obtain from this regression (which represents a summary measure of the individuals' unobserved 'ability'), for each party as well as for each group of legislators who were first elected to the

Table 3.3 The 'ability scores' of politicians

| | Quantiles | | | | | Interquartile | |
	10%	25%	50%	75%	90%	Range	Mean
Parties of the First Republic							
DC	−0.68	−0.04	0.64	1.60	2.45	1.63	0.76
MSI	−1.28	−0.42	0.44	1.29	1.79	1.70	0.37
PCI	−1.61	−0.63	0.23	1.08	1.79	1.71	0.17
PLI	−0.07	0.59	1.59	2.88	3.30	2.29	1.66
PRI	−0.81	0.10	1.12	2.00	3.01	1.91	1.10
PSDI	−0.60	0.08	0.88	1.99	2.80	1.91	1.07
PSI	−1.20	−0.48	0.34	1.33	2.12	1.82	0.43
All parties	−1.27	−0.47	0.39	1.28	2.17	1.63	0.42
Parties of the Second Republic							
AN	−2.44	−1.34	−0.45	0.33	1.11	1.67	−0.57
CCD	−2.02	−1.27	−0.46	0.37	1.08	1.64	−0.52
FI	−1.61	−0.83	−0.09	1.00	1.75	1.83	0.04
LN	−2.54	−1.47	−0.75	−0.21	0.44	1.27	−0.86
PDS	−1.73	−1.04	−0.33	0.29	1.22	1.32	−0.34
RC	−1.87	−1.31	−0.49	0.30	0.93	1.61	−0.51
ULIVO	−2.35	−1.35	−0.43	0.47	1.12	1.82	−0.51
All parties	−2.21	−1.32	−0.43	0.40	1.29	1.67	−0.47

Note: The rows that refer to all parties in the First and Second Republic also include minor parties.

House during the First Republic (Legislatures VIII–XI), and the Second Republic (Legislatures XII–XV).[3] The results are reported at Table 3.3.[4] Note that a value of zero denotes politicians who are 'average', while positive (negative) values denote politicians who are 'above (below) average'. Figure 3.2 plots the percentage of elected legislators of each party whose 'ability score' is positive.

[3] Recall that, although the First Republic also included Legislatures I–VII, we can perform this analysis only for Legislatures VIII–XV because of the lack of pre-1981 income data.

[4] Since, as we mentioned above, the fixed effects may also capture (labour supply) selection effects related to the fact that a proportion of the legislators does not report positive extra income while they are in Parliament, to assess the robustness of our findings we also performed a Heckman two-step estimation procedure. The procedure consists of a first step where we estimate a Probit model of the probability of reporting positive extra income as a function of all the individual variables, including party affiliation and cohort of first entry into the Parliament, and the parliamentary wage, and a second step where we regress the fixed effects on the individual-specific characteristics and an extra term (the inverse of the Mills ratio from the first step) that captures possible selection effects. The results we obtained from this alternative procedure are very similar.

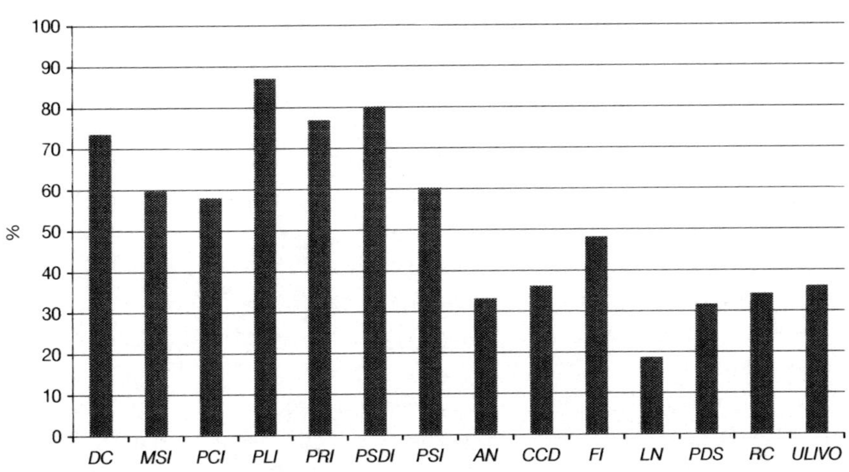

Fig. 3.2 Percentage of 'above-average' politicians: 'ability'

As we can see from Table 3.3, the median ability score of their elected representatives is positive for all the major parties of the First Republic, while it is negative for all the major parties of the Second Republic. The same is true with respect to the mean ability score, except that *FI* has a positive score, although very close to zero. Within each set of parties, their relative ranking based on their median (mean) ability scores is *PLI, PRI, PSDI, DC, MSI, PSI*, and PCI (*PLI, PRI, PSDI, DC, PSI, MSI*, and *PCI*) among the parties of the First Republic;[5] among the parties of the Second Republic, their relative ranking based on their median (mean) scores is *FI, PDS, ULIVO, AN, CCD, RC*, and *LN* (*FI, PDS, RC, ULIVO, CCD, AN*, and *LN*). With respect to how homogenous the quality composition of the group of legislators of each party is, measured by the interquartile range (that is, the distance between the 25th and the 75th percentile), the most homogenous (heterogeneous) parties of the First and Second Republics are *DC* and *LN* (*PLI* and *FI*), respectively. Looking at Figure 3.2, we observe that the party with the largest percentage of 'above-average' legislators in the First Republic is the *PLI* (with 87%), followed by *PSDI* (80%), *PRI* (76.8%), *DC* (73.5%), *PSI* (60%), *MSI* (59.7%), and *PCI* (58%).[6] Among the parties of the

---

[5] In interpreting these findings, it is worth recalling that, as noted in Chapter 1, the best Communist politicians were more likely to be members of the Central Committee rather than MPs, while holding a seat in Parliament was common practice within the *DC* leadership.

[6] These results confirm once more the potential perils of basing an analysis of the political parties' recruitment function solely on the socio-occupational characteristics of their MPs. For

Second Republic, the party with the largest percentage of 'above-average' legislators is *FI* (with 48%), followed by *ULIVO* and *CCD* (36%), *RC* (34.2%), *AN* (33%), *PDS* (31.6%), and a distant last *LN* (with only 18.6%). Overall, we observe that the switch from the First to the Second Republic led to a dramatic worsening of the quality of the cohorts of politicians who have entered Parliament after 1994. In fact, the percentages of 'above-average' new legislators who were elected to Parliament during the First and the Second Republics are equal to 61.9% and 35.2%, respectively.[7] This decline goes hand in hand with the dramatic decrease in the average level of education of the newly elected MPs, which, as we pointed out before, has been a staple of the Second Republic (see Figure 2.3).[8]

It is interesting to relate our findings on the deterioration of the quality of elected legislators (with respect both to their 'ability score' and to their level of education) in the period 1994–2006 relative to the earlier period (1981–94) to what happened to the parliamentary wage. As we described in Chapter 2, during the period 1981–2006 the (real) parliamentary wage displayed a monotonically increasing pattern (see Figure 2.5). Furthermore, while in the late 1980s and early 1990s it was comparable to the (real) congressional wage of US legislators, since 1994 it has become larger (see Figure 2.7). Thus, there appears to be a negative correlation between the quality of elected legislators and the parliamentary wage.

Recently, political economists have begun to investigate the relation between relative salaries in the political and private sectors and the behaviour of politicians. For example, Besley (2004), Caselli and Morelli (2004), and Messner and Polborn (2004) model the relationship between relative wages of elected officials and their average ability, in environments where ability is uni-dimensional (that is, common to the political and private spheres). Individuals decide whether to run for office based on their ability. In Caselli and Morelli (2004), individuals with relatively low ability have a lower opportunity cost of running, as they face worse opportunities in the

example, Figure 3.2 shows that *MSI* and *PSI* were equally able to select 'above-average' legislators, despite the fact that *MSI* was selecting politicians mainly from the legal sector and *PSI* from the industry and political sectors as well (see Figure 2.24). A similar argument applies to the three elite parties of the First Republic—i.e., *PLI*, *PRI*, and *PSDI*.

[7] It is useful to point out that there are no noticeable differences in the distributions of ability scores across the four different cohorts that first entered Parliament in 1994, 1996, 2001, and 2006, respectively, except for a slight improvement in the relative ability of the cohort elected in Legislature XV. For example, the percentages of 'above-average' new legislators who were elected to Parliament in Legislatures XII–XV are 33.7%, 35.8%, 34.2%, and 40%, respectively.

[8] Note that, if we rank all parties of the First and Second Republics based on the percentage of their legislators with a college degree and on the median quality score of their legislators separately, the correlation between the two rankings is 0.83.

private sector. This constrains the options available to voters, and may generate equilibria where only low-ability politicians are elected.[9] In their framework, increasing the relative wage of elected officials increases the average ability of politicians.[10] Similarly, in the model of Messner and Polborn (2004), lower-ability individuals are more likely to run for office in equilibrium. The equilibrium mechanism is different, however. It relies on the fact that, if salaries of elected officials are relatively low, high-ability individuals may free-ride by not running and letting low-ability types run instead. This implies a U-shaped relation between the salary of elected officials and their average ability.[11]

Mattozzi and Merlo (2008), on the other hand, propose a dynamic equilibrium model of the careers of politicians. In their model there are two dimensions of ability, political skills and market ability. Individual endowments of each type of skill, which are private information, are positively correlated. In equilibrium, there are both career politicians (who work in the political sector until retirement) and individuals with political careers (who leave politics before retirement and work in the private sector). Career politicians enter the political sector because of the non-pecuniary rewards from being in office, which include both ego rents and potential benefits from influencing policy. Individuals with political careers, on the other hand, enter the political sector in order to increase their market wages.[12] In equilibrium, individuals with political careers (that is, those who eventually plan voluntarily to leave politics to reap rewards in the private sector) have relatively better political skills than career politicians, although career politicians are still better than average.

Mattozzi and Merlo find that an increase in the salary a politician receives while in office decreases the average quality of individuals who become politicians, decreases turnover in office (as the proportion of career politicians goes up), and has an ambiguous effect on the average quality of career politicians. These results derive from the fact that a higher salary in the

---

[9] In their model, the prestige from holding office depends on the quality of the political class. If incompetent individuals are elected, politics becomes a low-status occupation, which further deters high-ability individuals from entering.

[10] Besley (2004) obtains a similar result in the context of a political agency model with moral hazard and adverse selection, and also provides some empirical evidence.

[11] While the probability that low-ability individuals run for office increases monotonically with the salary, for high-ability individuals it may decrease at relatively low levels of salary before it increases.

[12] Since political skills are positively correlated with market ability, and politics is a showcase (i.e., individuals who serve in office display their political skills), incumbent politicians may leave the political sector and work in the market sector at a higher wage than they would have anticipated receiving had they not become politicians.

political sector makes politics a relatively more attractive option for all levels of political skills, thus lowering the quality of the marginal politician (entry effect). At the same time, however, relatively better incumbent politicians are willing to remain in politics, since the salary in politics is now better relative to the market wages (retention effect).

From an empirical point of view, Keane and Merlo (2007) analyse how the career decisions of US legislators respond to monetary incentives. Their findings confirm the existence of the retention effect highlighted by Mattozzi and Merlo and show that it may be fairly sizeable. For example, they find that a 20 per cent reduction in the congressional wage would lead to a 14 per cent decrease in the average duration of congressional careers. Notably, however, the effect is not uniform across politicians of different types. In their analysis, Keane and Merlo distinguish between two latent characteristics of politicians: their political skills, which refer to the ability to win elections ('skilled type'), and their political ambition or desire for legislative accomplishment ('achiever type'). Their analysis shows that a reduction in the congressional wage would disproportionately induce skilled politicians to leave Congress, but not politicians who are the achiever type. They argue that whether a politician is the 'achiever type' is perhaps a better measure of his or her 'quality' than whether he or she is the 'skilled type' (which refers to a politician's electability). Thus, they conclude that the congressional wage does not differentially impact on the career decisions of high- versus low- quality members of Congress, although it does affect skilled politicians relatively more.

Borrowing some insights from this literature, we conclude that the sharp increase in the parliamentary wage in Italy has contributed to the decline of the quality of the elected legislators over time (via the entry effect pointed out by Mattozzi and Merlo, 2008). However, a drastic reduction in the parliamentary wage at this time may be counterproductive (because of the retention effect discussed above).[13] On the other hand, the historic circumstances that allowed elected Italian legislators to maintain additional

---

[13] Note, however, that the possible drawbacks of the retention effect would depend on the differential impact a reduction in the parliamentary wage would have on the behaviour of politicians of different types. If it could be shown, as pointed out by Keane and Merlo (2007) for the USA, that a reduction in the parliamentary wage would not disproportionately induce relatively better legislators to leave the Italian Parliament, then reducing the parliamentary wage might be a desirable policy. Also, note that, following a 10% reduction in the parliamentary wage in 2006, it appears that the new cohort elected to the Italian Parliament that year was of slightly better quality than the previous cohorts based on their ability score although not with respect to their average level of education. However, the electoral system was also different, thus making the interpretation of the comparison difficult.

sources of income from activities outside Parliament no longer apply. In 2005, the parliamentary wage of Italian legislators was larger than the average annual earnings of an Italian manager working in the private sector (see Figure 2.18), and their additional annual income was on average equal to another 38 per cent of their parliamentary wage. We therefore believe that a sensible policy would be to preclude Italian legislators from supplementing their parliamentary wage with additional earnings from sources outside Parliament (as is the case in the USA), and to index the parliamentary wage to the growth rate of the Italian economy.

Barring any discussion of the potential conflict of interest that arises when elected representatives can engage in income-earning activities outside their public office, there is another important reason why limiting these activities may be desirable: *de facto* 'part-time' legislators may not be as effective and/or as invested into the job of representing citizens as 'full-time' ones. Using our data, we were able to quantify the extent to which a legislator's involvement in income-earning activities outside Parliament affects his or her participation in parliamentary activities, or, more precisely, the extent to which earning additional income in excess of the parliamentary wage reduces a legislator's attendance rate at parliamentary voting sessions. To achieve this goal, we specify and estimate a panel regression model similar to the one we used to estimate the private returns to parliamentary experience, except that we now regress the attendance rate of legislators in each parliamentary term on their age and age squared, their parliamentary experience and experience squared, their average real annual extra income during the legislature (in thousands of 2005 euros), and a set of legislature-specific (time) dummy variables. As before, the role of the time dummies is to control for possible trends and all other effects systematically related to events occurring over time (as, for example, changes in the parliamentary majority that would make it more or less important for a legislator to attend the voting sessions during a legislature), and the role of the fixed effects in the error term is to control for all (observed and unobserved) legislators' characteristics that are related to their attendance behaviour. An important difference with the previous panel regression, however, is that the amount of extra income earned and the attendance of parliamentary sessions are simultaneously determined. In fact, both variables are presumably jointly endogenously determined as outcomes of each legislator's choice of how to allocate his or her time between parliamentary and extra-parliamentary activities. To address the endogeneity issue, we adopt an instrumental variable procedure where the annual

Table 3.4 Panel regression of attendance rates (N = 2,775)

Variable	Coefficient	Std error
Intercept	52.7191**	8.8674
Age	1.1436**	0.3410
Age^2	−0.0099**	0.0032
Experience	−0.8114**	0.3956
Experience^2	0.0077**	0.0223
Extra income (in thousands of 2005 Euros)	−0.0883**	0.0149

Note: The estimates of the first stage regression and of the 1,679 fixed-effect coefficients and the coefficients of the 7 time dummies that were included in the regression are not reported here to economize on space. **denotes significance at the 5% level; *at the 10% level.

income before entering Parliament is used as an instrument for the extra income earned while in Parliament. The results are reported in Table 3.4.[14]

As we can see from the estimates, holding everything else constant, an additional 10,000 euros of extra income earned outside Parliament decreases the attendance rate of a legislator by 1 per cent.[15] This result strengthens the case for precluding Italian legislators from supplementing their parliamentary wage with additional earnings from sources outside Parliament.

The analysis of legislators' attendance rates in parliamentary voting sessions also allows us to bring a new element into our discussion of the quality of the Italian legislators and how it has changed between the First and the Second Republics. As we mentioned above, Keane and Merlo (2007) raise the issue of whether, using their terminology, being a 'skilled' type is a better measure of the overall quality of a politician than being an 'achiever' type. More broadly, in addition to possessing the type of general skills that make an individual more likely to be successful in every occupation (for example, intelligence), the list of desirable traits for a politician typically include being 'public spirited' (for example, having a desire for public service and/or influencing public policy), as well as personal characteristics such as morality, integrity, and work ethic. Clearly, being involved in a scandal and/or being convicted of corruption or another crime is a direct

[14] Another important difference with the other panel regression we described above is that, unlike income, which is observed on an annual basis, attendance rates are available only for the entire duration of each legislature. Hence, the panel of attendance rates is much shorter (i.e., the number of observations for each individual is much smaller), which affects the performance of the fixed-effect estimator. We therefore use a random-effect estimator, which we then use to predict the individual fixed effects.

[15] Gagliarducci, Nannicini, and Naticchioni (2008) obtain a similar finding in their analysis of the behavior of Italian MPs in Legislatures XIII and XIV. We also find that, ceteris paribus, attendance rates decline with experience in Parliament, but increase with age.

indication of a lack of such desirable characteristics. On the other hand, although one could certainly not use attendance rates as a direct measure of public spiritedness, they may be positively correlated with such characteristics.[16] The data we presented in Chapter 2 provide some information in this regard and show, for example, that attendance rates have increased in the Second Republic relative to the First. An important limitation of our dataset, however, is that it does not contain any variable that would allow us to address this issue in a satisfactory manner, and provide a way for assessing the 'quality' of politicians and whether it has changed over time. In this regard, a data collection effort similar to the one undertaken by Diermeier, Keane, and Merlo (2005) for the United States, who compiled a record of major legislative achievements by members of Congress, may go a long way toward casting some light on these important questions.

3.2. Some closing remarks on the Italian electoral law

As we already pointed out in Chapter 1, Italy has experienced two changes of its electoral law since 1994. Until 1994 (Legislatures I–XI), elections were held according to an open-list proportional system. In 1994, a mixed-majoritarian system was introduced (the so-called *Mattarellum*), which was used to elect Legislatures XII–XIV. Finally, in 2005, a new closed-list proportional system was adopted (the so-called *Porcellum*), and this has been used to elect Legislatures XV and XVI (the legislature that was elected in April 2008).

Most of the public and scholarly debate on the relative merits of the different electoral laws focuses on their impact on the number of political parties and on government stability. With the adoption of the mixed-majoritarian electoral system, the average duration of the executive increased from slightly above one year in the First Republic to more than two years in Legislatures XII–XIV.[17] On the other hand, it has not been effective in reducing party fragmentation. In fact, while in 1994—the first election with the mixed-majoritarian electoral system—the number of

---

[16] Attendance rates obviously depend on party discipline. Furthermore, they are measured with error because of the pervasive phenomenon of the 'pianisti' (i.e., legislators who record roll-call votes not only for themselves but also for several other colleagues of their own party).

[17] Government duration is measured as the time elapsed between two changes in the partisan composition of the Cabinet. As a term of comparison, during the period 1945–96, government duration was over three and a half years in Germany, almost five years in Sweden, and eight and a half years in the UK.

parties in the Lower House decreased from sixteen to ten, in the next election in 1996 it went back to fourteen, and then down to eight in 2001 (see Figure 1.1). Under the closed-list proportional system, sixteen parties were represented in the 15th Legislature and five in the 16th Legislature.

However, a second issue that is equally important in the assessment of the relative desirability of different electoral systems is whether these systems differ in any systematic way with respect to the incentives they provide to politicians in terms of electoral accountability. In a pure majoritarian system, an incumbent typically reruns for office in the same district where he or she was first elected. Hence, at least to some degree, electors can evaluate the incumbent according to his or her own performance in office. In proportional systems, on the other hand, several incumbents run for office in the same district. Moreover, in a closed-list proportional system, such as the *Porcellum*, voters can vote only for the party list, but cannot choose a particular candidate on the list. As a result, the link between an incumbent's own political performance and the probability of being re-elected is weakened, and so is the electoral accountability. Although in an open-list proportional system—where voters vote for the party and for one (or more) candidate(s) on the list—there is some room for rewarding a good performance in office, the voters' control over the incumbent remains weaker than in a pure majoritarian system, both because electoral districts are larger and because candidates may run in more than one district. Unfortunately, the existing empirical findings on the effect of different electoral systems on ex-post electoral incentives are scant and inconclusive.

A third important element of the fundamental differences in electoral laws is the effect that alternative electoral systems may have on the selection of candidates by political parties. To this end, we can use the measure of legislators' quality we derived above (namely, their 'ability' scores), to analyse the consequences of changes of the electoral law on the selection of candidates and hence the quality of elected legislators. We document that the change from an open-list proportional system to the mixed-majoritarian system decreased the ability score of the cohorts of legislators who entered Parliament between 1994 and 2001. On the other hand, it appears that the new cohort that was elected to Legislature XV (that is, the first cohort elected with the *Porcellum*) was of slightly higher ability than those elected during the Second Republic with the mixed-majoritarian system. In fact, with respect to their ability scores, the proportions of 'above-average' new legislators who were elected to Parliament under the three electoral systems are equal to 62, 34, and 40 per cent respectively.[18]

Large differences emerge in the quality of legislators when we analyse the results at the party level (Table 2.3, Figure 2.2, and Figure 2.22). The small, elite parties of the First Republic (*PLI* and *PRI*) were better equipped to select good politicians in terms of their ability score and education level. Furthermore, in the case of the two largest parties of the First Republic, *DC* managed to select better politicians than the *PCI* in every dimension: the median (mean) candidate in the *DC* had an ability score of 0.64 (0.76) as compared to 0.23 (0.17) for the median (mean) candidate in the *PCI*, and almost 90 per cent of the *DC* legislators had a college degree compared to about 65 per cent in the *PCI*. Turning the attention to the Second Republic, the new recruits of the largest parties, *FI* and *ULIVO*, are systematically better than those of other parties with respect to their ability score and also their level of education. At the opposite end of the spectrum is *LN*, whose elected MPs fare the worst along several dimensions, which include their level of education as well as their ability scores. However, all parties of the Second Republic are worse than those of the First Republic in terms of their proportion of new legislators with 'above-average' ability scores.

These results portray a completely novel picture of the Italian electoral landscape. A better selection of politicians occurred under the open-list proportional system, where the recruiting of politicians was essentially done by the parties, with the control of the voters being limited to choosing the party and possibly a candidate in the party list. However, not all parties, when given this opportunity, were equally successful in recruiting the 'best' politicians. Moreover, the duration of governments was typically short. Placing the selection of the candidates even more under the control of party leaders, as it has been done since 2006 with the closed-list proportional system, reduced the overall quality of the legislators substantially below that of the legislators elected under the pre-1994 (open-list) system. Furthermore, the selection of politicians under the mixed-majoritarian law, which was strongly advocated during the 1990s, leading to the abolition of the proportional electoral system with the 1996 referendum, proved to be considerably worse.

---

[18] It is worth noting that the cohort elected in 2006 contained only 267 individuals compared to the 1,065 politicians who were first elected to the House between 1994 and 2001, and the 15th Legislature lasted only two years. Hence, we have to be very cautious in interpreting the effect of the *Porcellum*, and we need to revisit these findings after more cohorts of legislators have been elected with the new law. Also, recall that, with respect to the open-list proportional electoral system, we could calculate quality scores only for Legislatures VIII–XI because of the lack of pre-1981 income data.

These findings have interesting implications for the debate on electoral law. In fact, although the 2006 electoral system with closed-list proportional representation may not be undesirable *per se*, it is extremely risky, as its implications for the overall quality of Parliament critically hinge on the ability of individual parties to recruit the best possible politicians. As suggested by our analysis, this is not always the case.

Should we make a case for less party involvement in the selection of candidates? At least to some extent, the answer is yes. The open-list (proportional) system, which gives more choice to the voters, performed better than the closed-list (proportional) system. The worst selection occurred in a mixed-majoritarian system, where recruitment of candidates for the different districts was again under strict control of the party. Is an open-list proportional system the best possible electoral law for Italy? Should we then go back to the First Republic and (continue to) disregard the 1994 referendum? Not necessarily. A pure majoritarian system provides better incentives to discipline politicians, enhancing their electoral accountability, and it contributes to increased government duration. Moreover, a majoritarian system coupled with primary elections can also effectively reduce the control of party leaders over the selection of candidates.

APPENDIX

This study is based on a newly collected longitudinal dataset which contains detailed information on careers of all the 4,465 individuals who were elected to the House of the Italian Parliament from 1948 (the election of Legislature I) to 2006 (the election of Legislature XV). Our data end in 2008 (the end of Legislature XV), so we have complete histories of 4,078 members who left the Italian Parliament on or before 28 April 2008 (the date the legislators elected to Legislature XVI were sworn in). But histories are right-censored for the remaining 387 MPs who were re-elected to serve in Legislature XVI. To construct the dataset we used a variety of sources we now describe in detail.

For each individual in the sample, the dataset contains:

1. Biographical data (i.e., date and place of birth, gender, educational background, last occupation held prior to entering Parliament, party affiliation, and region or district where elected), and the full record of parliamentary service (with the exact dates of entry and, if applicable, exit), of committee and parliamentary group membership, of leadership positions within Parliament, and of all government posts held while in Parliament. We obtained this information from Camera dei Deputati (2007), the official website of the House, www.camera.it, and the official website of the government, www.governo.it.[1] To verify dubious entries we also consulted the transcripts of the relevant parliamentary sessions. As an additional source of information regarding the professional background of legislators we also consulted *La Navicella* (1949–2001) and Pasquino (1997).
2. Annual parliamentary wage since 1948. This information was provided by the Office of the Presidency of the House.
3. Attendance at parliamentary voting sessions for Legislatures VIII–XV. This information was provided by the office of the House that records the outcomes of all electronic voting sessions, which were introduced in 1979 at the beginning of Legislature VIII.

---

[1] At the beginning of our data collection effort we consulted the annals of the Italian Parliament better known as *La Navicella* (1949–2001). These annals have been the primary data source for previous works on Italian legislators (see, e.g., Anastasi 2004). The annals are published once for each legislature, typically during the first half of the term, and contain self-reported biographical information and parliamentary activities of all legislators. However, this source proved to be rather imprecise and unsuitable for our needs. First and foremost, since *La Navicella* prints information gathered at one point in time during a legislature, it cannot account for all the changes (such as premature exits, new entries, switches of groups and of committee memberships) that occur during the subsequent years. Second, being based entirely on self-reported information, these annals have a further degree of incompleteness because not all legislators report all their activities.

4. Mode of exit (i.e., voluntary exit, electoral defeat, or death). This information was obtained from the official electoral lists and the electoral results provided by the Ministry of the Interior for each of the sixteen general elections held between 1953 and 2008.

5. Annual before-tax declared income from 1981 to 2005. This information was obtained from the tax returns of each MP starting from his or her 1982 return (which contains information on the income in the previous calendar year), which can be found by visiting the archive at the *Servizio Prerogative e Immunità* of the House, where these returns can be consulted in accordance with the Italian Law n. 441, 5 July 1982, which established the publicity of the tax returns of all elected representatives.

6. Scandals from 1948 to 1994. To measure the involvement of a legislator in a scandal we used the dataset compiled by Golden (2007), which records all the instances where a request was put forward by the Italian judiciary to remove parliamentary immunity from a legislator in order to prosecute him or her. The data end in 1994 because of the constitutional change of November 1993, which eliminated the possibility of such requests and fully reinstated the notion of parliamentary immunity.

7. Post-Parliament employment. For a random sample of 860 MPs we were able to identify their main professional activity after exiting the Parliament. We focused on the first two-and-an-half years after the end of their last parliamentary term. The procedure we followed to construct a representative sample of former MPs is as follows. We first selected all individuals who were born in odd months (January, March, May, July, September, and November). For each of them we then gathered information from a variety of sources, which included books, datasets, the Internet, and phone interviews. Our starting point was two publications by the *Associazione Ex-Parlamentari della Repubblica* (2000, 2002) as well as the books by Martuscelli (1985) and Provantini (1997), which contain some information on the post-Parliament occupation of several former MPs. We then searched newspaper archives, the Web, and the House digital archives. In fact, by reading the transcripts of the House sessions, we found all the MPs who resigned from their seats in the Parliament to move into offices that, by law, are incompatible with a presence in the Italian Parliament (members of the CSM, European Parliaments, Constitutional Court, CNEL, and members of regional central administrations). The Web was used to match the list of legislators with existing datasets on individuals who held the above-mentioned offices. Last, we used phone interviews, through which we directly contacted ex-legislators and asked information about their career paths.

References

Aberbach, Joel, Putnam, Robert, and Rockman, Bert (1981). *Bureaucrats and Politicians in Western Democracies*. Cambridge, MA: Harvard University Press.

Anastasi, Antonio (2004). *Parlamento e Partiti in Italia dalla I alla XIV Legislatura*. Milan: Giuffrè.

Associazione Ex-Parlamentari della Repubblica (2000). *Gli ex Parlamentari della Repubblica*. Rome: La Navicella. Editoriale Italiana.

Associazione Ex-Parlamentari della Repubblica (2002). *Gli ex Parlamentari della Repubblica: Supplemento*. Rome: La Navicella. Editoriale Italiana.

Bartolini, Stefano, and D'Alimonte, Roberto (1996). 'Plurality Competition and Party Realignment in Italy: The 1994 Parliamentary Election', *European Journal of Political Research*, 29: 105–42.

Bertolino, Simone (2004). *Rifondazione Comunista: Storia e Organizzazione*. Bologna: Il Mulino.

Besley, Timothy (2004). 'Paying Politicians: Theory and Evidence', *Journal of the European Economic Association*, 2: 193–215.

Best, Heinrich, and Cotta, Maurizio (2000) (eds). *Parliamentary Representatives in Europe 1848–2000: Legislative Recruitment and Careers in Eleven European Countries*. Oxford: Oxford University Press.

Caciagli, Mario, and Barnes, Samuel Henry (1994). *L'Italia fra Crisi e Transizione*. Bari: Laterza.

Camera dei Deputati (2007). *I Deputati della Repubblica dalla I alla XIV Legislatura*. Camera dei Deputati.

Caselli, Francesco, and Morelli, Massimo (2004). 'Bad Politicians', *Journal of Public Economics*, 88: 759–82.

Colajanni, Napoleone (1996). *Mani Pulite? Giustizia e Politica in Italia*. Milan: Mondadori.

Cotta, Maurizio (1979). *Classe Politica e Parlamento in Italia: 1946–1976*. Bologna: Il Mulino.

Cotta, Maurizio, and Isernia, Pierangelo (1996) (eds). *Il Gigante dai Piedi di Argilla: la Crisi del Regime Partitocratico in Italia*. Bologna: Il Mulino.

De Rosa, Roberto (2007). 'Partito Democratico Della Sinistra—Democratici di Sinistra', in Luciano Bardi, Piero Ignazi, and Roberto Massari (eds), *I Partiti Italiani*. Università Bocconi Editore.

Diermeier, Daniel, Keane, Michael, and Merlo, Antonio (2004). 'A Political Economy Model of Congressional Careers: Supplementary Material', PIER Working Paper 04-038, Department of Economics, University of Pennsylvania.

Diermeier, Daniel, Keane, Michael, and Merlo, Antonio (2005). 'A Political Economy Model of Congressional Careers', *American Economic Review*, 95: 347–73.

Di Palma, Giuseppe (1977). *Surviving without Governing*. Berkeley and Los Angeles: University of California Press.

Di Palma, Giuseppe, and Cotta, Maurizio (1986). 'Cadres, Peones and Entrepreneurs: Professional Identities in a Divided Parliament', in Ezra Suleiman (ed.), *Parliaments and Parliamentarians in Democratic Politics*. Teaneck, NJ: Holmes and Meyer.

Dogan, Mattei (1975) (ed.). *The Mandarins of Western Europe*. New York: Halsted Press.

Dogan, Mattei (1989) (ed.). *Pathways to Power*. Boulder, CO.: Westview Press.

Doring, Herbert (1995) (ed.). *Parliament and Majority Rule in Western Europe*. Frankfurt am Mein: Campus Verlag.

Eldersveld, Samuel (1989). *Political Elites in Modern Societies*. Ann Arbor: University of Michigan Press.

Gagliarducci, Stefano, Nannicini, Tommaso, and Naticchioni, Paolo (2008). 'Outside Income and Moral Hazard: The Elusive Quest for Good Politicians', IZA Discussion Paper 3295, Institute for the Study of Labour, Germany.

Galli, Giorgio, and Prandi, Alfonso (1970). *Patterns of Political Participation in Italy*. New Haven: Yale University Press.

Gerth, Hans, and Mills, C. Wright (1946). *From Max Weber: Essays in Sociology*. Oxford: Oxford University Press.

Golden, Miriam A. (2007). 'Dataset on Parliamentary Malfeasance, Chamber of Deputies, Republic of Italy, Legislatures I–XI (1948–94)', www.golden.polisci. ucla.edu/italy. Version posted 21 Mar. 2007.

Gomez, Peter, and Travaglio, Marco (2006). *Onorevoli Wanted*. Rome: Editori Riuniti.

Henig, Stanley, and Pinder, John (1969) (eds). *European Political Parties*. New York: Praeger.

Ignazi, Piero, and Ysmal, Colette (1998) (eds). *The Organization of Political Parties in Southern Europe*. New York: Praeger.

Katz, Richard, and Mair, Peter (1994) (eds). *How Parties Organize*. London: Sage.

Keane, Michael, and Merlo, Antonio (2007). 'Money, Political Ambition, and the Career Decisions of Politicians', PIER Working Paper 07-016, Department of Economics, University of Pennsylvania.

Koole, Ruud (1996). 'Cadre, Catch-All or Cartel?' *Party Politics*, 2: 507–23.

La Navicella (1949–2001). *I Deputati e Senatori del I–XIV Parlamento Repubblicano*. Rome: Editoriale Italiana.

La Palombara, Joseph (1987). *Democracy Italian Style*. New Haven: Yale University Press.

La Palombara, Joseph, and Weiner, Myron (1966) (eds). *Political Parties and Political Development*. Princeton: Princeton University Press.

Mannheimer, Renato (1994). 'Forza Italia', in Ilvo Diamanti and Renato Mannheimer (eds), *Milano a Roma*. Rome: Donzelli.

Martuscelli, Vittorio (1985) (ed.). *Gli ex Parlamentari della Repubblica*. Rome: La Navicella. Editoriale Italiana.

Mattozzi, Andrea, and Merlo, Antonio (2008). 'Political Careers or Career Politicians?' *Journal of Public Economics*, 92: 597–608.

Merlo, Antonio (2006). 'Whither Political Economy? Theories, Facts and Issues', in Richard Blundell, Whitney Newey, and Torsten Persson (eds), *Advances in Economics and Econometrics, Theory and Applications: Ninth World Congress of the Econometric Society*, vol. I. Cambridge: Cambridge University Press.

Messner, Matthias, and Polborn, Mattias (2004). 'Paying Politicians', *Journal of Public Economics*, 88: 2423–45.

Morlino, Leonardo (1998). *Democracy between Consolidation and Crisis*. Oxford: Oxford University Press.

Morlino, Leonardo (2001). 'The Three Phases of Italian Parties', in Larry Diamond and Richard Gunther (eds), *Political Parties and Democracy*. Baltimore: Johns Hopkins University Press.

Norris, Pippa (1997). *Passages to Power: Legislative Recruitment in Advanced Democracies*. Cambridge: Cambridge University Press.

Norris, Pippa, and Lovenduski, Joni (1995). *Political Recruitment: Gender, Race and Class in the British Parliament*. Cambridge: Cambridge University Press.

Paolucci, Caterina (2007). 'Forza Italia', in Luciano Bardi, Piero Ignazi, and Roberto Massari (eds), *I Partiti Italiani*. Milan: Università Bocconi Editore.

Pasquino, Gianfranco (1997). *1945–1996: Profilo della Politica in Italia*. Bari: Laterza.

Patzelt, Werner (1999). 'Recruitment and Retention in Western European Parliaments', *Legislative Studies Quarterly*, 24: 239–79.

Poli, Emanuela (2001). *Forza Italia, Strutture, Leadership e Radicamento Territoriale*. Bologna: Il Mulino.

Provantini, Alberto (1997). *Onerevoli: Chi li ha Visti? La Sorte dei Seicento Deputati e Senatori della Prima Repubblica*. Rome: I Libri dell'Altritalia.

Putman, Robert (1976). *The Comparative Study of Political Elites*. Upper Saddle River, NJ: Prentice Hall.

Rizzo, Sergio, and Stella, Gian Antonio (2007). *La Casta*. Milan: Rizzoli.

Sartori, Giovanni (1966). 'European Political Parties: The Case of Polarized Pluralism', in Joseph La Palombara and Myron Weiner (eds), *Political Parties and Political Development*. Princeton: Princeton University Press.

Spotts, Frederic, and Wieser, Theodor (1986). *Italy: A Difficult Democracy: A Survey of Italian Politics*. Cambridge: Cambridge University Press.

Verzichelli, Luca (1994). 'Gli Eletti', *Rivista Italiana di Scienza Politica*, 24: 715–39.

Verzichelli, Luca (1996). 'La Classe Politica della Transizione', *Rivista Italiana di Scienza Politica*, 26: 727–68.

Vianello, Mino, and Moor, Gwen (2000) (eds). *Gendering Elites*. London: Macmillan.

Wertman, Douglas (1988). 'Italy: Local Involvement, Central Control', in Michael Gallagher and Michael Marsh (eds), *Candidate Selection in Comparative Perspective*. London: Sage.

Comments

Giuliano Amato

Generally speaking, allow me to observe that quantitative analyses are valuable, but they need to be framed in an explicative context that is also founded on other data. Moreover, the reciprocal is also of value, because many phenomena remain out of focus until the quantitative consistency is ascertained.

Based upon this premise, there are some points of research that merit comment and clarification. The first regards parliamentary wage, on which the consistent growth in the 1980s followed by a successive flattening out, is noted. This is indeed the case, but to appreciate the implication it is important to remember that Parliament has no discretion to fix the amount of the parliamentary wage. The Constitution prescribes that this occurs by law, but the law, precisely to avoid discretionary modifications, has anchored the parliamentary wage to the remuneration of magistrates, so that it grows when, and insofar as, magistrate remuneration grows. For those who do not know this, it could be amusing to add that these very magistrate salaries—a category that is too constitutionally noble to be involved in union negotiation—are subject to automatic changes. In short, we are dealing with an actual train, and members of Parliament are the last carriage. Certainly, as both hostility towards politics and a diffusion of disapproval for the 'caste system' that it embodies have grown, Parliament has exercised the only power it has, the negative power not to extend to its members the increases that are earned by magistrates. This is what has happened in recent years.

Similar observations seem necessary to me in order to appreciate the levels of participation in parliamentary activities, especially if one considers this participation as an indicator of dedication to public service. True, a parliamentarian who is never around and who, after election, continues to concern himself with other activities is not dedicated to public service.

However, attendance records (which are measured based upon the number of votes expressed every day) tell us only that the parliamentarian was indeed there, sitting for hours, pressing the vote button. These records do not tell us if the parliamentarian had actively participated in activities, if he was present only because he was constrained by the group leader, or if he was pushed by a desire to keep his full salary, as absences are deducted. The records also do not tell us if the vote came from his member card or the parliamentarian himself, as until recently it was technically possible for a parliamentarian to vote when not actually present.

I add that not even the other frequently used data, that is, the number of law proposals or questions presented, are an unambiguous key to determining dedication to public service. It depends on content, which in many cases reflects dedication, not to public spirit, but to a specific lobby or to the questions, whatever they may be, about a specific area. In short, even these data are quantitatively useful and nevertheless need to be read with tools of qualitative reading.

Educational qualifications are certainly a measure of the quality of parliamentarians, and their variations in time merit an attentive evaluation. Nevertheless, if these qualities are expressed across the professionalism with which the parliamentarian treats the subjects that are presented to him and also (and why not), in his capacity to frame a solution in a vision of general interest, then these depend also, and substantially, upon the channels across which the parliamentarian has been formed. The old parties had a curriculum that often started with local administrative experience. This experience accustomed one to the treatment of public affairs and only after this was there a passage to Parliament, where, moreover, there was a phase of specialization in a commission that made considerations for previous experience. It is certain that this process produced high-quality parliamentarians, regardless of educational qualifications. The *PCI* did this and had high-quality members in every commission. I do not know the educational qualifications of Senator Bollini. I know only that, as a young Minister of Treasury, when I found myself in front of the Senate Budget Commission in the late 1980s, I broke out in a cold sweat every time he asked me one of his well-articulated questions. And I know that, like me, my predecessors trembled. In turn, Luigi Spaventa, Budget Minister in Ciampi's government, who was dealing with the transition parliament between the First and so-called Second Republic, privately expressed his regret for the old parliamentarians of the *Democrazia Cristiana*, who, unlike the newcomers, knew how to read the state budget.

It is here that we discover that the idea that the capabilities provided by civil society for the government of public interest have a superior value is, in fact, an out-and-out myth. These capabilities are very useful, but, for them to be put to use in the government of the public interest, there is a need for a further and specific professionalism to be developed in some shape or form. Without this, the direct impact can be simply disastrous, whatever the educational qualifications or private professional experience that followed may be. The old parties provided for the necessary training that simply does not exist anymore.

Now, on the contrary, not only is this type of training missing, but a process of selection heavily based on image and the ability to gain consensus using means of mass communication is becoming increasingly frequent. Means of mass communication, as is noted, allow only for rapid, stentorian messages that preferably contain a strong emotional charge. And there is now, therefore, a new generation of politicians who are used to expressing their thoughts for no more than thirty seconds and who, little by little, shrink their thoughts to that thirty-second measure. They are not all like this, but it is often, if not the leaders, then the colonels whom the leaders choose who gain positions of prominence based upon their particular ability, in a negative sense, not to know what to say on a subject after having spoken on it for thirty seconds.

Research notes the inclination of parliamentarians to remain in Parliament and gives a Stiglerian interpretation for this; that is, self-preservation in what is, in its own way, a labour market. Undoubtedly this type of motivation exists, and, on the other hand, it is also essential that it exists, because it is noted that, without personal ambition, nobody gets anywhere. It must be said, however, that the permanence of parliamentarians is based not on their decisions but rather on the decisions of others on whom they wholly depend. It was like this in the old *PCI*, which had, for most of its members, the rule of two legislatures, sufficient enough to do a good job in Parliament, but also enough to accrue a reasonable annuity, which allowed them to return to party activities at the expense of the state. It was less so with the old *DC* and with other parties that were less organized, in which election was entrusted to the abilities of each person to procure preferences. The capacity to get oneself voted, and therefore self-entrepreneurship, was quite important in the years of Mattarella's uninominal district electoral, while, in the latest legislatures, based upon frozen lists presented by parties, the re-election of everyone was placed wholly in the hands of other people. Of course, there is also the courting of greats such as Umberto Veronesi, and, in his case, the decision to stand as a candidate (or better, to accept the candidature that was offered to him) and eventually the decision to stay were his. But I also remember the conversation that I overheard in *Transatlantico* between two colleagues who were taken up with the amendment to stabilize a group of public employees. 'See,' said one to the other. 'Here we are, straightening out these people, and maybe in a few months we'll be in their same situation.' The average MP is visible more in this conversation than in the case of Veronesi.

The fact that there are numerous parliamentarians who remain connected to political activities can have different interpretations. Their expectations in this sense and most of all the affirmation of the principle that a suitable job is their right after leaving parliament are not to be shared. It is in this way that castes are created, and it is in this way that one negates the meaning of public service, which, because of its nature, is a life experience and not a career above and beyond the age of retirement. This being said, it is also true that the experience of Parliament provides a wider wealth of knowledge and teaches one to stay in public life, thanks to that great school, which consists of being guided in all ways by parliamentary procedures (listen to others, respond to the arguments of others, and so on). Therefore, a recourse that is not generalized but rather specific and motivated to who has left Parliament for other public appointments is not in itself a bad thing. Here, the quantitative datum, that also considers the type of appointment, is very important to understand in which of the two situations one finds oneself.

There is, instead, a single evaluation, and it is always and only negative, for the muddle between parliamentary activities and previous activities. It is necessary to keep in mind that the problem exists, but by now it exists only for the private sector. Public employees certainly do not lose their jobs, but they are kept on leave and stop any activity and for several years they have had to choose between a parliamentary career and a public-sector job, and, if they choose a parliamentary career, they must, rightly, pay contributions towards the pension they will receive according to their job. I remember when the option of 1993 arrived and I chose a professor's position, and I remember also the difficulty I had in convincing my colleagues who instead chose a parliamentary career, to pay the contributions that their universities had stopped paying.

With the private sector we are much further behind; there are only the constraints derived from law on the conflict of interest. These constraints do not impede, however, a parliamentarian from continuing his career, for example, as a lawyer—having as such, a pre-eminent role in promoting laws that determine a new and different outcome in his trials (there have been considerable examples of this in Italy in recent years) and in any case favour his clients. This really is not good. And has to be changed.

Lucrezia Reichlin

I would like to start my comments by congratulating the authors and the Fondazione Rodolfo Debenedetti for this project, which has produced a sober and very informative documentation on the socio-economic profile of the Italian members of Parliament (MPs). The authors have gathered a very rich dataset based on the curricula of MPs elected between 1948 and 2008 and, since 1982, their tax returns. Not only is the dataset unique, but the analysis is thorough and sophisticated, a first important step for a quantitative assessment of the profile of Italian legislators.

Who were the Italian politicians and what have they become?

Before commenting on the more analytical aspects of Part I of this book, let me summarize what, in my view, are the main stylized facts emerging from the data.

The Parliament of the First Republic had a high percentage of lawyers, mostly males, relatively young. The parliamentary wage (*indennità parlamentare*) was low by international comparison, and so was the income earned outside the Parliament, especially in relation to what was earned by the MPs of the Second Republic. The First Republic MP also had a relatively high level of education, but his or her attendance rate in parliamentary voting sessions was lower than for MPs of the Second Republic.

Over time, the average age has increased and there has been a decrease in the number of lawyers in favour of managers, in line with national demographic and socio-economic trends. On the other hand, unlike what has been true for the Italian population, the number of college graduates has decreased and so has the number of female representatives. Other characteristics have remained the same: although the number of college graduates has decreased, the number of MPs coming from the education sector has remained very high. Moreover, in both Republics, the MP, once elected, has remained in Parliament for several legislatures, which suggests that joining Parliament is a career choice: 'who gets in does not get out'.

But there are other developments with respect to the post-war years that are not gradual and represent instead an abrupt change that has determined an entirely new profile of the Italian legislators of the Second Republic. Since the Second Republic, the income distribution among MPs has become less equal, and this is mainly due to differences in earning capacity in extra-parliamentary activities. The new MP is not only richer because the parliamentary wage has gradually increased over time but, especially, because the capacity of earning extra income increases once one has been elected. This is particularly true for those MPs who had relatively high income prior to election. The data show that joining the Parliament has always induced an improvement in income status. However, it is important to distinguish between an increase in income because of the low pre-entry income level of the MP and one that is due to the increase in the remuneration of extra-parliamentary activities once one has been elected. On this particular aspect we recognize some heterogeneity across political parties, with *Forza Italia* comprising the bulk of the 'new riches' and the *Lega Nord* and *Rifondazione Comunista* showing an income trajectory similar to that of the Partito Comunista Italiano of the First Republic—that is, an increase in income explained by the difference between the low pre-entry wage and the parliamentary wage. Clearly, these parties fish in different ponds, and the economic perspectives of the political career depend largely on the pre-entry economic status.

Who, in sum, are the legislators of the Second Republic? Relative to the First, they are older, less educated, better paid, less equal, with more managers and more women. Moreover, they have a higher attendance rate at parliamentary voting sessions than their predecessors.

The analysis

The authors have collected a longitudinal dataset, and this has allowed them to assess key questions on the selection of Italian politicians and their performance. With longitudinal data, it is possible to define an econometric model and, under some assumptions, extract information on unobserved characteristics such as the intrinsic quality of the legislators and their 'public spiritedness'. In particular, given what the data show, it is interesting to understand whether there is a nexus between quality and income and public spiritedness and income. Results lead to the conclusion that 'quality' has decreased in the Second Republic (the 'ability score' is positive for almost all parties in the First Republic, but negative in the Second) and that there is a negative correlation between the 'ability score' and the parliamentary wage. However, the index of 'public spiritedness' increases in the Second Republic, and this explains why there is a negative correlation between 'quality' and 'public spiritedness'.

These results are a bit puzzling. The typical MP of the Second Republic seems to be mediocre but hard working. What is really behind this conclusion? What is the selection process that explains that Italians remunerate public spiritedness but not quality?

To understand it, let us take a closer look at the econometric analysis.

Let me first comment on the way the 'ability score' measure is constructed (quality).

The analysis is in two steps. In step 1, the authors run the panel regression where real annual extra earnings are regressed against age, experience, years in parliament, and fixed effects. In the second step they run the cross-section regression of fixed effects against education, gender, and the sectors of employment prior to election. Under the assumption that extra earnings measure individual skills and that individual skills are positively correlated with ability, the authors interpret the residual of the second regression as a measure of 'unobserved ability'.

For 'public spiritedness' the idea is the same. The analysis is again in two steps. In the first step the authors run a panel regression of attendance rate against the same variables as the regression of extra earnings and, in the second step, the same cross-section regression of fixed effects. Under the assumption that the attendance rate in Parliament measures public spiritedness, the residual of the second regression is interpreted as measuring 'unobserved public spiritedness'.

The exercise is ingenious, but there are some problems that can affect the interpretation of the results. In particular, we may ask whether it is reasonable to assume that the ability to earn extra income is correlated with individual ability. Here it seems that there is a bit of circular reasoning: we are outraged about the increase of extra income over time but we associate it with an index of quality! Does the ability to earn beyond what is explained by control variables really reflect ability or just corruption? As far as public spiritedness is concerned, I believe that the attendance rate is a very rough approximation, likely to change with different political cultures and internal functioning of political parties. The anecdotal evidence presented by President Amato in his comments goes in this direction.

Finally, but importantly, results suggest that the main characteristics that are identified by the analysis are quite heterogeneous across political parties. Clearly, more work has to be done to understand this heterogeneity, since it is likely to shed some light on the nature of the selection process.

Heterogeneity suggests that the data indicate something potentially more interesting than just a negative causal link between ability and public spiritedness. My reading is that we can identify at least three profiles for MPs. A group of professional politicians, typically coming from the public sector or the education sector, quite old and not very representative of Italian society. A new group, coming from the top of the managerial class, composed of people for which money and politics go in tandem, and finally a group, which is similar to the *Partito Comunista Italiano* of the post-war years, where members come from lower-income classes, do not have college degrees, and are typically younger. This group seems to be mainly in the *Lega Nord* and in *Rifondazione Comunista*.

This diversity, however, tends to disappear, since, as we have seen, all of them, once elected, tend to stay in Parliament for several legislations and therefore form potentially a class of professional politicians. Is this the right form of democratic representation?

What is to be done?

This discussion is too complex for this short comment. My message is that it would be a mistake to criticize the political class as a whole for its excessive parliamentary wage. It is, however, disturbing that being elected to Parliament increases the ability to earn from extra activities, and this applies, in particular, for those MPs who had a higher income before being elected.

What is this extra-parliamentary activity? To what extent does it reflect corruption? Should extra-parliamentary activity be banned?

Whatever is the answer to these questions, there is a need for a higher degree of transparency. This study is a first step, but it would be desirable to go beyond and provide systematic information to the public about who represents them. One obvious minimal measure would be to publish information on the income of MPs online, as, for example, is done by the House of Commons in the UK. The publication of this study should serve to put some pressure in this direction. However, the problem seems to be larger than an economic one, and it is one of lack of representativeness. On one side we have a class of people who want to get elected to make money, but on the other side we have a class of professional politicians, mainly coming from the public sector, which seems to represent poorly the more dynamic elements of Italian society.

Clearly, policy responses should focus on guaranteeing higher turnover and more representation.

Part II

Italian Managers: Fidelity or Performance?*

Andrea Prat, Oriana Bandiera, Luigi Guiso, and Raffaella Sadun

* This research is funded by Fondazione Rodolfo Debenedetti. We thank Nick Bloom, Tito Boeri, Vittorio Colao, Daniel Ferreira, Guido Friebel, Luis Garicano, Barbara Petrongolo, Steve Pischke, Fabiano Schivardi, John Van Reenen, and Luigi Zingales for useful discussions. We are grateful to Enrico Pedretti for his help with the ManagerItalia Survey, to Valentina Adorno and Paola Monti for help with the INPS database, and to a number of people at Fondazione Debenedetti for their help with the CEO time-use survey. Marcello Sartarelli provided valuable research assistance.

Introduction

There is increasing awareness that the success of an economic system
depends not only on the availability of factors of production such as
physical and human capital—traditionally highlighted in the growth literature—but also on assets that are less tangible and more difficult to measure, including the quality of its institutions, the underlying culture, and,
last but not least, firms' managerial and entrepreneurial talent. While
institutions and culture have recently received attention as drivers of
long-term growth (see Acemoglu, Robinson, and Johnson 2001, 2002;
Guiso, Sapienza, and Zingales 2008; Tabellini 2008), much less is known
about the role of managerial capabilities. There is a growing consensus that
the presence of capable and motivated managers can be an important
ingredient in the success of an economic system (Bloom, Sadun, and Van
Reenen 2008); in a calibration exercise, Caselli and Gennaioli (2005) argue
that dynastic selection of firms' managers can go a long way in explaining
differences in aggregate total factor productivity (TFP) across countries. Yet,
not much empirical evidence is available about the role of managerial and
entrepreneurial talent. One reason is that, if it is hard to measure human
capital, it is even more difficult to obtain measures of such a complex
concept as managerial and entrepreneurial talent.

The goal of this work is to provide systematic information about the
selection of managers, their efforts, and their managerial styles, to help us
understand (a) how such a critical factor as how to select managers is
chosen and developed; (b) what features of capitalism shape the selection
of managers; and (c) how this selection can contribute to a firm's productivity. For this we draw on data from a country—Italy—that, besides allowing access to a number of sources of information that are relevant but
not always easy to obtain, has considerable heterogeneity in the nature of
firms, which range from tightly family-owned ones to widely held public

companies. Thus, within a setting that shares common institutions, legal frameworks, and uniform tax incentives, we are able to obtain information from firms that vary in nature and organization, and thus that can be taken as representative of the various forms of capitalism that prevail worldwide.

But why are managerial capabilities so critical for economic success and why do they deserve so much attention? One could argue that, after all, a manager is no different from any other type of worker and all that matters is the overall quality of the human capital that is available to a firm. A simple answer would be that not all workers contribute equally to a firm's productivity. Actually, if we were to infer contributions to productivity from observed pay (and, to a certain extent, in a market economy we can), we already have the answer: managers' pay is a multiple of that of white-collar workers of otherwise similar age and education, because managers are key assets for a firm, as they are critical for its total factor productivity. The leadership they provide, the strategic steering of the firm, the organizational capital that they are meant and are able to create are what make them different from standard workers. In a famous paper on the size distribution of firms, Robert Lucas (1978) identified a link between the size of a firm and the talent of its managers, which defined the ability of a firm to expand. Some evidence consistent with this idea has started to appear. For instance, Bennedsen, Pérez-González, and Wolfenzon (2008) test for the impact of CEOs on performance by using well-informed data from Denmark and find that such accidental (and thus exogenous) shocks as the death of the CEO or of one of his parents (which arguably affects the CEO's focus) are strongly correlated with declines in a firm's operating profitability, investment, and sales growth.

This is consistent with managers being a key determinant of firm performance and suggests that firm owners should pay a lot of attention to selecting and motivating them.

In a frictionless but heterogeneous world where managers can be perfectly monitored, capitalists (the owners of a firm) interested in maximizing the value of a firm should select the manager with the highest ability to extract surplus from the production factors of that particular firm. This may not necessarily work when there are frictions or when owners also derive other forms of benefit from the firm. In this chapter, our key hypothesis is that there are two 'models' of managerial career development: a performance model and a fidelity model.

In the performance model, managers are hired on the basis of their expected performance, inferred from all available signals (education, success in past jobs, and so on). Their performance is assessed regularly on the basis of predetermined, measurable outcomes. Assessments are used to determine the bonus they receive, which is a significant part of their compensation package, and to make promotion decisions. Managers who systematically underperform are dismissed.

In the fidelity model, there is instead an important relational component. Rather than focusing on predetermined outcome measures, the manager is expected to implement faithfully the wishes of the owner of the firm. Managers are hired on the basis of their expected fidelity; hence, direct personal knowledge is highly valued. Objective performance measures are used less often. Instead, managers are promoted or dismissed on the basis of the quality of their relationship with the owners.

These two models, we argue, are associated with the firm ownership structure. Family firms—that is, firms with a strong ownership concentration and heavy involvement of the owners in the direct management of the firm—prefer the fidelity model, while public companies, possibly operating in highly competitive international markets, find the performance model more appealing.

Of course, no firm uses a pure form of fidelity model or a pure form of performance model. There is always a personal relationship component, even for positions with highly measurable outcomes. A performance component is also always there: even the most dictatorial owner is likely to reward talent. However, as we will soon show, the fidelity/performance model will be able to offer a consistent account of what we see in the data we have collected. In particular, we will use our interpretative scheme to ask the following research questions:

- *Question 1*: How are managers selected? How are they assessed? How are they rewarded, promoted, and dismissed?
- *Question 2*: What do the fidelity and performance models imply about the selection of managerial talent? What are the characteristics of managers that tend to work in fidelity-based firms? Do they put forth more or less effort? How do they use their time?
- *Question 3*: Are the policies we observe more consistent with a fidelity model or a performance model? Which firms are more likely to use a fidelity model?
- *Question 4*: Does the choice of the managerial policy model explain firm performance, in terms of both growth and return on capital?
- *Question 5*: Do Italian firms rely more on the fidelity model than comparable firms in other countries?

For this purpose we rely on four main data sources:

1. a new survey that we ran on a sample of 600 managers belonging to ManagerItalia (the trade association for managers who work in the service sector);
2. a new, unique survey of 121 top CEOs, selected from among the largest Italian firms and banks;
3. administrative pay information over the working lives of managers from the Italian Social Security Agency (INPS);
4. an international management practices survey covering over 4,000 manufacturing firms in twelve countries.

The datasets (1)–(4) are described in detail in Chapter 5. For the purpose of the analysis, the observations in our datasets have been matched to the Italian Company Accounts and Amadeus databases, both of which contain standard firm balance sheet and income statement information. Even though, as said, we rely mostly on information on Italian managers, our study should be viewed as a first step towards answering some questions of general interest. Our managers' survey is indeed the first to combine extensive personal data on managers with detailed information on firms. Our CEOs' study is, to the best of our knowledge, the first time-use survey conducted among top managers.

The remainder of Part II is organized as follows. Chapter 4 reviews the relevant literature on managers' incentive schemes and selection practices. Chapter 5 describes our data sources in detail. Chapters 6, 7, and 8 report our findings: Chapter 6 focuses on managers' characteristics; Chapter 7 describes firms' policies; and Chapter 8 analyses the link between managers' characteristics, firms' policies, and observable outcomes. Chapter 9 concludes.

4

Overview

This research is related to several literatures. A first strand contains studies on HR and management practices, which look at heterogeneity of practices across firms and at their relationship with firm performance. A second relevant strand of the literature focuses on family firms. Finally, we contribute to the literature on CEO selection and its impact on firm performance. We briefly review each of these literatures below.

4.1. Incentives, management practices, and family firms

4.1.1. Incentives

Several studies have analysed the factors behind the adoption of specific HR practices and incentive (for example, piece-rate) contracts. Gibbons and Waldman (1999) survey the theoretical literature on careers in organizations, focusing on human-capital acquisition, job assignment, incentive contracting, efficiency wages, and tournaments. They apply these models to explain issues such as wage growth in the absence of promotions, promotions used for job assignment, promotions used to provide incentives, and separation. Demougin and Siow (1994) present a theoretical model that links the probability that an unskilled worker can be successfully trained or screened to the efforts put in by a firm. This, in turn, depends on the presence of positive hiring costs—which tilt the firm's preference towards internal training/screening—and optimal firm size—which might conflict with efficient managerial husbandry. The model generates a number of predictions on layoffs, lateral mobility, promotions, and wages.

On the empirical side, Baker, Gibbs, and Holmstrom (1994a) use data on the workforce, including its managers, of a single firm, observed between 1969 and 1988, to provide evidence on the existence of internal labour markets, showing that employees have careers in firms that follow more-or-less defined paths in the organization. They show that these career paths are stable through time and result in long-term worker–firm attachments, and that wages are tied to the characteristics of jobs, rather than individuals. The paper also documents the existence of promotion 'fast tracks', which reveals that tenure with the firm does not result in better career attainment, and that the importance of levels to pay is largely driven by selection of individuals through promotion. In a companion paper (Baker, Gibbs, and Holmstrom 1994b) the authors focus more specifically on wages. Their main finding is a cohort effect—that is, cohorts who earn more maintain their advantage over time—suggesting that firms may shield their employees from some of the market-induced variation in marginal product.

A second type of contributions looks at HR policies using large datasets with employee details for numerous firms. Abowd, Kramarz, and Roux (2006), for example, use longitudinally linked employer–employee data from France to look at the simultaneous determination of worker mobility and wage rates using an econometric model that allows for both individual- and firm-level heterogeneity. The results show remarkable heterogeneity, with both positive and negative duration dependence present in a significant proportion of firms. They show that average structural returns to seniority are essentially zero, but positive seniority returns are found in low starting-wage firms. With a similar approach, Lazear and Oyer (2004) use a very rich Swedish dataset with detailed and accurate job classifications, which make it possible to determine whether job openings are filled internally or externally, and to follow employees as they change jobs. They show evidence that firms fill a large number of jobs internally, especially within higher managerial ranks. In terms of wages, external labour markets seem to be relatively more important than idiosyncratic firm effects.

Prendergast (1999) provides an excellent review on the subject of incentive contracts, which are specific types of management/HR practices used to encourage employees' effort and correct time allocation. A recurring theme in this context is the trade-off between risk and incentives—that is, that the provision of incentives is aided by the use of pay-per-performance, but their provision imposes additional risk on workers, which is costly to firms through higher wages. In this context, pay-per-performance should be less frequent with imprecise performance measures, or when agents are less able to handle risk. Empirical research has tested the relationship between pay-for-performance and observed measures of uncertainty or risk aversion, with mixed results. Aggarwal and Samwick (1999) use a large dataset of executives at large American corporations and find that pay sensitivity to performance decreases with firm volatility, supporting the insurance/incentive trade-off theory. Using matched worker–firms data for Italy, Guiso, Pistaferri, and Schivardi (2005) find that only transitory idiosyncratic shocks to firm performance leave compensation unaffected, while permanent variations are shared by a firm's workers; furthermore, they find that managers receive less insurance than other employees—a finding that is consistent with managers having a higher marginal value of effort than other types of workers (differences in risk aversion being already controlled for). They also find that firms with higher variability in performance do provide more insurance, supporting one of the fundamental implications of agency theory.

Ackerberg and Botticini (2002) test for risk sharing in sharecropping by considering how farmer wealth, a proxy for ability to handle risk, affects contract choice. They find that, after they have controlled for matching issues, more wealth is correlated with a greater likelihood of renting, consistent with the usual risk-sharing story. However, observed measures of uncertainty have rarely been found to be positively correlated with incentive provision. Prendergast (2002) reviews evidence that was available at the time and suggests that the allocation of responsibility to employees may play an important role in the relationship between uncertainty and incentives. When workers operate in certain settings, firms are content to assign tasks to workers and monitor their inputs. By contrast, when the situation is more uncertain, they delegate responsibility to workers but, to limit their discretion, base compensation on observed output. This may induce a positive relationship between uncertainty and performance pay.

4.1.2. Management practices

A second relevant strand of literature focuses on management practices (in terms of both HR and operations), and their implications for firm performance. Data availability dictates the type of methodology used, with the focus gradually shifting from samples of a single or a few firms, to large samples of firms active within a single country, to large samples of firms observed in multiple countries.

Lazear (2000) relates the effects of monetary incentives on output using data from a single firm. He tests the existence of a positive correlation between piece rates and average worker productivity, workforce ability, and variance in output across individuals. The shift towards incentive pay is associated with a 44 per cent increase in output per worker, and a significant rise in profits. Bandiera, Barankay, and Rasul (2007) design a field experiment to identify the causal effect of high-powered managerial incentives on firm's productivity. They find that offering managers performance bonuses instead of fixed pay increases productivity by 22 per cent, half of which is due to the fact that, when they are paid performance bonuses, managers select more productive workers.

Ichinowsky, Casey, and Shaw (1997) investigate the productivity effects of employment practices using data from a sample of thirty-six homogenous steel production lines owned by seventeen companies. They show that specific HR practices—such as incentive pay, teams, flexible job assignments, employment security, and training—achieve substantially higher levels of productivity than firms with more 'traditional' HR policies.

Among large-sample, single-country studies, Black and Lynch (2001) estimate the effect of workplace practices, information technology, and human capital investments on productivity using a large sample of US firms. They estimate an augmented Cobb–Douglas production function with both cross-section and panel data covering the period of 1987–93, and find that it is not whether an employer adopts a particular work practice but rather how that work practice is actually implemented within the establishment that is associated with higher productivity. For example, unionized establishments that have adopted human resource practices that promote joint decision making coupled with incentive-based compensation have higher productivity than other similar non-union plants, whereas unionized businesses that maintain more traditional labour management relations have lower productivity. Furthermore, they show that plant productivity is higher in businesses with more-educated workers or with greater computer usage by non-managerial employees.

Bloom and Van Reenen (2010) collect synthetic measures of management practices for 800 medium-sized manufacturing firms in France, Germany, the UK, and the USA.[1] They report evidence of significant heterogeneity in management practices even within narrowly defined sectors. The study shows the existence of strong positive correlations between management quality and measures of firm performance (total factor productivity, sales growth, return on capital, and Tobin's q) and between management quality and competition.[2] Bloom, Sadun, and Van Reenen (2008) extend the previous analysis, augmenting the original sample with a set of 200 Italian firms. They

---

[1] See Chapter 6 for details on the methodology.

[2] They employ three alternative measures of competitive pressure: the inverse of the Lerner index, the share of imports on industry production, and the number of competitors reported by the managers during their interviews.

show the relative managerial weakness of Italian firms vis-à-vis those in the USA and, to a lesser extent, in France, Germany, and the UK.

4.1.3. Family firms

Family firms are a central theme of this research. From a theoretical perspective, Burkart, Panunzi, and Shleifer (2003) provide a model of family ownership, which focuses on the founder's trade-off between more professional management and risk of expropriation. A very relevant point of the paper is the observation that the founder's decision is shaped by the legal environment,[3] which may rationalize the different patterns of corporate governance between Anglo-Saxon and continental European firms.

A recent strand of the literature has focused on the role of family ownership for firms' growth and performance.[4] Bloom and Van Reenen (2010) document that family firms where the CEO is chosen on a *primogeniture* basis show significantly lower management scores than other family- and non-family-owned firms. Bloom, Sadun, and Van Reenen (2008) discuss the role of first-generation family firms—that is, firms where the founder still acts as CEO of the company and other family members play key managerial roles—and show that these specific types of family firms account for a relevant proportion of the Italian managerial gap vis-à-vis the USA.

Villalonga and Amit (2006), using proxy data on all Fortune 500 firms during 1994–2000, find that family ownership creates value only when the founder serves as the CEO of the family firm or as its Chairman with a hired CEO, while firm value is destroyed when descendants serve as CEOs. Consistent with this finding, Pérez-González (2008) uses data from CEO successions to examine the impact of inherited control on firms' performance, finding that firms where incoming CEOs are related to the departing CEO, to a founder, or to a large shareholder by either blood or marriage underperform in terms of operating profitability and market-to-book ratios relative to firms that promote unrelated CEOs. These findings are confirmed in Bennedsen, Pérez-González, and Wolfenzon (2006), where variation in CEO succession decisions that result from the gender of a departing

---

[3] Specifically, in legal regimes that successfully limit the expropriation of minority shareholders, the widely held professionally managed corporation emerges as the equilibrium outcome. In legal regimes with intermediate protection, management is delegated to a professional, but the family stays on as large shareholders to monitor the manager. In legal regimes with the weakest protection, the founder designates his heir to manage, and ownership remains inside the family.

[4] See Betrtand and Schoar (2006) for a survey.

CEO's firstborn child is used as an instrumental variable (IV) for the probability of encountering a family CEO. Using this strategy, they show that family successions have a large negative causal impact on firm performance and that the negative impact of family CEOs is underestimated by standard ordinary least squares (OLS) techniques. In a recent contribution, Bertrand et al. (2008) study the family trees and the business groups of seventy of the largest business families in Thailand. They find a positive relationship between family size and involvement of family members in the business group, especially when the ultimate control has passed from the founder to one of his descendants, and document that groups that are run by larger families tend to have lower performance.

4.2. CEOs' characteristics and activity

Evidence on CEOs' characteristics and working environment is remarkably thin. To the best of our knowledge, ours is the first survey on CEOs' use of time.[5] One of the few studies that focuses on CEOs' characteristics is Kaplan, Klebanov, and Sorensen (2008), who use a detailed dataset with assessments of CEO candidates for companies involved in private equity (PE) transactions to study how CEOs' characteristics and abilities relate to hiring decisions, PE investment decisions, and subsequent performance. They highlight the importance of 'soft' or team-related skills for hiring decisions, in spite of the fact that these skills are not necessarily associated with greater success.[6] Frydman and Sakes (2010) investigate the market for managers from the 1930s to the 2000s. The paper documents that, until the 1970s, the market for CEOs was characterized by relatively stable pay and low inequality among executives, while these patterns have reversed since the 1970s. Furthermore, using biographical sources to construct a consistent panel dataset following the education, career paths, and compensation of top executives from 1936 to 2003, she documents the rapid increase in business education and greater occupational mobility within the firm since the 1970s, and notes that the proportion of executives who worked at one corporation throughout their entire career was about 20 percentage points higher in the 1960s than in the 1990s.

---

[5] The only other study on the use of time by managers that we are aware of is Luthans (1988).

[6] See Graham and Harvey (2001) for a survey of 392 CEOs about the cost of capital, capital budgeting, and capital structure.

Relatively little is known about the impact of CEOs on firm performance. Westphal (1998) shows that CEOs with more independent boards spend time 'ingratiating and persuading' board members, while Adams, Almeida, and Ferreira (2005) document that firms whose CEOs have more powers display more variable performance. Bertrand and Schoar (2003) construct a manager–firm matched panel dataset to track top managers across different firms over time and find that manager-fixed effects matter for a wide range of corporate decisions, including investment, financial, and organizational practices. Furthermore, managers with higher performance fixed effects receive higher compensation and are more likely to be found in better-governed firms. They show that executives from earlier birth cohorts appear on average to be more conservative, while managers who hold an MBA degree seem to follow on average more aggressive strategies.

5
Data Sources

Our analysis relies on four datasets. The first two were collected for the purpose of this study, and contain information on a cross section of Italian managers and CEOs. We complement these with two further pre-existing datasets to shed light on the evolution of key variables over time and on the comparison between Italian managers and their foreign counterparts.

5.1. Survey of ManagerItalia members

The aim of this new survey was to collect information on the character-istics of Italian managers and the firms they work for, and to obtain a rich description of the incentives managers face, both explicitly (for example, performance bonuses) and implicitly (for example, importance of person-al relationships for career progress). In particular, we collected informa-tion on:

1. managers' demographics, education, family background, and risk aversion;
2. firms' ownership structure and multinational status;
3. firms' hiring and firing practices;
4. managers' career progression path within the firm, including appraisals and promotion tracks;
5. the structure of pay schemes.

Our sample of managers was selected from the member directory of ManagerItalia, a professional association of managers operating in the trade and services sectors. ManagerItalia members accounted for 96 per cent of all managers in the trade and service sectors in 2008. These, in turn, made up 20 per cent of all Italian managers.[1]

In 2008 the ManagerItalia member directory contained 22,100 managers employed by 8,739 firms. Of these, we took details from the 2,012 firms that could be matched with the Italian Company Accounts Database—a firm-level dataset containing information on balance sheets, firm demographics, and employment. The information is provided by commercial banks and covers all the banks' largest clients.[2] The Company Account Database and, a fortiori, our sampling universe are skewed towards large firms.

To select our sample, we started with the 2,012 firms for which balance-sheet data were available. We further restricted the list to managers employed in the three main operational areas—general directorate, finance, and sales—and randomly drew one manager per firm in one of these areas. The final sample contained 605 each of general directors, finance directors, and sales directors, for a total of 1,815 observations.

The administration of the survey was outsourced to Erminero & Co.—an established survey firm located in Milan. All 1,815 sample managers were contacted by phone to schedule a phone interview, which was then administered by a team of thirty-five analysts trained by Erminero & Co. The response rate was 33 per cent, with an average duration of 21 minutes per interview. The data thus contain 603 observations, split equally across the three operational areas.

The average size of the firms included in our sample was 240 employees (50 at the median). In terms of ownership, 48 per cent of the firms in our sample were family or founder owned, 12 per cent were privately owned, and 8 per cent were state owned. We also had a sizeable proportion of firms owned by dispersed shareholders (that is, no party retains more than 25 per cent of the company's shares) and private equity-backed firms (8 per cent). Most of the firms included in the sample (58 per cent) were affiliated with a multinational. In 21 per cent of the cases, the multinational was head-quartered in Italy.

---

[1] Social security data indicate that in 2006 the number of individuals employed on a 'manager contract' in the private sector was 117,000. Of these, 23,000 belonged to the trade and private service sectors, and 22,100 belonged to ManagerItalia. Managers working for Italian branches of multinational firms belong to the trade and service sectors, even if the firm itself is classified as industry—e.g. car manufacturers—as long as no production plants are located in Italy.

[2] The data are collected by the Centrale dei Bilanci, an organization established in the early 1980s by the Bank of Italy and Italian Banks with the purpose of recording and sharing information on borrowers.

The ManagerItalia dataset covers only the service sector. Among services, specific industries are over-represented, such as wholesale (45 per cent of the sample) and business services (11 per cent), and retail and specialized IT services (4 per cent). The survey is also skewed in terms of location. Most of the sample refers to firms situated in Lombardy (58%). However, the survey also includes a fairly high number of firms from other northern and central regions, such as Veneto (8 per cent), Piedmont (5 per cent), Emilia (9 per cent), Tuscany (5 per cent), and Lazio (9 per cent).

5.2. CEOs' time-use survey

The aim of this survey is to shed light on the activities CEOs engage in on a day-to-day basis. To this purpose we designed a 'time-use' questionnaire that allowed the CEOs' personal assistants (PAs) to record information on the nature of and time involved in all activities performed over the course of a day over a five-day week.

The questionnaire was divided into three parts. The first part asked the PA to record the information on all activities that lasted 15 minutes or longer for each day of the week. We collected detailed information on the following:

1. the type of activity the CEO was engaged in (e.g., meetings, phone calls, etc.);
2. the duration of the activity;
3. whether the activity had been scheduled in advance and if so when;
4. whether the activity was held regularly and if so how often;
5. where the activity took place (e.g., own firm headquarters, other firm);
6. the number of participants;
7. the type of insider participants (e.g ,finance, marketing, etc.);
8. the type of outsider participants (e.g., suppliers, consultants, etc.).

The second part of the questionnaire asked the PA to list the type and duration of all activities that lasted less than 15 minutes and all other activities not listed in the first part.

The third part asked the PA to record whether scheduled activities had to be cancelled, whether the CEOs took some days off during the week, and basic demographic information on the CEO—namely, age and gender.

CEOs in our sample were selected from the largest Italian firms and banks. Size was measured as yearly revenue for firms and as the average of (1) employment, (2) stock-market capitalization, and (3) total value of loan portfolio for banks. The master sample contains the top 850 Italian firms from the Dun & Bradstreet database and the top 50 Italian banks from the list of all major Italian financial groups compiled yearly by the Research Division of Mediobanca, a leading Italian investment bank.

The administration of this survey was also outsourced to Erminero & Co. All 850 institutions were contacted to ascertain the identity and contact details of the CEO; this procedure yielded 720 complete records. Out of these, 50 were randomly selected for a pilot survey and the remaining 670 formed the final sample.

Sample CEOs received an official invitation letter from the Fondazione Rodolfo Debenedetti, which sponsors this project, followed by a personal phone call explaining the purpose of the survey and the relevant confidentiality clauses. Upon acceptance, the survey was mailed to the PA identified by the CEO, who was asked to record the information and send back the completed forms via either fax or mail.

The acceptance rate was 18 per cent; the final sample contained information on the time use of 121 CEOs, belonging to 110 firms and 11 financial institutions.

5.3. INPS database

Our third dataset was the INPS database, which contains information on the entire population of workers registered with the social security system. The Italian National Institute for Social Security (Istituto Nazionale della Previdenza Sociale (INPS)) requires firms to file a yearly report (form O1M until 1998 and form SNA-770 since 1999) for each worker on the payroll. The data are used to compute the tax liabilities and social contributions of individual employees, which are then paid directly by the firm on behalf of the employees. This database covers the universe of employees in the private sector—thus excluding the self-employed, public employees, and off-the-books work.

Our dataset was a subsample of the universe, based on workers born on any one of four particular days of the year. Our data refer to 1985–2004. Data were extracted for each of the years between 1985 and 2004. If a worker was extracted in a year, information was then provided for all the years covered by the sample, provided the worker contributed to INPS in previous or subsequent years. Hence, the dataset is a longitudinal panel, with different career lengths, which is particularly suited to making comparisons over time. Since only employees in the private sector contribute to

INPS, a worker can leave the sample because he retires, becomes self-employed, joins the public administration, or moves to work abroad. Movers within the private sector, on the other hand, can be tracked.

The form reports information on annual earnings and on the number of weeks and days worked. Earnings are divided into two components: normal and occasional. Occasional earnings include sums drawn from the wage supplementation fund for laid-off or short-time workers, seniority and loyalty premia, one-time bonuses, relocation expenses and business travel refunds, the monetary value of goods in kind, and allowances for lost tips and commissions. The bulk of the occasional earnings should be one-time bonuses, and their incidence on total pay has been increasing over the years. We will distinguish between the two components and their sum, which corresponds to total pay. Since misreporting is prosecuted, reporting error should be negligible.

Given the nature of the dataset, each observation represents a single job—the relationship for which the employer has paid at least one contribution to INPS on behalf of its employee during the reference year (what is called the 'contributive position')—and not a single individual. As a consequence, for the same worker multiple observations can be found in the same year for different positions opened with the same or different employers. To obtain total pay components for a given individual year we aggregate across different employers. INPS has made the data available in an anonymous format to guarantee privacy, but, apart from that, data are not subject to top coding. Hence, information is available also for workers at the top percentiles of the pay distribution, making the data particularly useful to explore pay-structure issues.

The dataset also has information on job categories, albeit with a rough breakdown: apprentices, production workers, clericals, and executives. Some demographic information on the worker is also available; in particular, gender, year, and province of birth. Unfortunately, no information on education attainment is available.

5.4. CEP Management Survey

Finally, in order to contrast Italian managers and managerial practices in Italy with those prevailing in other countries, we have relied on a fourth database, the CEP Management Survey. In the summer of 2006 the Centre for Economic Performance at the London School of Economics, in cooperation with a private consultancy firm, employed a team of 51 MBA-type students to collect data on management practices on more than 4,000 firms in 12 countries (for a full description, see Bloom, Sadun, and Van Reenen 2008). Following the methodology in Bloom and Van Reenen (2010), the survey was based on a grid of eighteen questions, which relate to key aspects of workplace management.

Four of these questions relate to 'people' management, and these are the questions we will focus on throughout.[3] The questions are open rather than tick box, and the interviewers are trained to probe with follow-up questions in order to ascertain what is actually going on in the firm. They relate to the promotion system, the fixing/firing of poor performers, the rewarding of high performers, and the incentives and importance given to attracting and retaining talented workers. Each question is scored on a scale of 1 ('worst practice') to 5 ('best practice'), and the basic composite measure z-scores each individual question, averages across the four questions, and then z-scores this average. For example, on the promotion question a low score indicates that employees are promoted solely on the basis of tenure, whereas a high score reflects firms that promote on the basis of effort and ability.

In sum, the scores reveal whether the firm devotes much effort to promoting, rewarding, and retaining its most talented workers.

To avoid the well-known sample bias arising from the psychological reflex to give an answer that the interviewee thinks the interviewer wants to hear, the survey was 'double blind'. First, the interviewees did not know that they were being scored. Second, the interviewers had no information about the firm's performance before the interview. This was achieved by selecting medium-sized manufacturing firms and by providing only firm names and contact details to the interviewers (but no financial details). These smaller firms (the median size was 270 employees) would not be known by name and are rarely reported in the business media.

The survey was targeted at plant managers in firms randomly drawn from the population of all public and private firms with between 100 and 5,000 employees in the manufacturing sector. The response rate was 45 per cent and uncorrelated with firm performance. The interviews took an average of 50 minutes, with the interviewers running an average of 78.5 interviews each, over a median of three countries.[4]

---

[3] The other management practice questions related to shop-floor operations (lean manufacturing techniques), monitoring (tracking and reviewing of individual and factory performance), and targets (the breadth, realism, and interconnection of goals).

[4] Detailed information on the interview process was also collected, including the interview duration, date, time of day, day of the week, and self-assessed reliability score, plus information

The overall sample consisted of approximately 4,000 firms in Europe (France, Germany, Greece, Italy, Poland, Portugal, Sweden, and the UK), Asia (China, India, and Japan), and the USA. The Italian sample consisted of 202 firms, with an average of 606 employees.

on the interviewees' tenure in the company, tenure in the post, seniority, and gender. Robustness tests including these plus interviewer fixed effects yield results extremely similar to the ones reported here.

6

Managers' Characteristics

This chapter combines information from the four datasets to shed light on the characteristics of Italian managers. We present evidence on basic demographics, education, and social background and a novel measure of attitudes towards risk.

In each section, we focus on the differences across different types of ownership structures (for example, family versus dispersed shareholders), and between firms with international exposure versus purely domestic companies. For the sake of simplicity, we focus our discussion on the differences emerging from the raw data (that is, unconditional correlations). Most of the results that we discuss still hold if one adds a battery of controls. In Chapter 7, Tables 7.2 and 7.4 explore the robustness of our results to the inclusion of additional controls for firm (for example, size and industry) and manager characteristics (for example, area of work and seniority).

6.1. Demographics

6.1.1. Age

The average age of Italian managers appears to be in line with the average age of their colleagues in other countries (Figure 6.1). The average Italian manager is 45 years old, which is similar to the age of the average manager employed in the UK and the USA. Italian managers are younger than their Japanese counterparts (who are 50 years old on average).

The ManagerItalia dataset allows us to disaggregate age by type of manager and type of firm. Average age in the ManagerItalia sample is 47 years (Table 6.1). Unsurprisingly, individuals with more senior roles tend to be older (49 years) (Figure 6.2). People in finance are slightly younger than

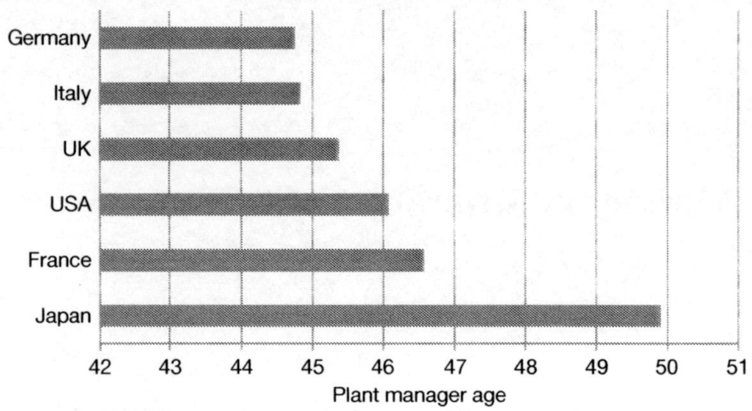

Fig. 6.1 Age of managers
Source: CEP survey.

Table 6.1 Basic characteristics

Managers			
Variable	Frequency	Mean	SD
Age	603	46.98	7.12
Male (%)	603	89.88	0.30
Degree (%)	603	50.08	0.50
Honours (%)	302	11.92	0.32
Managers' fathers			
Variable	Frequency	Mean	SD
Father's degree (%)	603	15.92	0.37
Father blue-collar worker (%)	545	21.47	0.41
Father teacher, retailer, clerk	545	35.05	0.48
Father manager, entrepreneur	545	43.49	0.50
Foreign managers			
	Frequency	Mean	SD
Domestic	255	0.02	0.15
Italian MNE	125	0.04	0.20
Foreign MNE	233	0.07	0.26

people in sales and general management (46 versus 47 years old). Multinationals tend to have slightly younger managers (Figure 6.2), but the differences are not statistically significant. The survey also shows that managers are significantly younger if the firm is owned by a family, *and* the manager is a member of the family. The average age of this specific type

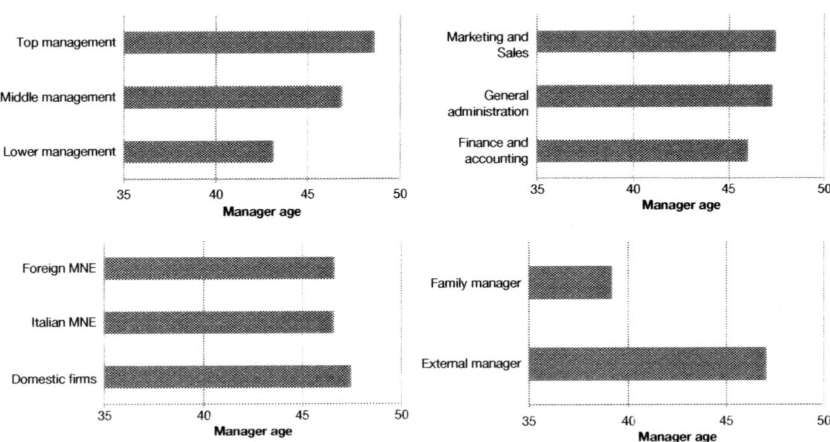

Fig. 6.2 Age of Italian managers
Source: ManagerItalia survey.

of family manager is 39 years old, versus 47 for managers working in a family firm who are not members of the family.[1]

The CEO questionnaire sheds some light on the age distribution of managers at the top of the largest Italian firms. Figure 6.3 shows that CEOs in the sample exhibit considerable variation in age. The average age is 54, while the youngest 5 per cent of CEOs is younger than 41 and the oldest 5 per cent is older than 67.

The extent of variation in the age distribution is consistent with previous findings in Prat and Sadun (2006), who compare the age profile of the CEOs of the top forty Italian firms and the top forty US firms. In their sample the average age is 58 in Italy and 56 in the USA. However, the striking difference is in the dispersion: Italian top companies are much more likely to be headed by managers who are quite young or quite old. While in the USA most CEOs are between 50 and 60, in Italy there are twenty CEOs who are over 60 and thirteen in their forties.[2]

---

[1] The difference between family managers and the others is statistically significant at the 5% level.

[2] Lippi and Schivardi (2007) argue that the relatively large proportion of above-retirement-age managers in Italy reflects the importance in Italy of relations and networks in business and the fact that the supply of relations increases with age. Hence, firms may be willing to trade off efficiency against access to networks in their managerial turnover decisions. Lippi and Schivardi also document a negative relation between manager age above a certain threshold and a firm TFP.

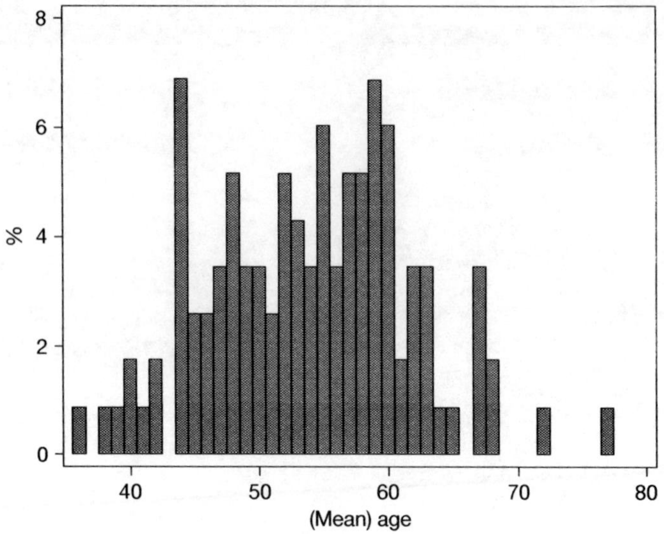

Fig. 6.3 Age of Italian CEOs

The INPS data (see Figure 6.4) display a slight upward trend in the age of Italian managers from 1985 to 2004: the median age goes from 45 in 1985 to 47 in 2004. Instead, age dispersion goes down: there are fewer young managers but the same share of older managers.

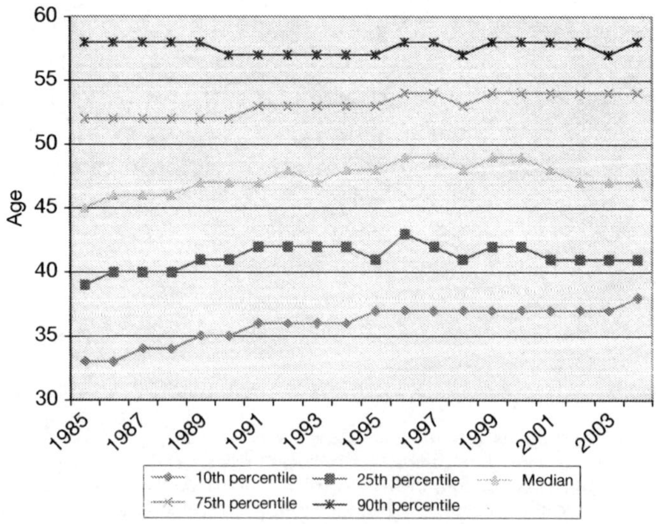

Fig. 6.4 Age distribution of Italian managers, 1985–2004

6.1.2. Gender

As in all the countries for which we have data, most managers are men.

In the CEP international comparison, Italy appears to be one of the worst performers in terms of gender equality (Figure 6.5). For example, only 1 per cent of the managers interviewed in Italy were female. This is very close to the proportion of female managers in France and Japan, but significantly lower than the figure in the UK and the USA (5 per cent).

However, the proportion of female managers is much higher in the INPS data (to be discussed below) and the ManagerItalia sample (10 per cent (see Table 6.1)), perhaps reflecting the different female participation in service versus manufacturing industries. Interestingly, the ManagerItalia dataset (Figure 6.6) shows that the gender gap is much smaller in finance than in sales or general management: the proportion of female managers is 20 per cent in finance versus 6 per cent in sales and general administration. This observation is somewhat surprising, as finance is, at least in Anglo-Saxon countries, often perceived to be a male-oriented discipline, in comparison with marketing and strategy.[3]

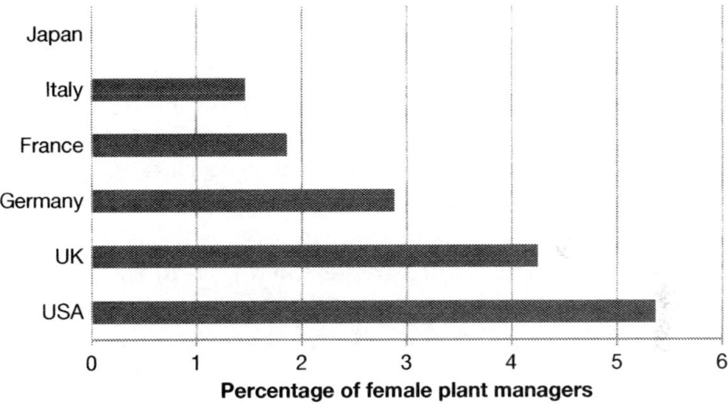

Fig. 6.5 Female managers
Source: CEP survey.

[3] See, e.g., *Wall Street Journal* (2005). This article, entitled 'Men Do Numbers, Women Do Strategy', built from interviews with recruiters and some statistics, concludes that female MBA students are less likely to take finance courses and to apply to jobs in finance. The other trend that appears from the ManagerItalia data is that family firms are less likely to have female managers. On the other hand, managers who are family members are more likely to be female. This seems to indicate that family-run firms are less likely to hire women unless they are part of the family.

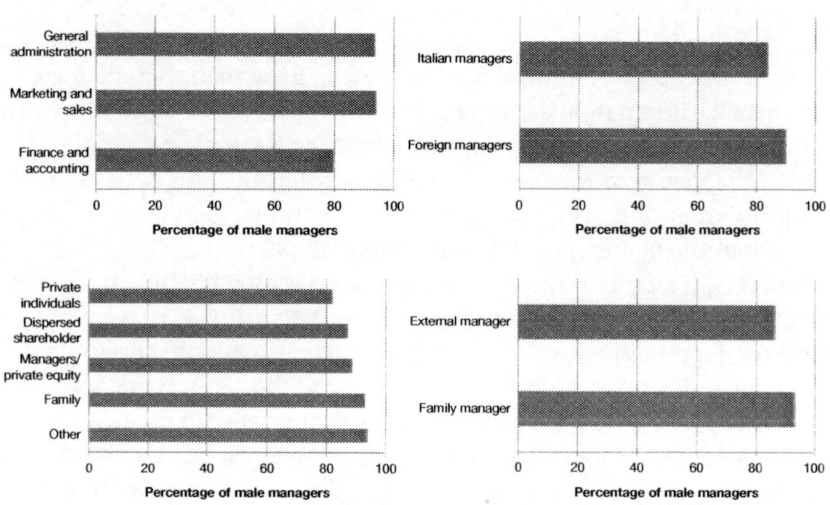

Fig. 6.6 Gender of Italian managers
Source: ManagerItalia survey.

In our sample of 121 top CEOs, only 2 are women. Such a strong gender imbalance at the top is found in most countries: for instance, only two of the US top-100 Fortune CEOs are women.[4]

Finally, according to INPS data, the importance of women in Italian management has improved markedly since the mid-1980s. As Figure 6.7 shows, the ratio of women managers went from 6 or 7 per cent in the late 1980s to over 12 per cent in 2004. Do women face a glass ceiling? Are they 'allowed' into managerial positions only as long as they are low-ranking ones? If we restrict attention to the top quartile of mangers (defined by total pay), we find that women are less represented than in the profession at large. However, the share of women in the top quartile has grown tremendously in relative terms, going from 1 per cent in 1985 to 8 per cent in 2004.

6.1.3. National origin

We know the place of birth of the ManagerItalia members. About 4 per cent of them were born outside Italy. Regarding regional origin, the INPS data show that individuals are more likely to become managers if they are born in regions that have a high density of firms. For instance, 20 per cent of the

---

[4] See Gamba and Goldstein (2009) for an in-depth study of gender imbalance in Italian boards of directors. The share of female directors is much lower in Italy than in the USA and in north European countries.

(a)

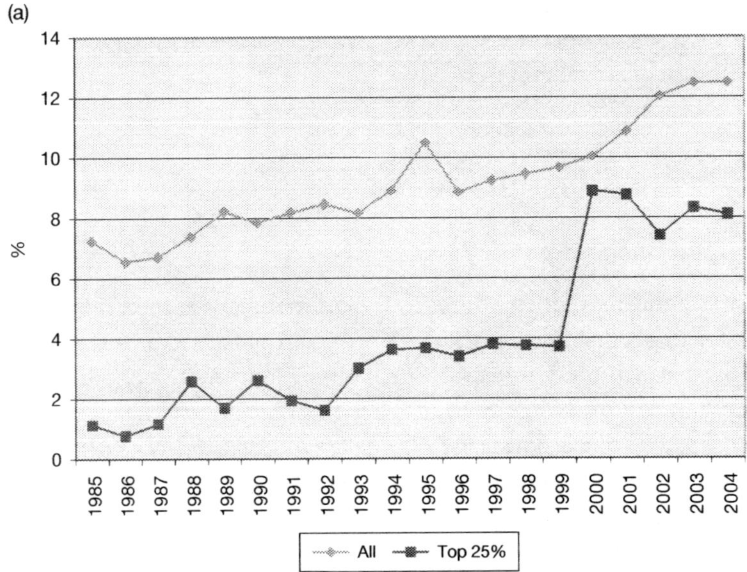

Fig. 6.7a Share of female managers
Source: INPS.

(b)

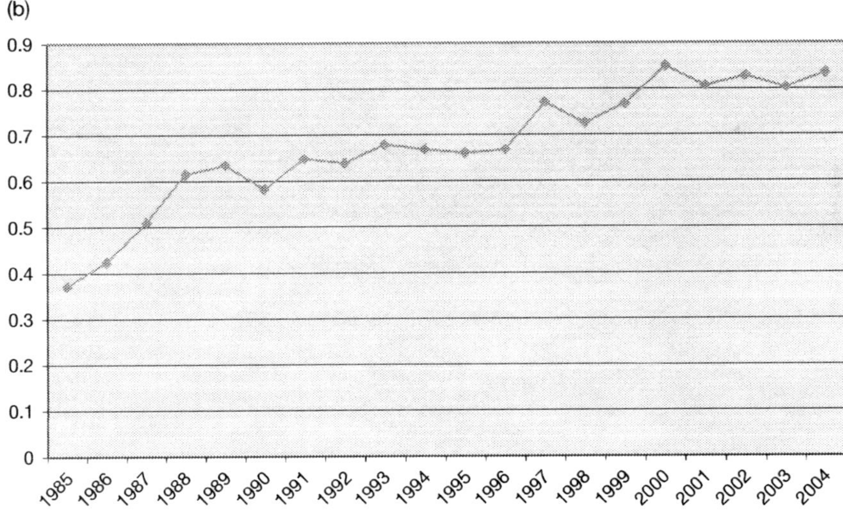

Fig. 6.7b Ratio of women's median total pay to men's total pay
Source: INPS.

managers in the INPS records were born in Lombardy, where 38 per cent of
the firms are registered. This suggests a strong local learning component in
acquiring managerial abilities.

6.2. Managers' background

6.2.1. Education

One of the most striking features of Italian managers is their relatively low
level of formal education: just over 50 per cent of the managers working in
firms who were interviewed in the CEP survey had an undergraduate degree
(Figure 6.8). Among large European countries, only the UK has a similar
proportion of college graduates in management (44 per cent), while all
other countries are characterized by a much higher proportion of college
graduates. For example, French and US firms report, on average, 60 per cent
of college graduates in management.

This is only in part a reflection of the fact that Italian workers are on average
less educated than workers in other countries. For instance, the average
proportion of workers with degrees who are not in managerial positions is
14 per cent in Italy (Figure 6.8). The figure is lower in Germany (12 per cent)
and France (13 per cent) and almost the same in the USA (15 per cent).

The proportion of ManagerItalia members with an undergraduate degree
is almost exactly 50 per cent. The percentage goes down for people working

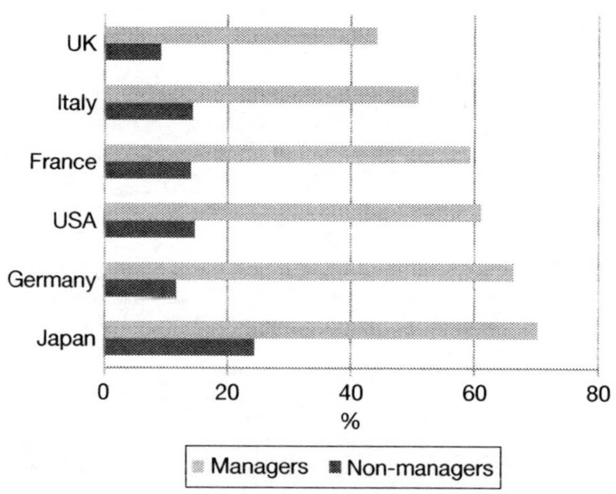

Fig. 6.8 Percentage of workforce with a college degree
Source: CEP survey.

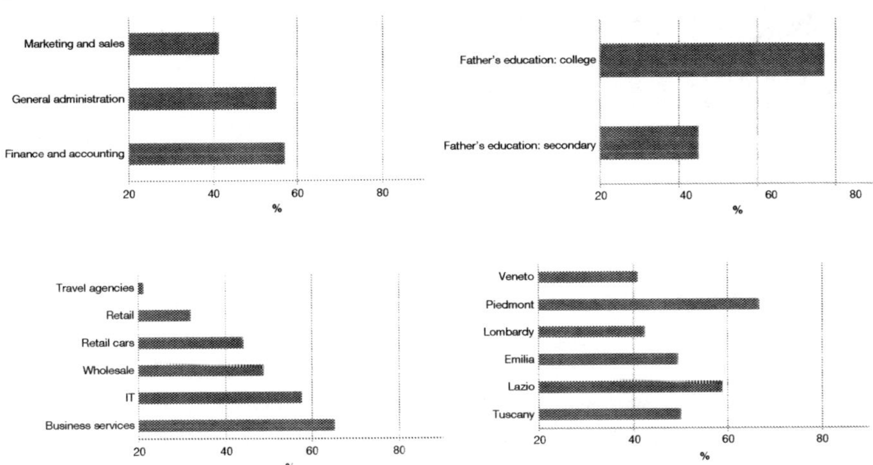

Fig. 6.9 Percentage of managers with a college degree
Source: ManagerItalia survey.

in sales and marketing (Figure 6.9). There appear to be important sectoral and regional differences. The proportion of managers with an undergraduate degree is as low as 20 per cent in the travel industry and goes up to 65 per cent in business services. The figure is lowest in northern regions, especially Veneto and Lombardy.

Whether a manager holds a college degree is correlated with a well-specified socio-economic background. For example, the occupation of the manager's father seems to be a good predictor for the presence of a college degree. Only 30 per cent of the 117 managers who reported that their father was a blue-collar worker held a degree, versus the 65 per cent of managers who reported that their father was a manager, entrepreneur, or another professional figure. Similarly, the proportion of managers with a college degree is 77 per cent of those who reported that their father held a college degree, versus the 44 per cent of those who reported that their fathers stopped their education before university. The data also show that the presence of a college degree is more likely among foreign and younger managers,[5] as well as for family managers (that is, managers working for a family firm and belonging to the owning family).

Apart from the fact that only a small number of managers hold a college degree, among those with a degree the grade obtained is comparable only

---

[5] For example, 76% of foreign managers have a college degree (versus 49% of Italian managers) and the percentages of managers with a college degree is 73% for managers below 40 years, 53% for managers between 40 and 50 years, and 30% for managers above 50 years.

with the mean grade of all graduates. Managers' average grade is 101.8 (the maximum grade being 110 with honours), slightly below the mean grade among the graduates in a representative survey.[6] Hence, in so far as college degree grades are correlated with ability, managers do not seem to be selected from among the most able college graduates.

It is instructive to compare managers' demographic traits and education levels with those of other close categories such as executives (clerical employees with administrative tasks), professionals and self-employed, and entrepreneurs. For this we have relied on data from the Survey of Household Income and Wealth (SHIW)—a biannual survey run by the Bank of Italy on a large sample of Italian families. To obtain a reasonable number of observations on these categories we have pooled observations from the last three waves (years 2000, 2002, and 2004). Comparisons are shown in Table 6.2.[7] Managers are about five years older than other executives and professionals, and they are more educated than these two categories (the share of managers with a degree is 15 percentage points larger than among executives and professionals), but they are more male oriented. On the other hand, compared to entrepreneurs, managers are a bit older and have a smaller share of women (10 per cent versus 20 per cent) but are much more educated: among entrepreneurs the share with a college degree is only 8 per cent.

6.2.2. Family and origin

Family firms are a key feature of the Italian economy. La Porta, Lopez de Silanes, and Shleifer (1999), for example, report that 60 per cent of Italian medium-sized publicly traded firms belong to a family (including both founders and second-generation firms), versus 10 per cent in the USA and 40 and 50 per cent in France and Germany, respectively. The importance of family firms in the Italian economy is confirmed in the CEP survey. Table 6.3 shows that the proportion of family-owned firms in Italy recorded in the CEP survey is 62 per cent, significantly higher than for Germany, France, the UK, and the USA, which range from 38 per cent to 28 per cent. First-generation (that is, firms where the CEO still has an active role) and

---

[6] In the 2004 Survey of Household Income and Wealth (SHIW), a representative household survey, the average grade among college graduates is 102 and the median is 104.

[7] Mean characteristics of managers in SHIW are very similar to those in the ManagerItalia dataset; mean age is 47 years, the share of male managers is 89.9%, and 42.6% hold a degree.

Table 6.2 Basic characteristics: executives, professional, and entrepreneurs (SHIW sample)

Executives			
Variable	**Frequency**	**Mean**	**SD**
Age	540	42.58	921
Male (%)	540	74.26	0.44
Degree (%)	540	30.00	0.46

Professionals and self-employed			
Variable	**Frequency**	**Mean**	**SD**
Age	462	43.97	11.17
Male (%)	462	82.90	0.30
Degree (%)	462	34.60	0.50

Entrepreneurs			
Variable	**Frequency**	**Mean**	**SD**
Age	374	44.14	11.68
Male (%)	374	79.68	0.40
Degree (%)	374	8.02	0.27

Note: The data from the Survey of Household Income and Wealth (SHIW) pool the last three waves, 2000, 2002, and 2004, and refer to the private sector.

Table 6.3 Family ownership in the CEP survey

	Italy	**France**	**Germany**	**Japan**	**UK**	**USA**
Family ownership (founder and family)	62	28	38	26	32	28
Founder	37	23	33	23	24	18
Family	25	5	5	3	8	10

second-generation family firms are both over-represented in Italy compared to other countries, although the proportion of founder-owned firms is slightly higher (37 per cent versus 25 per cent).

The proportion of family firms is also very high in the ManagerItalia survey (47 per cent),[8] as we can see from Table 6.4. As one would expect, the manager is more likely to be a family member if the CEO is part of the family that owns the company and the firm is not a multinational. Senior

---

[8] Of these, 19% are founder-owned and 28% are second-generation family firms.

Table 6.4 Firm characteristics

Ownership		
	Frequency	**%**
Cooperative	22	3.65
Dispersed shareholders	147	24.38
Government	27	4.48
Managers	13	2.16
Private equity	31	5.14
Private individuals	78	12.94
Founder	116	19.24
Family	169	28.03

Family firms (169)		
	Mean	**SD**
Family CEO (%)	0.66	0.47
Family members in management (number)	1.83	1.00

Multinational firms		
	Frequency	**%**
Domestic	255	42.29
Italian MNE	125	20.73
Foreign MNE	223	36.98
Country of Origin of Foreign MNEs		
France	30	13.51
Germany	51	22.97
Netherlands	13	5.86
Japan	16	7.21
UK	16	7.21
USA	60	27.03
Other	36	16.21

Note: Australia (1), Austria (1), Belgium (7), Denmark (4), Finland (1), Israel (1), South Africa (1), South Korea (1), Spain (3), Sweden (7), Switzerland (5).

managers are also more likely to be family members. Interestingly, the probability that the manager is part of the family goes down drastically if the firm is a multinational—less so if the multinational is headquartered in Italy.

Multinationals are more likely to employ foreign-born managers, although the difference is not large. The proportion of foreign managers is 2 per cent in domestic firms, and 4 per cent and 6 per cent respectively in Italian and foreign multinationals. Non-Italians tend to concentrate in senior positions and in the finance area. For example, 6 per cent of managers in the finance area are foreign versus 3 per cent in sales and marketing.

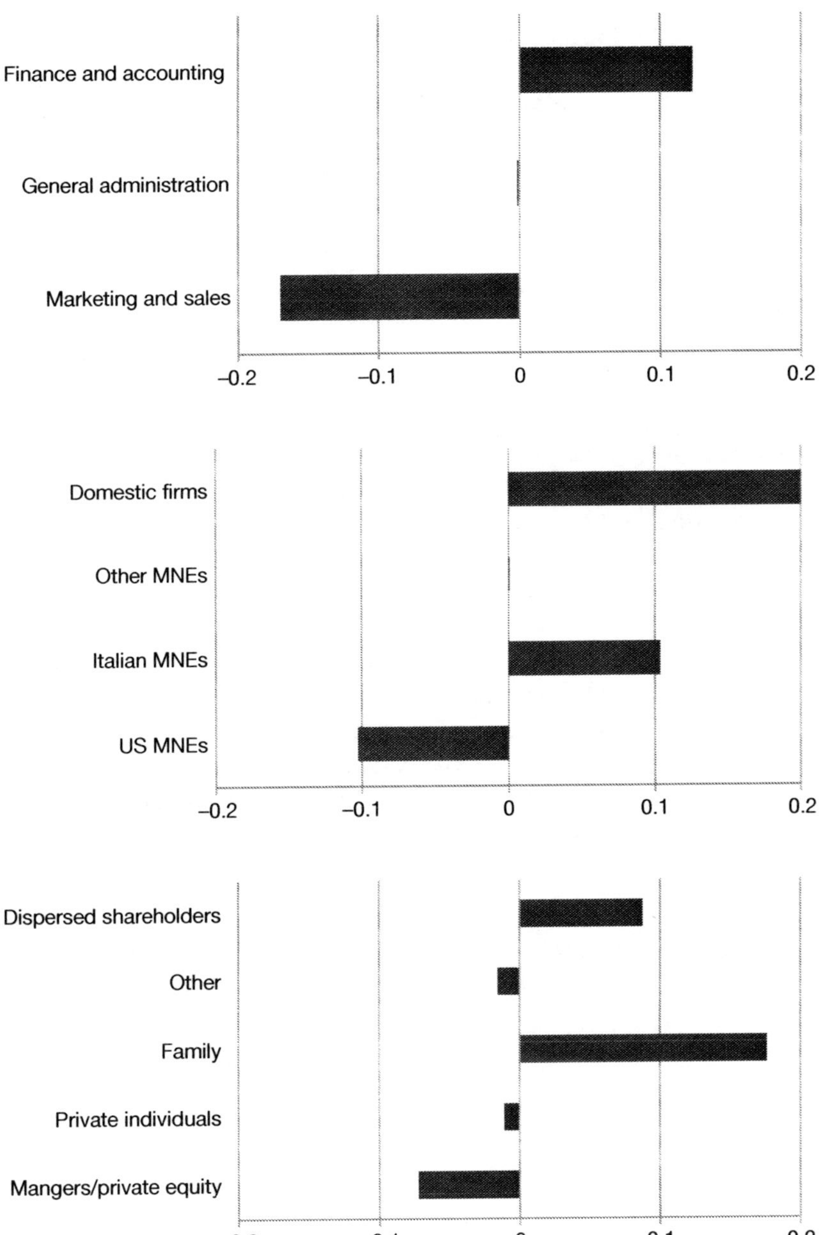

Fig. 6.10 Risk tolerance
Source: ManagerItalia survey.

6.2.3. Attitude towards risk

Managers tend to be involved in larger, more complex, and risk-intensive decisions than other workers. They also tend to operate within a complex web of formal and informal professional interactions. Their attitude to risk taking and to interpersonal trust may be useful in gauging their management style.

In order to identify their attitudes towards risk, we asked the managers two distinct questions. In the first question, we asked the managers to state explicitly their preference towards risk, choosing between four possible combinations of risk and profits (from low risk, low profit, to high risk, high profit). The second question differed, because the managers were asked to state their preference between ten different pairs involving a safe prospect and a risky one with differing combinations of risk and return, but they were not told explicitly which combination was riskier. In the analysis we use a principal factor component of the two variables, and define as 'risk' the resulting standardized variable.

With respect to risk, there are three clear patterns. The most risk-tolerant managers are in US multinational firms or in firms owned by private equity groups and tend to be employed in the sales area (Figure 6.10). In Chapter 9 we will come back to the pattern of risk tolerance and its relation to firm/job characteristics and we will show that it can be interpreted as an equilibrium selection phenomenon: more risk-tolerant managers are matched to jobs that involve steeper incentive schemes. Instead, the only pattern that emerges with respect to trust is that managers specializing in finance are less trusting than those in general management and sales.

7

Firms' Managerial Policies

The next step in our analysis sheds light on the incentive structure faced by Italian managers. We present evidence on several dimensions of incentives, ranging from explicit short-term incentives related to objective measures of performance (that is, bonus pay) to implicit long-term incentives such as the role of personal relationships on the managers' career prospects.

As in the previous chapter, the discussion relates mostly to the differences emerging from the raw data. Table 7.2 and Table 7.4 explore the robustness of our results to the inclusion of additional controls for firm (e.g. size and industry) and manager characteristics (e.g. area of work, seniority).

7.1. International comparison

The CEP management survey allows a direct comparison of the type of management practices adopted by medium-sized Italian manufacturing firms. When we look at the overall scores of the various indicators of managerial practices, the direct comparison with their international peers shows that Italian firms are similar to UK and French firms, but significantly worse than Japanese, German, and US firms (Figure 7.1a).

However, the overall management scores hide an interesting heterogeneity between practices geared towards operational excellence, and those related to people management—that is, the selection, reward, hiring, and promotion of the workforce.

All countries except the USA score higher on operational rather than on people management (Figure 7.1b) and the difference is highest for France and Italy. Analysing the different components of the people management

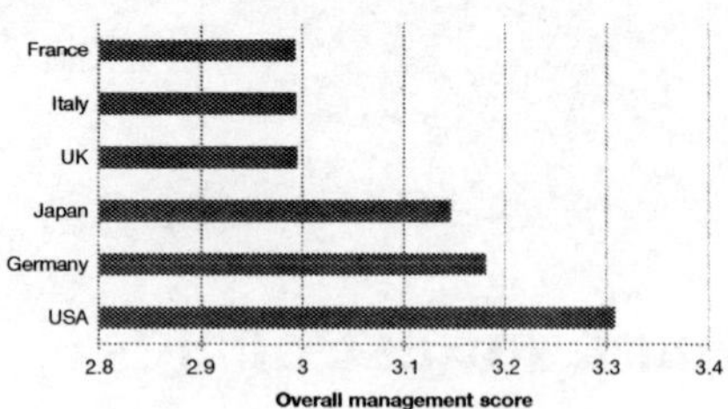

Fig. 7.1a Overall management score
Source: CEP survey.

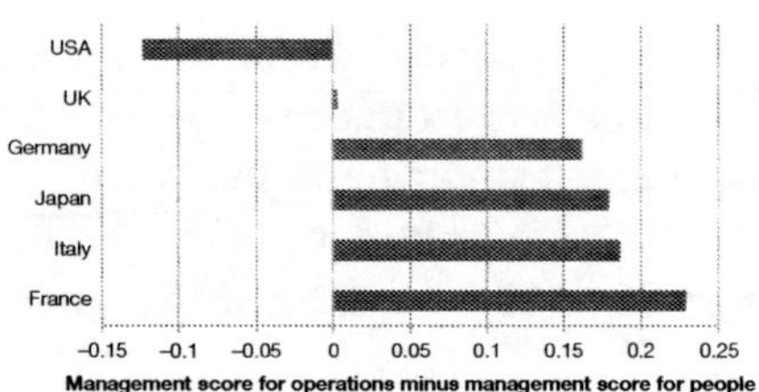

Fig. 7.1b Operational versus people management
Source: CEP survey.

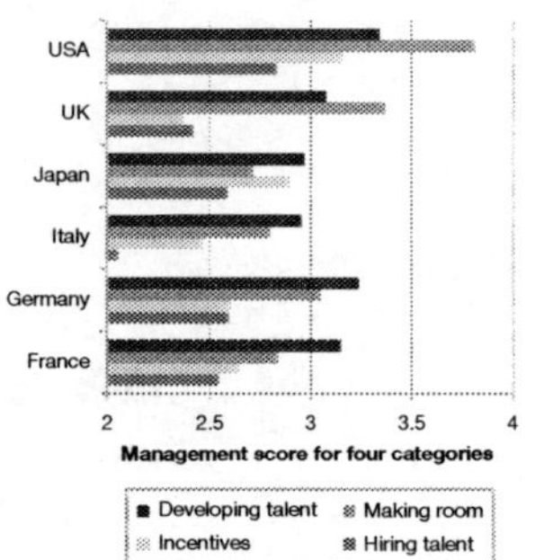

Fig. 7.1c Components of people management

variable separately reveals that Italy ranks lowest or second lowest on several personnel policies, ranging from hiring practices, to the use of appraisals and bonuses, and to talent management (Figure 7.1c).[1]

---

[1] It is worth noting the Italian gap in people management persists even when we control for firms' size and sector of activity.

7.2. Analysing people management with the ManagerItalia survey

7.2.1. Recruitment

We define three classes of hiring channels based on the experience of the managers in our sample: the most impersonal one (head hunters, agencies, advertisements, or taken away from competitors) accounts for about 26 per cent of the sample; a less impersonal one but still based on professional contacts (business contacts, self-referrals, recommendations) accounts for over 50 per cent of the cases; finally, sample managers got their job through contacts with family and friends in 20 per cent of cases (Table 7.1).

Figure 7.2 and Table 7.2 show that firm ownership, nationality, and international exposure correspond to specific hiring practices.

In particular, the unconditional correlations in Figure 7.2 suggest that:

1. Compared to other ownership structures, firms with insider ownership (founder, family, or other private individuals) are more likely to hire through informal networks and less likely to hire through market channels.
2. Compared to foreign multinationals, Italian firms (both domestic and multinational) are more likely to hire through informal networks and less likely to hire through market channels.

Table 7.1 Managerial labour market, hiring and turnover

Variable	Frequency	%	Standard deviation
Managers hired through (%):			
Professional contacts	603	52.24	0.50
Family or friends	603	20.07	0.40
Head hunter, hiring agency, advertisement	603	26.20	0.44
Other	603	1.49	0.12
Frequency of managerial turnover due to:		0.00	
Poor market conditions	603	13.76	0.34
Problems with owners	603	33.17	0.47
Failure to meet objectives	603	26.04	0.44
Better offer	603	47.43	0.50
Personal reasons	603	36.15	0.48
Number of firms previously worked by the manager	603	0.95	1.07
Manager received job offer in the past three years (%)	603	70.81	0.46

Source: ManagerItalia.

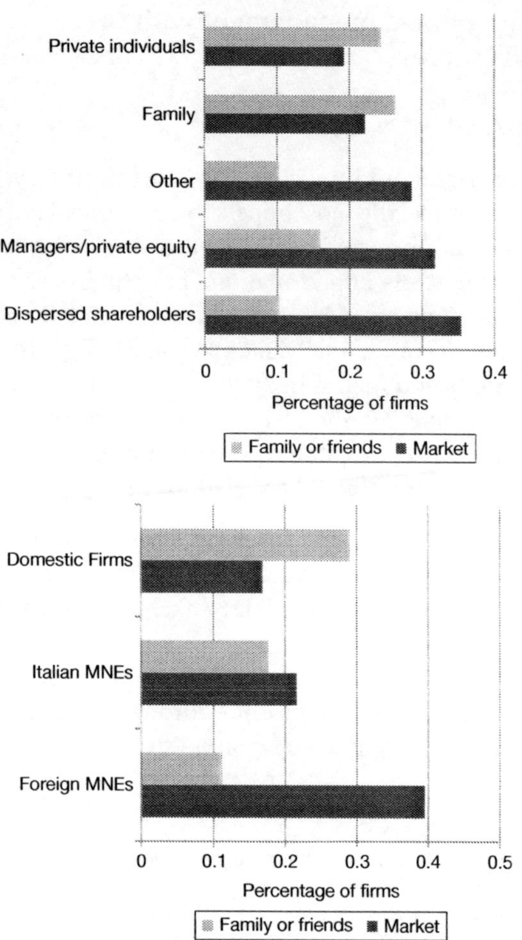

Fig. 7.2 Hiring practices

Recruitment practices thus appear to depend on the company's national origin, with Italian firms more likely to use personal or even professional channels. Our data does not make clear whether this is due to different corporate cultures or to the relative lack of contacts of non-Italian firms.

7.2.2. Appraisals

A key element of human resource management is a system to evaluate the performance and the professional growth of employees. This applies a fortiori to managers. We asked managers in our ManagerItalia sample: (1)

Table 7.2 Recruitment, appraisal, and bonuses

Dependent variable	(1) Manager hired through market	(2) Manager hired through family or friends	(3) Presence of appraisals	(4) Yearly frequency of appraisals	(5) Importance of appraisals	(6) Presence of bonus	(7) ln(Bonus percentage+1)
ln(Employment)	0.009	0.004	0.025	0.023	0.062*	0.034**	0.078*
	(0.014)	(0.012)	(0.016)	(0.041)	(0.037)	(0.014)	(0.043)
Area = General administration	−0.044	0.017	−0.012	0.027	−0.060	0.014	0.136
	(0.056)	(0.048)	(0.061)	(0.154)	(0.136)	(0.061)	(0.184)
Area = Sales and marketing	−0.090*	0.015	0.013	0.151	−0.032	0.108**	0.376**
	(0.052)	(0.042)	(0.053)	(0.142)	(0.120)	(0.048)	(0.149)
Seniority	0.013	0.031	0.105**	0.267**	0.301***	0.038	0.245*
	(0.042)	(0.037)	(0.048)	(0.131)	(0.111)	(0.049)	(0.145)
MNE	0.160***	−0.140***	0.224***	0.027	0.371***	0.252***	0.739***
	(0.054)	(0.043)	(0.059)	(0.147)	(0.130)	(0.051)	(0.154)
USA MNE	0.033	0.011	0.126*	0.608***	0.454**	0.044	0.155
	(0.081)	(0.056)	(0.069)	(0.204)	(0.180)	(0.051)	(0.180)
Italian MNE	−0.132**	0.042	−0.063	0.108	−0.123	−0.087*	−0.294*
	(0.057)	(0.046)	(0.064)	(0.156)	(0.144)	(0.052)	(0.162)
Ownership = State	0.008	0.008	−0.018	−0.165	0.087	−0.037	−0.233
	(0.084)	(0.062)	(0.087)	(0.230)	(0.213)	(0.076)	(0.227)
Ownership = Family	−0.014	0.095**	−0.126**	−0.406**	−0.250*	−0.037	−0.174
	(0.062)	(0.046)	(0.064)	(0.168)	(0.147)	(0.054)	(0.168)
Ownership = Founder	−0.060	0.083	−0.013	0.056	−0.087	0.014	−0.048
	(0.063)	(0.051)	(0.070)	(0.190)	(0.156)	(0.061)	(0.188)
Ownership = Private equity	0.136	0.078	−0.038	−0.050	0.019	0.016	0.211
	(0.100)	(0.076)	(0.109)	(0.279)	(0.274)	(0.074)	(0.241)
Ownership = Manager	−0.228***	−0.015	−0.117	−0.374	−0.292	0.075	0.315
	(0.067)	(0.116)	(0.156)	(0.314)	(0.306)	(0.119)	(0.413)
Ownership = Private individuals	−0.097	0.112*	−0.006	−0.031	−0.051	−0.081	−0.334*

(continued)

Table 7.2 *(continued)*

Dependent variable	(1) Manager hired through market	(2) Manager hired through family or friends	(3) Presence of appraisals	(4) Yearly frequency of appraisals	(5) Importance of appraisals	(6) Presence of bonus	(7) ln(Bonus percentage+1)
	(0.068)	(0.058)	(0.069)	(0.190)	(0.160)	(0.063)	(0.197)
Family manager	−0.331***	0.646***				0.124	0.254
	(0.071)	(0.097)				(0.113)	(0.380)
Male	0.018	−0.064				0.009	0.213
	(0.062)	(0.061)				(0.065)	(0.196)
Degree	0.032	−0.049				0.000	0.011
	(0.041)	(0.037)				(0.040)	(0.126)
ln(Age)	−0.321**	−0.145				−0.312**	−1.346***
	(0.127)	(0.131)				(0.135)	(0.429)
Observations	603	603	603	603	603	603	603
Dummies regions	yes	yes	yes	yes	yes	yes	yes
Dummies sectors (sic 2)	yes	yes	yes	yes	yes	yes	yes

Note: *** denotes significance at the 1% level; ** at the 5% level; * at the 10% level.

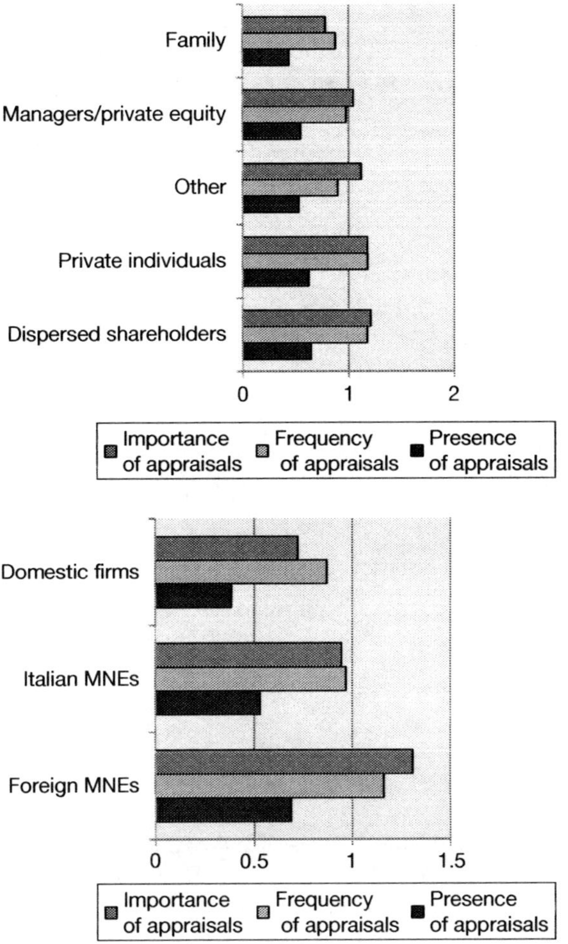

Fig. 7.3 Appraisals

Note: variables expressed in % deviations from the mean.

Source: ManagerItalia survey.

whether there are regular appraisal meetings to evaluate their performance; (2) how often the meetings are held; and (3) how important those meetings are to determine promotions, bonuses, salary, and firing decisions. The answers to the three questions are reported graphically in Figure 7.3 and analysed in more detail in Table 7.2.

A first and—in our view—stunning result, is that almost half of the managers in our sample *never* face appraisal meetings. This is particularly striking in light of the fact that, as our time-use survey (Section 5.2) shows, top executives spend a large amount of time in meetings. Given the presence of a meeting-oriented culture, it is surprising that half of the firms decide to devote no meeting time at all to evaluating the path of their managers' talent.

Patterns of assessment vary tremendously by class of firms, and these patterns are similar across the three questions. Figure 7.3 shows that:

1. The likelihood, frequency, and importance of appraisals is lower in family firms. In contrast to the earlier findings regarding hiring channels, firms owned by the founder or other private individuals differ from family firms.
2. Compared to domestic firms, multinational firms put more emphasis on all three aspects of appraisals.
3. Among multinationals, US firms put the strongest emphasis on all three aspects of appraisals.

Table 7.2 further shows that the likelihood, frequency, and importance of appraisals increase with managers' seniority. This is a somewhat surprising result, as one would expect junior managers to be more monitored (by senior managers). One interesting result is that the emphasis on appraisals does not depend on the functional area the manager belongs to. Firm size does not seem to matter either, once sector controls are included.

7.2.3. Bonuses

We asked managers whether their compensation package included a bonus and how large that bonus was. Table 7.3 shows that 73 per cent of our managers received a bonus and the average bonus (including those who got zero) amounted to 15 per cent of total compensation.

Figure 7.4 shows that firm ownership, nationality, and international exposure matter for both the existence and the size of bonus payments. The figure highlights that:

1. Compared to other ownership structures, firms with insider ownership (founder, family, or other private individuals) are less likely to offer performance bonuses, and these account for a smaller share of total compensation.
2. Compared to multinational firms—especially if they are foreign— domestic firms are less likely to offer performance bonuses, and these account for a smaller share of total compensation.

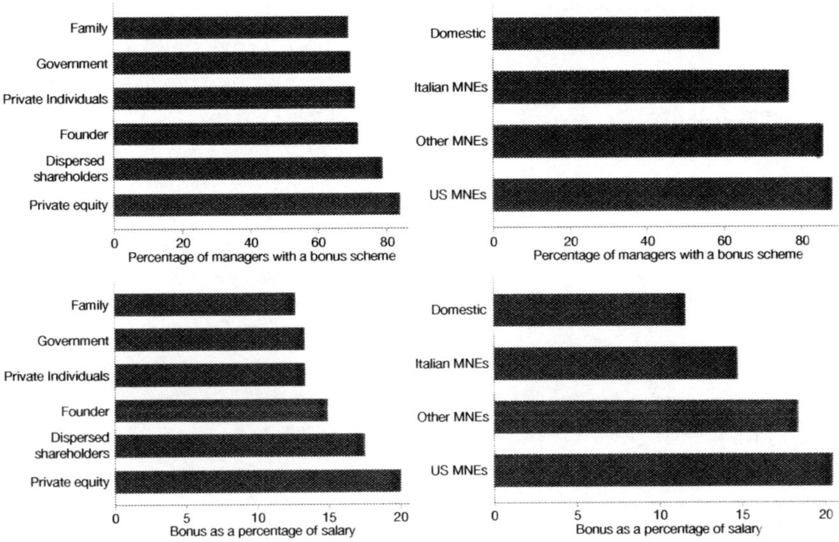

Fig. 7.4 Bonus schemes

The regression analysis in Table 7.2 allows us to compare the relative importance of ownership versus multinational status. The evidence indicates that the latter dominates—that is, there is no significant difference between insider and outsider ownership once multinational status is controlled for.

Table 7.2 also shows that bonuses are more important in larger firms and for younger managers. Finally, managers employed in sales are offered more powerful incentive schemes. This result should be interpreted together with the findings, regarding appraisals, that the emphasis on assessment is the same across the three functional areas. One possible explanation is that, compared to finance and general management, sales performance is easier to measure.

7.2.4. Promotions and dismissals

Our survey contains a number of questions about the criteria for promotions and for dismissals.

Let us look first at promotions (Table 7.3 and Figure 7.5). Reassuringly, 95 per cent of managers in our sample report that performance is an important

Table 7.3 Managers at work

Variable	Frequency	Average	Standard deviation
Effort			
Weekly hours worked	603	53.71	7.87
Monthly weekends worked	603	1.19	1.10
Promotions			
Factors relevant for promotions (%)			
Tenure	603	36	0.48
Performance	603	95	0.22
Relationship with the owners	603	84	0.37
Fast track for star performers (%)	603	37	0.48
Managers promoted internally (%)	603	39	0.49
Remuneration			
Wage	603	98963.52	29548.15
% firms with bonus scheme	603	73	0.45
Percentage bonus	603	14.93	14.63
Appraisals			
% firms with appraisals	598	53	0.50
Yearly appraisals frequency	598	1.00	1.29
Appraisals important for:			
Promotions	323	63	0.48
Bonus	323	62	0.49
Wage	323	58	0.49
Firing	323	43	0.50
Other	323	20	0.40
Job satisfaction			
Manager is very happy (%)	603	50	0.50

factor in managerial promotions. This high level of positive responses means that this question has limited ability to discriminate among firms (except in certain cases of inside ownership). Other important factors are tenure—namely, the number of years in the firm (36 per cent of managers)—and the quality of the relationship with the owners (85 per cent). A signal of a strong implicit incentive structure is the presence of a fast-track promotion system for promising young managers, which can be seen as the opposite of promotion by tenure. Fast-track systems are present in 37 per cent of our firms.

Figure 7.5 highlights systematic differences between classes of firms. In particular:

1. Multinationals are less likely to promote on the basis of tenure, while no clear pattern emerges in terms of ownership types.
2. Multinationals are more likely to offer fast-track promotions to star performers.

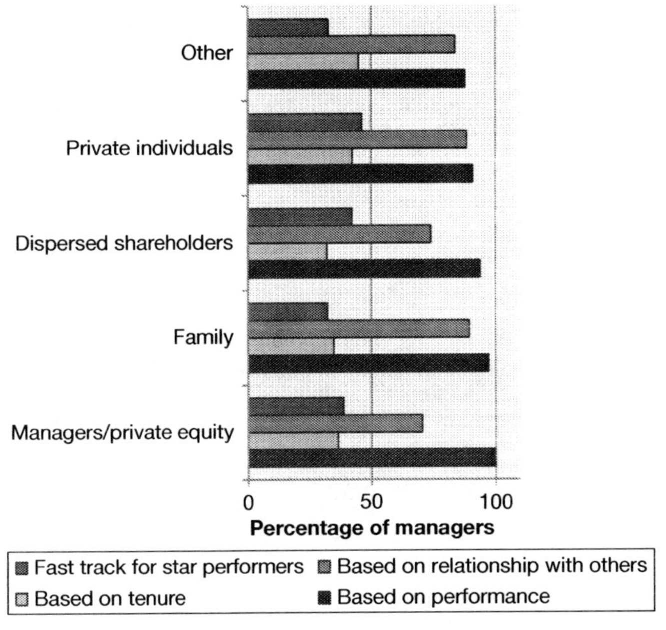

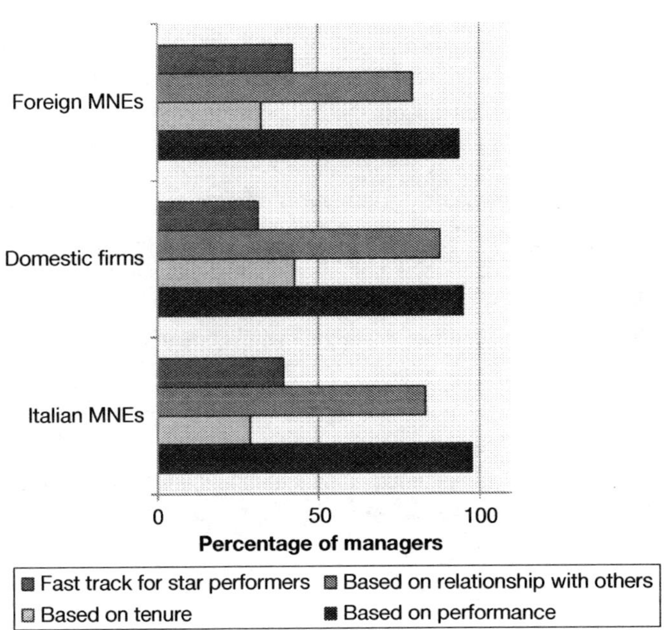

Fig. 7.5 Promotions

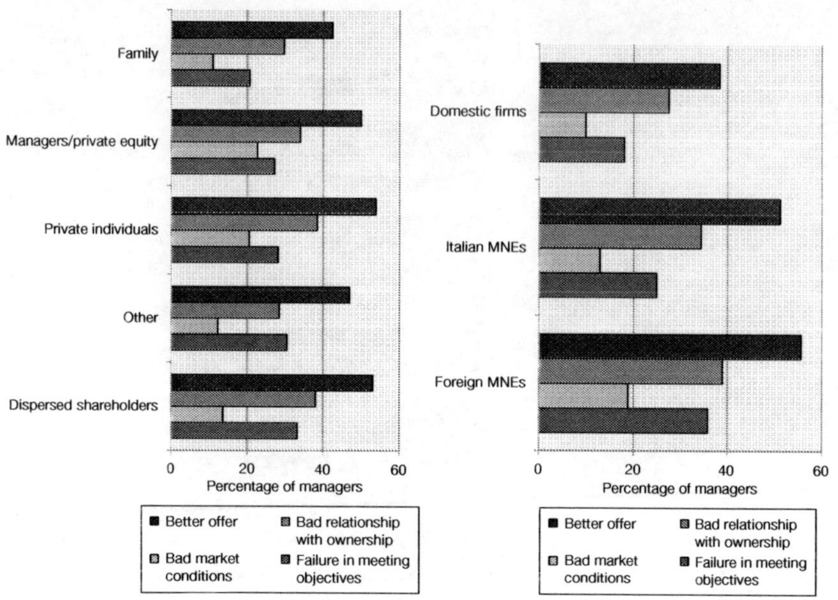

Fig. 7.6 Dismissals

3. As one would expect, promotions depend on the relationship with the owners when the owners are insiders, with no significant difference between family, founder, and privately owned firms.

Managerial turnover is analysed in Table 7.1 and in Figure 7.6. A manager may leave the firm voluntarily (better job or personal reasons) or involuntarily (poor market conditions, problems with the owners, and poor performance).[2] It is interesting that the most common cause of involuntary separation is neither the state of the market (13 per cent) nor the performance of the manager (26 per cent) but the relationship with the owners (33 per cent).

Figure 7.6 shows that there is a stark difference among firm classes. The state of the market and managerial performance are significantly more important in multinational firms, especially if they are American (managers employed by US multinationals are 28 percentage points more likely to be

---

[2] Obviously, we expect the majority of our involuntary separations to take the form of a resignation rather than an actual dismissal, which in Italy occurs only in extreme conditions.

Table 7.4 Promotions and dismissals

Dependent variable	(1)	(2)	(3)	(4)	(5)	(6)	(7)	(8)
	Promotions are based on:			*Fast tracks for star performers (0/1)*	*Manager dismissals are due to:*			
	Performance	Tenure	Relationship with owners		Failure to meet objectives	Bad market conditions	Bad relationships with owners	Better offer
ln(Employment)	−0.001	−0.014	0.001	0.006	0.011	0.008	0.050***	0.046***
	(0.005)	(0.016)	(0.010)	(0.017)	(0.015)	(0.010)	(0.015)	(0.015)
Area = General administration	−0.042	−0.001	−0.064	0.129**	0.077	0.037	0.108*	0.073
	(0.038)	(0.064)	(0.047)	(0.063)	(0.056)	(0.049)	(0.059)	(0.062)
Area = Sales and marketing	0.027	−0.017	0.017	−0.002	−0.034	−0.006	−0.071	0.028
	(0.026)	(0.053)	(0.039)	(0.052)	(0.048)	(0.041)	(0.050)	(0.054)
Seniority	0.061**	−0.023	−0.041	0.077	−0.025	−0.057	−0.084*	−0.086*
	(0.029)	(0.048)	(0.039)	(0.049)	(0.042)	(0.039)	(0.046)	(0.050)
MNE	−0.010	−0.129**	−0.036	0.100*	0.093*	0.033	0.068	0.129**
	(0.024)	(0.059)	(0.044)	(0.058)	(0.053)	(0.043)	(0.054)	(0.059)
USA MNE	0.002	0.009	0.006	−0.038	0.281***	0.056	0.057	0.128***
	(0.038)	(0.075)	(0.066)	(0.079)	(0.077)	(0.069)	(0.080)	(0.077)
Italian MNE	0.026	−0.011	0.011	−0.020	−0.019	−0.034	0.003	−0.010
	(0.022)	(0.062)	(0.050)	(0.062)	(0.059)	(0.049)	(0.063)	(0.065)
Ownership = State	−0.072	0.100	0.085	−0.111	−0.002	0.003	−0.082	−0.033
	(0.055)	(0.080)	(0.066)	(0.090)	(0.083)	(0.066)	(0.084)	(0.092)
Ownership = Family	0.011	−0.031	0.136***	−0.059	0.008	0.008	−0.002	−0.007
	(0.023)	(0.064)	(0.051)	(0.063)	(0.058)	(0.046)	(0.063)	(0.063)
Ownership = Founder	0.006	−0.057	0.135**	−0.035	−0.051	−0.012	−0.056	−0.003
	(0.028)	(0.070)	(0.055)	(0.069)	(0.062)	(0.048)	(0.067)	(0.069)
Ownership = Private equity	0.043*	0.043	0.013	−0.090	−0.046	0.146	−0.094	−0.062
	(0.025)	(0.098)	(0.087)	(0.097)	(0.100)	(0.093)	(0.105)	(0.110)
Ownership = Manager	0.085**	−0.019	−0.222	−0.035	−0.082	−0.060	0.051	0.135

(continued)

Table 7.4 (*continued*)

Dependent variable	(1)	(2)	(3)	(4)	(5)	(6)	(7)	(8)
	Promotions are based on:			*Fast tracks for star performers (0/1)*	*Manager dismissals are due to:*			
	Performance	Tenure	Relationship with owners		Failure to meet objectives	Bad market conditions	Bad relationships with owners	Better offer
	(0.035)	(0.168)	(0.147)	(0.162)	(0.137)	(0.089)	(0.137)	(0.146)
Ownership = Private individuals	−0.065	0.064	0.111*	0.044	−0.015	0.068	0.020	0.043
	(0.041)	(0.071)	(0.060)	(0.078)	(0.068)	(0.060)	(0.069)	(0.075)
Observations	603	603	603	603	603	603	603	603
Dummies regions	yes	yes	yes	yes	yes	yes	yes	yes
Dummies sectors (sic 2)	yes	yes	yes	yes	yes	yes	yes	yes

Note: ***denotes significance at the 1% level; ** at the 5% level; * at the 10% level.

dismissed because of poor performance than managers in other multinationals).

Managers in multinational firms are also much more likely to leave their firm because they find a better job. At this stage, this finding might admit both a negative interpretation (they are more likely to leave because they are less happy) and a positive one (they face more opportunities, either because they have more talent to start with or because they have more chances of growing). As we shall see in Section 8.4, the evidence on job satisfaction militates against the negative interpretation. Figure 7.6 also reveals that firm ownership is correlated with reasons for dismissal. In particular we see that managers are less likely to leave the firm because of poor performance and more likely to leave the firm because of poor relationships with the owners when the firm is owned by a family or its founder.

The regression analysis in Table 7.4 again allows us to assess the relative importance of ownership versus multinational status. The evidence indicates that the latter dominates—that is, there is no significant difference between insider and outsider ownership once multinational status is controlled for.

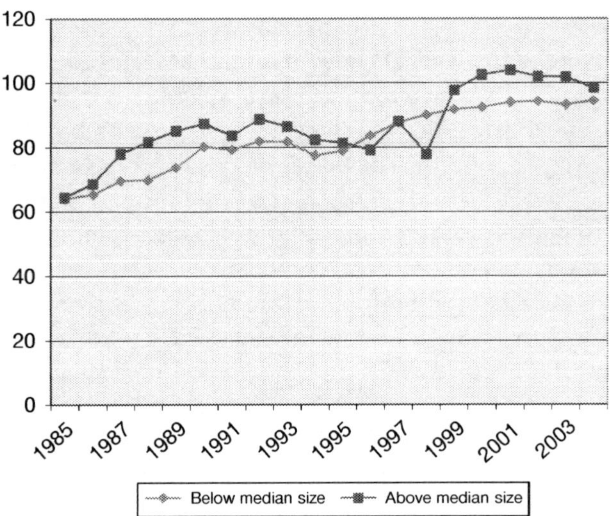

Fig. 7.7 Total pay by firm size (median total pay, 2004 euros)

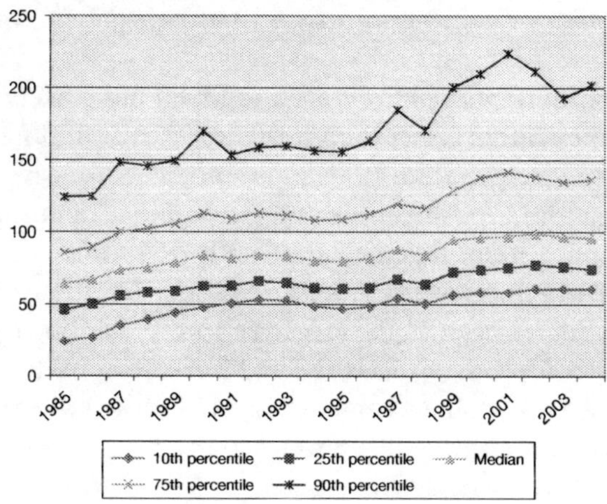

Fig. 7.8 Total pay (2004 euros, thousands)

7.3. The evolution of the incentive structure: evidence from INPS

According to the INPS database, the pay (in real terms) of Italian managers has increased between 1985 and 2004 by about 70 per cent, while the pay of managers at the bottom deciles has more than doubled (Figure 7.8). Compensation does not seem to be significantly different across firm size classes (Figure 7.7).

The structure of managerial compensation has changed dramatically. In 1985, almost no Italian manager received a variable pay component (Figure 7.9). At the end of the 1980s the share of managers with bonuses increased quickly to over 80 per cent. The bonus has also become a more important part of total pay, at around 15 per cent for the median manager; furthermore, for 10 per cent of the sample, bonus shares account for more than one-third of total pay.

To gain additional insight into the dynamics of incentives, we focused on two cohorts of managers: those who were 35–44 years old in 1985 and those who were 35–44 years old in 1995. We followed them for ten years.

One important point to bear in mind is that we know only whether an individual paid contributions to the INPS. When a manager leaves our sample, there are two possibilities: (1) he is no longer working (in which case, he may draw a pension); (2) he is still working but he does not appear in the INPS database (because he is either self-employed, has a job in the government sector, or works abroad). The interpretation of the findings in

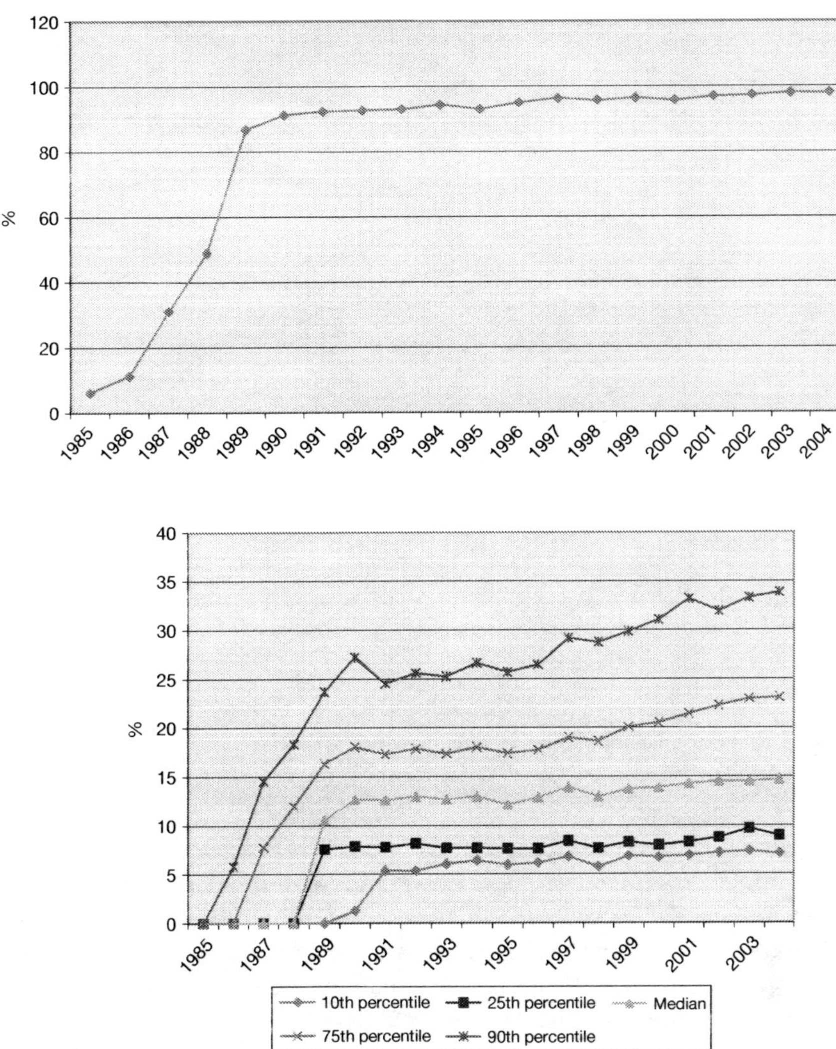

Fig. 7.9 Bonus as percentage of total pay

this section depends in part on what one thinks that a manager does when he drops out of the INPS sample. While some of the individuals who leave management do become successful entrepreneurs, we hypothesize that this accounts for a small fraction. The others—those who retire (we are focusing on relatively young managers) or those who downsize to freelancing—are likely to suffer a monetary loss.

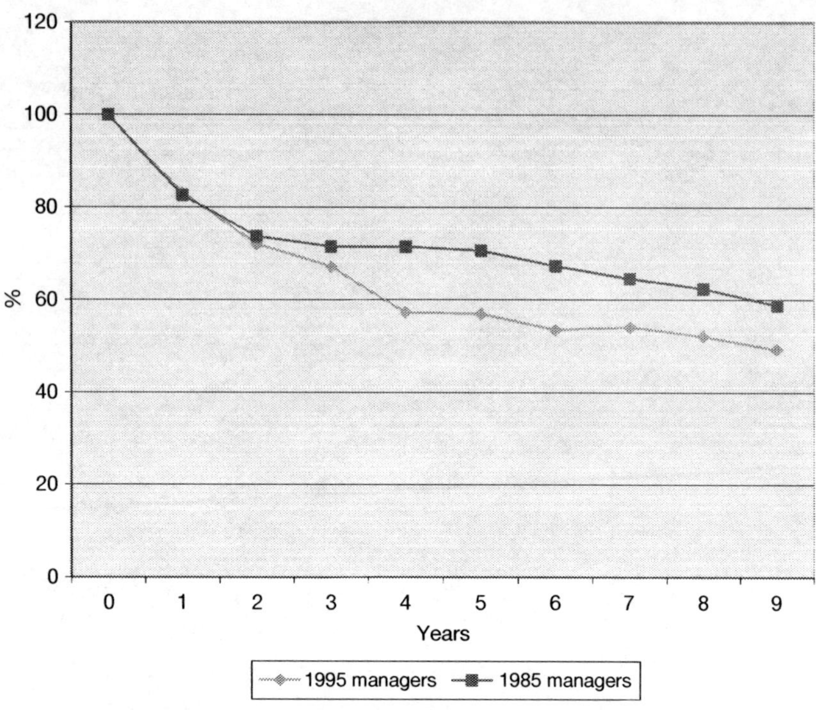

Fig. 7.10 Percentage of managers still employed as managers
Note: base years = 1985 or 1995.

Figure 7.10 depicts the proportion of managers in a given cohort who are still employed (as managers or as other kinds of non-independent workers) after n years. The hazard rate is high: after five years, 30–40 per cent of our managers have disappeared from the sample. The survival rate was systematically higher for the 1985 managers than for the 1995 managers.

We also compute the pay dynamics for the two cohorts under consideration (Figure 7.11 and Figure 7.12). The two graphs in Figure 7.11 are obtained under the (optimistic hypothesis) that managers who drop out of the sample face the same salary distribution as those who stay in the sample: this means that we can just drop the missing observations. The two graphs in Figure 7.12 instead correspond to the most pessimistic scenarios: managers who leave the INPS sample receive a zero salary. We normalize the total pay of a manager in the base year (either 1985 or 1995) and we study its evolution in the next ten years.

The first point to note is that, in both cohorts, managers faced strong intertemporal incentives. In the optimistic scenario, a top-quarter

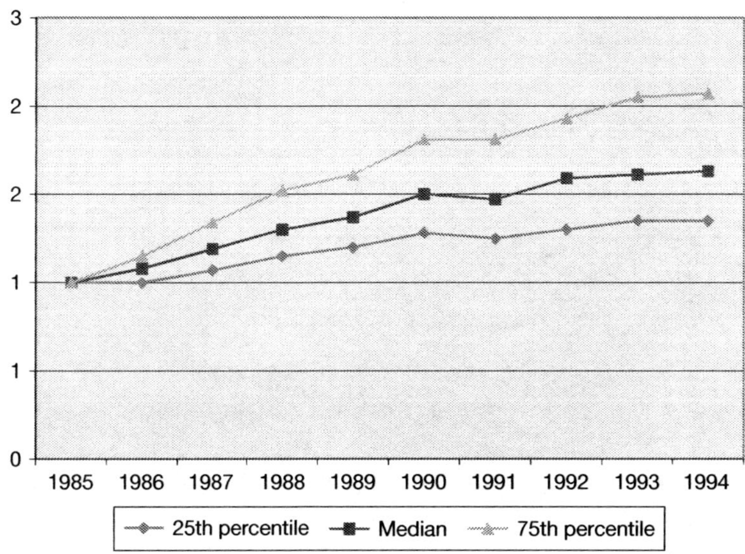

Fig. 7.11a Total pay profile of 1985 managers aged 35–44, missing observations dropped (constant euros)

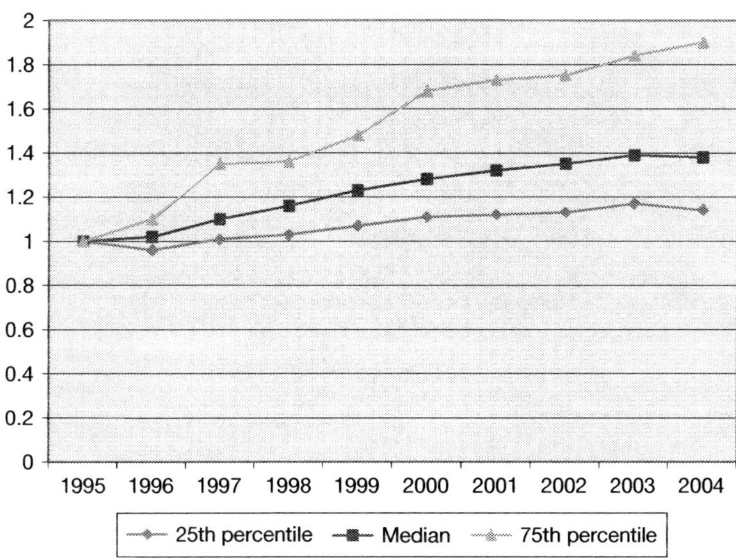

Fig. 7.11b Total pay profile of 1995 managers aged 35–44, missing observations dropped (constant euros)

Note: 1995 pay = 1.

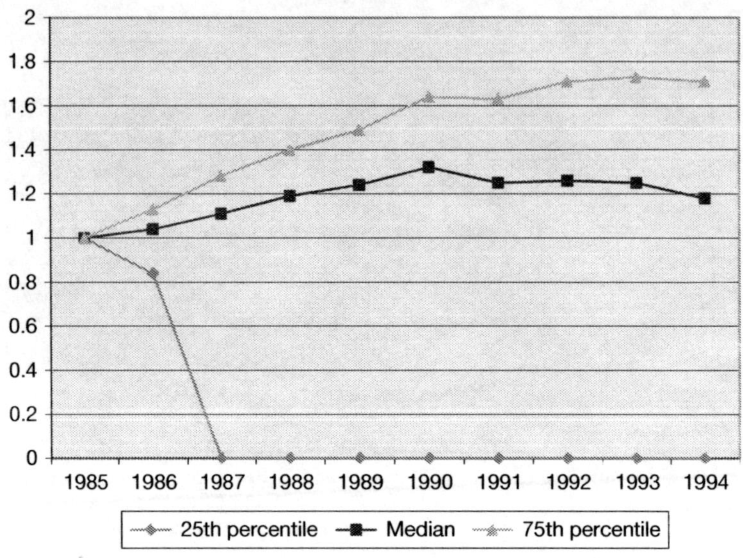

Fig. 7.12a Total pay profile of 1985 managers aged 35–44, missing observations set to zero (constant euros)

Note: 1985 pay = 1.

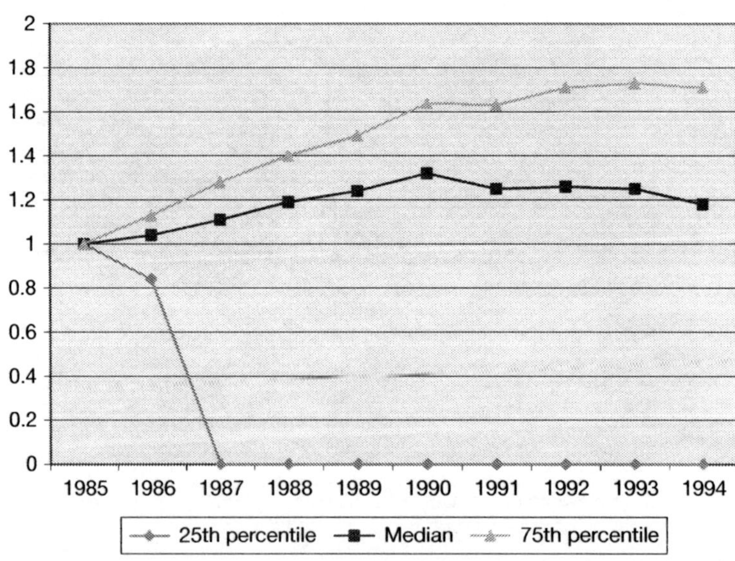

Fig. 7.12b Total pay profile of 1995 managers aged 35–44, missing observations set to zero (constant euros)

performer (manager at the 25th percentile of total pay) earned, after ten years, over 50 per cent more than a bottom-quarter performer. In the pessimistic scenario, a bottom-quarter performer ends up very quickly (after two years) with a zero salary.

In either case, this kind of dynamic variation appears to be larger than year-by-year variation in bonuses. For instance, in 1995 top-quarter performers received a 17 per cent bonus, while bottom-quarter performers received an 8 per cent bonus. Compare this 7-point difference to the 50 per cent difference (minimum) that is due to dynamic effects.

There is a notable difference in the pay dynamics for the two cohorts. In both the optimistic and the pessimistic scenarios, the same pattern emerges: the 1985 cohort had a more favourable income profile than the 1995 cohort, possibly reflecting different overall growth rates of the economy over the two decades. In the period under consideration, a median performer in the 1985 cohort could expect a 60 per cent pay increase (in the good scenario) and a 10 per cent pay increase (in the bad scenario). A median performer in the 1995 cohort faced a 40 per cent increase in the good scenario and would find himself without a job in the bad scenario.

8

Fidelity versus Performance

The analysis of personnel policies among our sample firms reveals two distinct models. Some firms adopt a *performance model*, whereby managers are hired through formal channels, they are assessed regularly and rewarded, promoted, and dismissed on the basis of objective measures of performance. Other firms instead adopt a *fidelity model* of managerial talent development: they hire managers on the basis of personal or family contacts, they do not assess the managers' performance formally, and managers' rewards are based on the quality of their relationship with the firm's owners.

The analysis also reveals that non-family firms and multinationals are more likely to adopt the performance model, whereas family firms and firms that operate exclusively in the domestic market tend to adopt the fidelity model.

In this chapter we assess whether and how the type of managerial model affects the selection of managers into a firm, their effort and behaviour, their income and job satisfaction, and ultimately the firm's performance.

We have shown that personnel policies vary across firms on four key dimensions—namely, hiring practices, appraisals and promotions, bonuses, and dismissals. Within these, we can distinguish between incentives that are explicitly based on managers' performance, such as bonuses and fast-track promotions, and those that are based on the relationship between the managers and the firm owners, such as hiring through the informal network of family and friends.

For brevity we develop two indexes that summarize our personnel policy variables. The first index is the principal component of all performance-related measures, such as bonuses, appraisals, and merit-based promotions. The variable increases with the intensity of use of performance rewards. We label this 'performance index'.

The second index, which we label 'fidelity index', captures the importance of a good personal relationship with the owners of a firm for the professional career of the managers. This is defined as the principal component factor of the variables recording the role of personal relationship with the owners for promotion and firing decisions, and the cases in which the manager was hired through personal (family or friends) contacts. The fidelity index is higher for firms that rely more heavily on personal contacts and relationships with the owners.

Table 8.1 and Table 8.2 show summary statistics of the two incentive indexes. In Table 8.1, moving from the 25th to the 75th percentile of the performance index coincides with an increase in the probability of having an explicit incentive scheme and with the proportion of the bonus, which goes from 9.48 per cent to 16.70 per cent of the salary. There is also a significant increase in the probability of having a formal appraisal system in place (from 23 per cent to 75 per cent of the firms) and a slight increase in the relevance of the appraisals. Table 8.2 reports a similar exercise for the fidelity index. Moving from the 25th to the 75th percentile of the variable implies a significant increase in the frequency of managers' leaving because of a bad personal relationship with the owners, and a dramatic increase in the proportion of managers being hired through family or friends, while there is no change in the relevance of a good personal relationship with the owners for promotions.

Table 8.1 Components of the performance index

Percentile performance index	Existence bonus	Percentage bonus	Existence appraisals	Fast track for star performers
1st–25th	0.00	0.00	0.27	0.12
26th–50th	0.86	9.48	0.23	0.31
51st–75th	1.00	16.70	0.75	0.34
76th–100th	0.99	32.78	0.86	0.70

Table 8.2 Components of the fidelity index

Percentile fidelity index	Turnover for bad relationship with ownership	Hiring through informal contacts	Importance of relationship with owners for promotions
1st–25th	0.26	0.09	0.00
26th–50th	0.00	0.00	1.00
51st–75th	1.00	0.00	1.00
76th–100th	0.30	1.00	1.00

8.1. Selection

We start by analysing whether different managerial policies attract managers who differ systematically on key characteristics, such as education and risk aversion. Table 8.3 shows that the fidelity model and the performance model are indeed associated with different selection methods.

Performance-based firms hire on the basis of observable signals of quality rather than personal connections, and hence they put a premium on education, both university degrees and executive training. Table 8.3, columns (1)–(6) clearly indicate that managers who are hired by firms with high performance indexes are more likely to have a college degree and more likely to have completed executive education.

A performance-based incentive scheme involves a certain risk, because it rewards success and punishes failure. Highly risk-averse individuals prefer to work for fidelity-based firms. Table 8.3, columns (7)–(9) support this conjecture. Risk attitudes are strongly linked with the matching of managers to firms. More risk-tolerant managers are found in firms with higher performance indexes. For example, from column (9) we can see that a standard deviation change in the performance index is associated with a 9.1 per cent standard deviation change in the variable risk. On the other hand, the fidelity-index measure typically enters the regression with much smaller and insignificant coefficients.

It is interesting to know that—with two exceptions to be discussed shortly—firm ownership is not correlated with the managers' risk aversion coefficients in column (9). This means that firm-specific differences appear to work only through the choice of incentive schemes.

The two exceptions to the last statement are manager-owned firms and Italian multinationals: they both seem to attract more risk-tolerant individuals. While for the first exception there is an obvious explanation that has to do with the equity stake, the reason behind the second exception is not clear.

8.2. Effort

Next, we analyse the impact of different personnel policies on managerial effort. To measure effort we asked managers how many hours a week they worked and how often they worked over the weekend. Table 7.3 above

Table 8.3 Education and incentives

Dependent variable	(1)	(2)	(3)	(4)	(5)	(6)	(7)	(8)	(9)
	College degree (0/1)			Executive education (0/1)			Risk tolerance		
ln(Employment)	0.019	0.017	0.033**	0.031**	0.023	0.024	−0.015	−0.024	−0.031
	(0.014)	(0.014)	(0.016)	(0.015)	(0.015)	(0.017)	(0.029)	(0.029)	(0.032)
Area = General administration	−0.049	−0.055	−0.039	0.032	0.013	0.003	0.195	0.177	0.131
	(0.059)	(0.059)	(0.061)	(0.060)	(0.060)	(0.063)	(0.121)	(0.121)	(0.129)
Area = Sales and marketing	−0.131***	−0.139***	−0.129**	0.035	0.010	0.008	0.336***	0.311***	0.307***
	(0.050)	(0.050)	(0.052)	(0.053)	(0.052)	(0.055)	(0.104)	(0.105)	(0.110)
Seniority	0.103**	0.097**	0.121**	0.032	0.010	0.039	−0.006	−0.029	0.020
	(0.047)	(0.047)	(0.048)	(0.047)	(0.047)	(0.050)	(0.099)	(0.098)	(0.107)
MNE	0.049	0.029	0.065	0.181***	0.120**	0.154**	0.137	0.082	0.054
	(0.051)	(0.053)	(0.059)	(0.053)	(0.055)	(0.062)	(0.108)	(0.116)	(0.132)
USA MNE	−0.027	−0.032	−0.046	0.023	0.007	−0.019	0.244*	0.231	0.205
	(0.070)	(0.070)	(0.075)	(0.074)	(0.073)	(0.077)	(0.146)	(0.147)	(0.156)
Italian MNE	−0.076	−0.069	−0.071	−0.166***	−0.139**	−0.175***	0.073	0.101	0.130
	(0.056)	(0.056)	(0.060)	(0.059)	(0.059)	(0.062)	(0.123)	(0.125)	(0.133)
Ownership = State	0.003	0.011	0.023	0.009	0.030	−0.012	0.104	0.119	0.231
	(0.079)	(0.079)	(0.080)	(0.083)	(0.082)	(0.088)	(0.188)	(0.189)	(0.200)
Ownership = Family	−0.045	−0.036	0.015	0.020	0.045	0.064	−0.003	0.014	0.048
	(0.059)	(0.059)	(0.063)	(0.060)	(0.061)	(0.062)	(0.126)	(0.126)	(0.132)
Ownership = Founder	−0.041	−0.040	−0.013	−0.043	−0.042	−0.047	0.169	0.168	0.197
	(0.064)	(0.065)	(0.069)	(0.066)	(0.066)	(0.070)	(0.142)	(0.141)	(0.149)
Ownership = Private equity	−0.146	−0.146	−0.091	0.196**	0.191**	0.186**	0.111	0.101	0.196
	(0.093)	(0.092)	(0.095)	(0.089)	(0.088)	(0.093)	(0.196)	(0.196)	(0.205)
Ownership = Manager	−0.118	−0.122	−0.130	0.052	0.035	0.039	0.689**	0.668**	0.711**
	(0.128)	(0.126)	(0.123)	(0.148)	(0.144)	(0.163)	(0.270)	(0.270)	(0.286)
Ownership = Private individuals	−0.073	−0.069	−0.102	0.041	0.054	0.044	0.137	0.149	0.155

(*continued*)

Table 8.3 (*Continued*)

	(1)	(2)	(3)	(4)	(5)	(6)	(7)	(8)	(9)
Dependent variable	College degree (0/1)			Executive education (0/1)			Risk tolerance		
	(0.068)	(0.068)	(0.072)	(0.069)	(0.070)	(0.074)	(0.136)	(0.138)	(0.142)
Family manager	0.045	0.027	−0.053	0.076	0.070	−0.054	−0.015	0.038	0.010
	(0.135)	(0.147)	(0.148)	(0.135)	(0.141)	(0.167)	(0.306)	(0.307)	(0.314)
Male	0.110*	0.107*	0.117*	−0.019	−0.036	−0.013	0.079	0.056	0.014
	(0.064)	(0.064)	(0.069)	(0.068)	(0.070)	(0.075)	(0.125)	(0.124)	(0.132)
Degree							0.016	0.007	0.008
							(0.087)	(0.087)	(0.093)
ln(Age)	−1.000***	−0.971***	−0.974***	−0.184	−0.070	−0.123	−0.847***	−0.725**	−0.911***
	(0.126)	(0.131)	(0.142)	(0.136)	(0.139)	(0.153)	(0.289)	(0.292)	(0.321)
Performance index		0.033	0.018		0.097***	0.085***		0.083*	0.090*
		(0.021)	(0.022)		(0.022)	(0.023)		(0.049)	(0.052)
Fidelity index		0.001	0.007		0.004	0.013		0.004	−0.008
		(0.021)	(0.022)		(0.021)	(0.022)		(0.043)	(0.044)
N	603	603	603	603	603	603	603	603	603
Dummies regions and sectors	No	No	Yes	No	No	Yes	No	No	Yes

Note: *** denotes significance at the 1% level; ** at the 5% level; * at the 10% level.

Table 8.4 Manager effort

Dependent variable	(1)	(2)	(3)	(4)	(5)	(6)
	Monthly weekends worked			Weekly hours worked		
ln(Employment)	0.045	0.047	0.039	0.622***	0.576***	0.611**
	(0.034)	(0.034)	(0.039)	(0.219)	(0.222)	(0.251)
Area = General administration	0.386***	0.366***	0.375***	2.185**	1.884*	1.590
	(0.133)	(0.133)	(0.137)	(0.996)	(0.988)	(1.000)
Area = Sales and marketing	0.408***	0.390***	0.325***	2.275***	1.972**	2.057**
	(0.117)	(0.118)	(0.123)	(0.804)	(0.804)	(0.830)
Seniority	0.121	0.110	0.115	1.273*	0.984	1.275
	(0.103)	(0.102)	(0.110)	(0.770)	(0.761)	(0.779)
MNE	−0.216*	−0.295**	−0.364***	0.554	−0.554	0.239
	(0.116)	(0.120)	(0.135)	(0.841)	(0.868)	(0.941)
USA MNE	0.143	0.132	0.231	−0.906	−1.075	−1.367
	(0.176)	(0.175)	(0.184)	(1.114)	(1.102)	(1.103)
Italian MNE	0.018	0.035	0.092	−0.450	−0.077	−0.715
	(0.131)	(0.132)	(0.146)	(0.927)	(0.918)	(0.949)
Ownership = State	−0.212	−0.175	−0.224	−2.903**	−2.467*	−2.188
	(0.180)	(0.178)	(0.194)	(1.341)	(1.324)	(1.390)
Ownership = Family	−0.224	−0.158	−0.228	0.172	0.926	0.532
	(0.138)	(0.140)	(0.151)	(0.973)	(0.964)	(1.012)
Ownership = Founder	−0.149	−0.120	−0.158	0.485	0.839	0.969
	(0.148)	(0.148)	(0.159)	(1.008)	(1.007)	(1.047)
Ownership = Private equity	0.378*	0.398*	0.285	1.183	1.328	0.823
	(0.211)	(0.216)	(0.222)	(1.578)	(1.557)	(1.579)
Ownership = Manager	−0.226	−0.254	−0.252	0.592	0.083	−0.044
	(0.335)	(0.321)	(0.344)	(2.210)	(2.085)	(2.067)
Ownership = Private individuals	−0.289**	−0.246*	−0.317**	−0.926	−0.339	−1.391
	(0.144)	(0.145)	(0.158)	(1.131)	(1.124)	(1.103)

(continued)

Table 8.4 *(Continued)*

	(1)	(2)	(3)	(4)	(5)	(6)
Dependent variable	Monthly weekends worked			Weekly hours worked		
Family manager	0.418	0.349	0.290	−0.410	0.093	0.271
	(0.309)	(0.308)	(0.342)	(1.877)	(1.871)	(2.144)
Male	0.286*	0.290*	0.266*	2.632**	2.410**	2.367**
	(0.152)	(0.153)	(0.161)	(1.146)	(1.153)	(1.204)
Degree	0.007	−0.009	0.038	−0.676	−0.851	−1.160
	(0.094)	(0.093)	(0.100)	(0.672)	(0.659)	(0.717)
ln(Age)	−0.272	−0.287	−0.265	−2.542	−1.782	−2.899
	(0.325)	(0.332)	(0.364)	(2.236)	(2.262)	(2.412)
Performance index		0.102**	0.087*		1.386***	1.255***
		(0.048)	(0.051)		(0.333)	(0.358)
Fidelity index		−0.077*	−0.055		−0.929***	−0.793**
		(0.045)	(0.047)		(0.318)	(0.333)
N	603	603	603	603	603	603
Dummies regions and sectors	No	No	Yes	No	No	Yes

Note: *** denotes significance at the 1% level; ** at the 5% level; * at the 10% level.

shows that the average manager works 54 hours per week and works a little over a weekend a month.

Table 8.4 reveals that the incentive policy of the firm affects managers' effort. Managers with higher-powered incentives work longer hours and are more likely to be at work over the weekend. For example, one standard deviation change in the performance-index variable is associated with 1.3 more hours worked per week (2.3 per cent of mean hours worked) and 0.08 more weekends worked per month (8 per cent of mean number of weekends worked). For hours, the coefficients on the type of the firm are not significantly different from zero, indicating that the only effect that the type of firm has is through the incentive scheme offered. On the other hand, in the case of weekends, there is a direct effect: managers in multinationals and firms with family CEOs are significantly less likely to be at work at weekends.

Interestingly, managers' effort (in terms of both hours and weekends worked) is negatively correlated with the fidelity index. A standard deviation change in the variable is associated with a decline of almost one hour's work per week, and a decline of 0.05 weekends worked per month. Other variables that affect effort are: functional area (higher effort in sales, and partly general management), nationality (foreign-born managers put in more hours), and gender (men are more likely to work weekends). Contrary to what one might expect, younger managers do not seem to work harder.

8.3. Use of time

Our findings indicate that managers who work for firms that reward on the basis of performance tend to work more hours per week. A key question is whether they essentially do more of the same type of work or whether their 'style' differs substantially. In this section we describe and analyse a survey that was purposely designed to collect detailed information on the managers' use of time.

8.3.1. Data description

Our questionnaire contained detailed information on CEOs' use of time every day over a five-day week. This allowed us to compute the number of hours worked in a week, the number of activities performed, and the allocation of time across different types of activities.

Figure 8.1 shows that most CEOs work between 40 and 60 hours per week, with an average of 47.8. Figure 8.2 shows that this time is divided across several activities. The average CEO engages in thirty-five different activities per week—that is, about seven per day. There is, however, substantial variation in the number of activities performed by different CEOs. At one end of the distribution, the 5 per cent of CEOs on the left tail engage in twenty activities per week; at the other end, the 5 per cent of CEOs on the right tail of the distribution engage in fifty-four different activities per week.

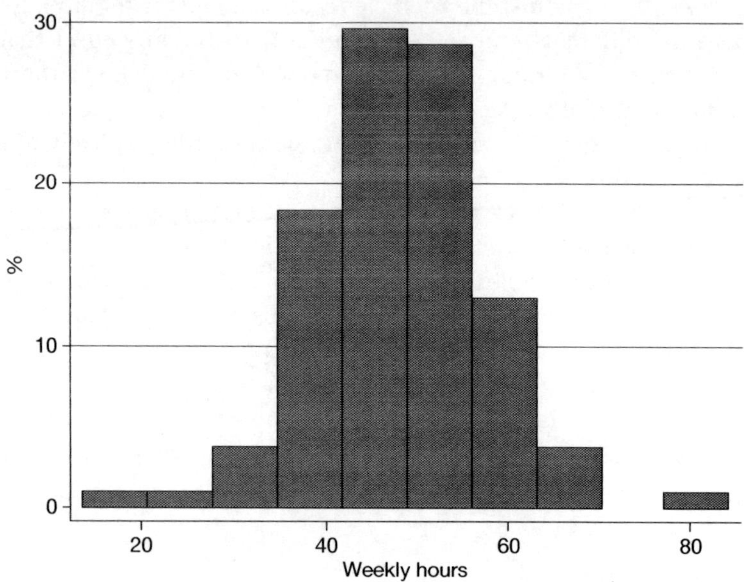

Fig. 8.1 CEOs' working hours

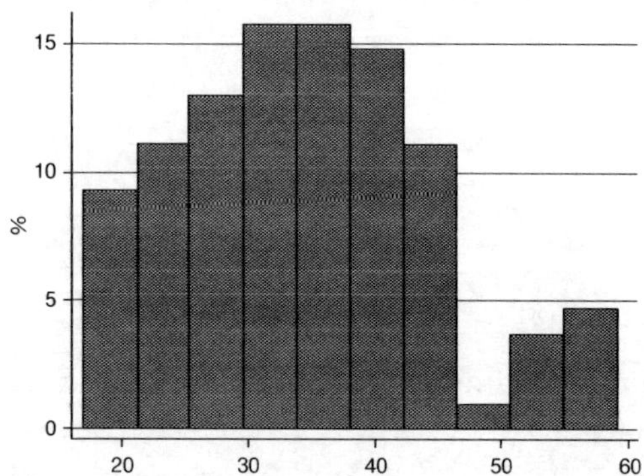

Fig. 8.2 CEOs' total activities

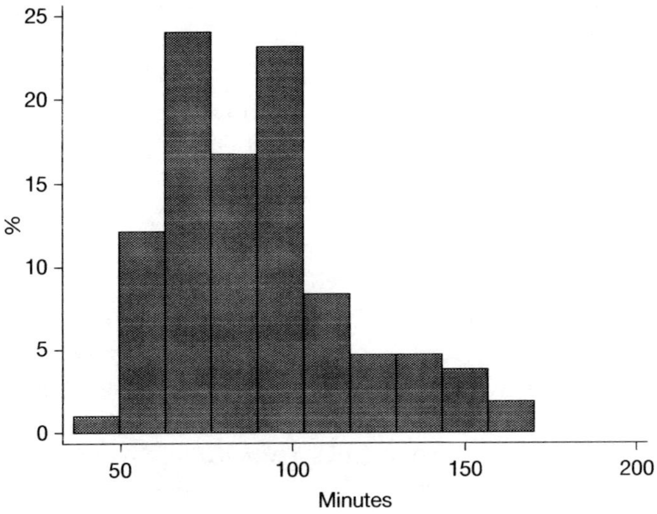

Fig. 8.3 Mean duration of CEOs' activities

Figure 8.3 shows that most activities last between 50 and 100 minutes, with an average of just under one and a half hours. Taken together, Figure 8.1 and Figure 8.2 show that the variation in total hours worked is explained mostly by a larger number of activities. Namely, CEOs who work longer hours engage in more activities rather than devoting longer to each of a similar number of activities.

Figure 8.4 shows how CEOs allocate their working hours across different types of activity. CEOs spend half of their time in meetings, with the average meeting lasting just over one and a half hours (94.5 minutes).

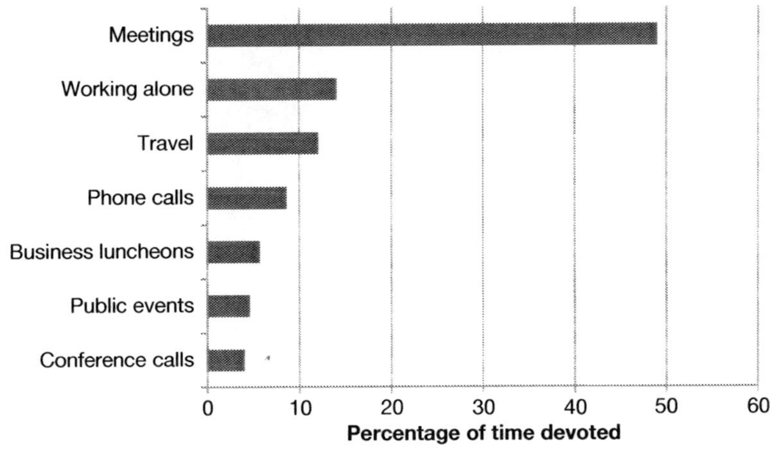

Fig. 8.4 Allocation of CEOs' working hours

The analysis of individual observations reveals substantial variation across different CEOs. For the 5 per cent of CEOs who engage in the fewest meetings, these take only 26 per cent of their time. On the other hand, the 5 per cent of CEOs who engage in the most meetings devote 76 per cent of their time to these. The second most common activity, taking 14 per cent of the average CEO time, is 'working alone', an umbrella-type activity that brings together all working tasks the CEO performs alone, such as reading documents or preparing materials for a meeting. For this activity, too, we note that there is substantial variation across different CEOs. At the bottom of the distribution, 5 per cent of CEOs spend no time working alone. At the top, 5 per cent of CEOs spend 36 per cent of their time working alone. The third most common use of time is travel, with an average share of 12 per cent. The remaining 25 per cent of time is almost equally split between phone calls, video and teleconferences, participation in public events, and business luncheons. All of these exhibit substantial variation across different CEOs.

As discussed in Section 5.2, the questionnaire collected detailed information on all the activities the CEO was engaged in for longer than 15 minutes. For these 'main' activities we know the number of participants, their type, the location, the planning horizon, and the frequency. We

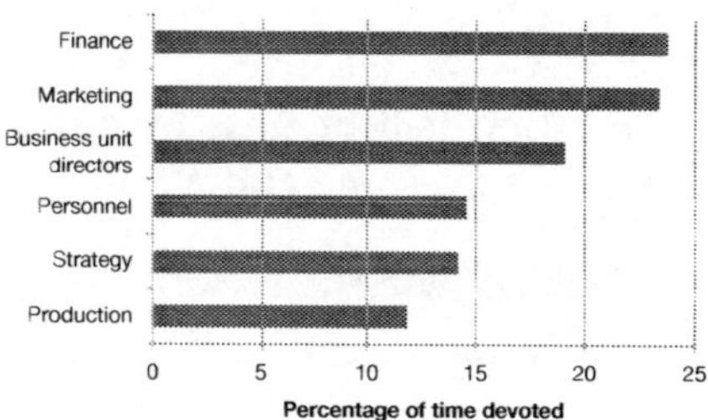

Fig. 8.5a Other parties involved in CEOs' activities: insiders

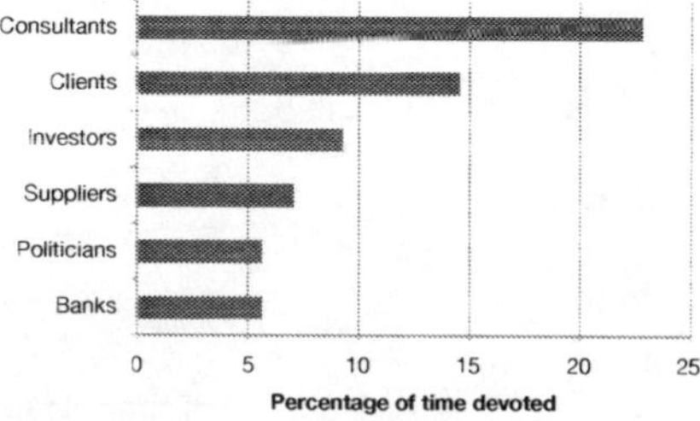

Fig. 8.5b Other parties involved in CEOs' activities: outsiders

describe this information in Figure 8.5. For activities that involve other parties, we classify these as 'insiders' if they are employees of the firm and 'outsiders' if they are not. Activities can be undertaken alone, with insiders, with outsiders, or with both. On average, CEOs spend 62 per cent of their time with insiders and 38 per cent with outsiders. Among insiders, CEOs on average spend most of their time with representatives of finance (24 per cent) and marketing (23 per cent). Among outsiders, the two top categories are consultants (22 per cent) and clients (15 per cent); interestingly, CEOs spend an equal amount of time dealing with financial intermediaries and politicians, which each absorb 7 per cent of their time.

Not surprisingly, most of the CEOs' activities take place at the firms' headquarters rather than in other locations. CEOs indeed spend two-thirds of their time at the headquarters. A further quarter is equally divided between time spent in other offices of their firm and in other firms located in Italy. The remaining 6 per cent is spent abroad.

Figure 8.6 shows that CEOs devote half of their time to activities that are not held regularly. The remaining half is almost equally split between activities that are held weekly, monthly, and annually.

Figure 8.7 shows that, if other parties are involved, there tend to be only a few of them. On average, CEOs spend 80 per cent of their time in activities that involve fewer than ten people, and half of this is spent on activities that involve only one or two participants.

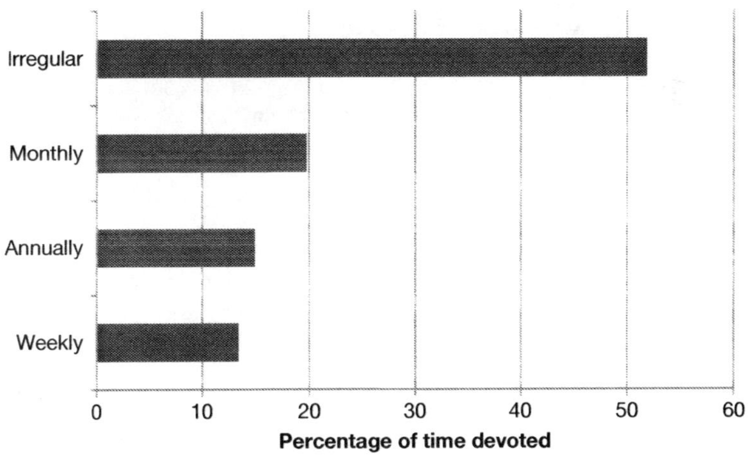

Fig. 8.6 Regularity of CEOs' activities

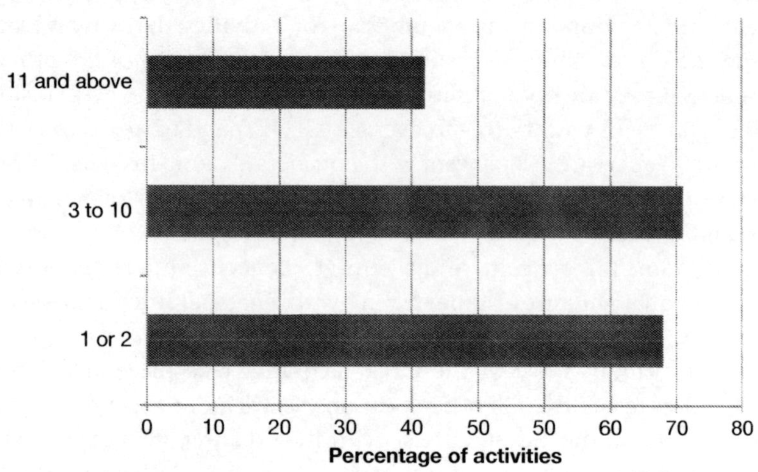

Fig. 8.7 Number of people involved in CEOs' activities

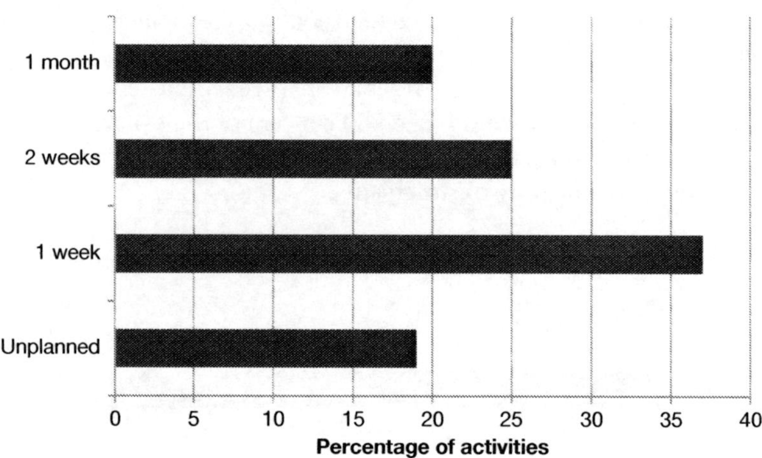

Fig. 8.8 Planning of CEOs' activities

Figure 8.8 shows that most of the CEOs' time is spent in activities that are not planned far in advance—that is, only one week or less. Interestingly, about one-fifth of the CEOs' time is devoted to activities that are not planned at all.

8.3.2. *Do CEOs of different age cohorts use their time differently?*

We used regression analysis to investigate whether CEOs of different age cohorts differ systematically in hours worked and use of time. We state that we find evidence of differences by age only when we can reject the hypothesis that the estimated coefficient of age is equal to zero at the 90 per cent confidence level or higher.

We first addressed the questions of whether CEOs work longer hours because they engage in more activities or because they spend a longer time on each activity. The answer is negative. We did not find a statistically significant effect of age on either variable. The magnitude of the estimated effects is very small. For instance, we found that, compared to a 54-year-old (the average age of CEOs in the sample), a 64-year-old works 20 minutes less per week, is engaged in one less activity, and spends 2 more minutes on each activity.

Next, we analysed whether age affects the allocation of time across different types of activities. This and all other results are reported in Table 8.5.

We found that for the main activities—that is meetings, travel, and time spent working alone—CEOs of different cohorts behaved similarly. We observed some variation only in the use of communication devices. Younger CEOs use video and teleconferencing more frequently and phone calls less frequently, compared to their older counterparts. The difference is substantial: the share of time spent on video and teleconferencing is twice as large for CEOs who are ten years younger than average (44-year-olds) compared to CEOs who are ten years older than average (64-year-olds).

A rather interesting pattern emerges when we compare the share of time spent with different categories of people. Older CEOs spend relatively less time with insiders, especially with those belonging to the areas of marketing and finance. The estimates indicate that a CEO who is ten years younger than average spends 21 per cent of his time with finance and 20 per cent with marketing representatives. This difference can reflect differences in managerial styles across cohorts or a more pronounced need for younger, less experienced managers to collect information about the firm by meeting insiders. In comparison, the same figures for a CEO who is ten years older than average are 15 per cent and 12 per cent. In contrast, we find that CEOs of different ages allocate their time across different categories of outsiders in a similar way.

Our analysis also revealed that younger CEOs are also more likely to spend more time at the firm's headquarters rather than at other firms' sites. The differences between CEOs of 44 and 64 years is 12 percentage points.

Finally, we found no evidence that age is correlated with the frequency at which activities take place or the time horizon over which they are planned. Regardless of their age, CEOs devote the majority of their time to activities that are not held regularly and are either unplanned or scheduled in for a week or less.

8.3.3. Do CEOs who work longer hours use their time differently?

The final part of our analysis aims to establish whether CEOs who work longer hours exhibit a systematically different time-use pattern. As in the previous section, we employ regression analysis, and we state that we find evidence of differences only when we can reject the hypothesis that the estimated coefficient of weekly hours is equal to zero at the 90 per cent confidence level or higher. All results are reported in Table 8.5.

The analysis of time spent on different type of activities reveals a striking difference on the division between meetings and time spent working alone. CEOs who work longer hours spend relatively less time in meetings and more time working alone. The estimates indicate that a CEO who works 10 hours longer than average per week spends 56 per cent of his time in meetings and 18 per cent working alone. In comparison, a CEO who works 10 hours less than average per week spends 64 per cent of his time in meetings and 12 per cent working alone.

Differences also emerge when we compare the share of time spent with different categories of people. CEOs who work longer hours spend relatively less time with outsiders. The estimates indicate that a CEO who works 10 hours longer than average per week spends 35 per cent of his time with outsiders. In comparison, a CEO who works 10 hours less than average per week spends 47 per cent of his time with outsiders. The difference is mostly driven by the fact that CEOs who work longer hours spend relatively less time with consultants. The estimates indicate that a CEO who works 10 hours longer than average per week spends 19 per cent of his time with consultants, whereas this share increases to 27 per cent for CEOs who work 10 hours less than average.

The analysis reveals no significant difference in the frequency with which activities are held and in their geographical location. Regardless of the length of their working week, CEOs spend most of their time on

Table 8.5 CEOs' use of time by age cohort and working hours

Dependent variable:		(1) Age coefficient	(2) 'Average' CEO	(3) CEO who is 10 years younger than average	(4) CEO who is 10 years older than average	(5) Hours coefficient	(6) CEO who works 10 more hours per week than average	(7) CEO who works 10 fewer hours per week than average
				Implied values for:			Implied values for:	
Activities:								
	Total number	−0.103 (0.090)	26.5	27.5	25.5	0.480* (0.092)	31.3	21.7
	Mean duration	0.219 (0.323)	90	88.2	92.2	0.886* (0.313)	99	81
Share of time spent in:								
	Meetings	−0.002 (0.002)	0.60	0.62	0.58	−0.004* (0.002)	0.56	0.64
	Working alone	0.003 (0.002)	0.15	0.12	0.18	0.003* (0.001)	0.18	0.12
	Phone calls	0.001* (0.001)	0.07	0.06	0.08	0.001 (0.001)	0.08	0.06
	Conference calls	−0.002* (0.001)	0.05	0.07	0.03	−0.001 (0.001)	0.04	0.06
Share of time spent with:								
	Insiders	−0.002 (0.002)	0.62	0.64	0.60	0.004* (0.002)	0.66	0.58
	Finance	−0.003* (0.002)	0.18	0.21	0.15	−0.001 (0.002)	0.17	0.19
	Marketing	−0.004*	0.16	0.20	0.12	−0.002	0.18	0.14

(continued)

Table 8.5 (*Continued*)

Dependent variable:		(1) Age coefficient	(2) 'Average' CEO	(3) CEO who is 10 years younger than average	(4) CEO who is 10 years older than average	(5) Hours coefficient	(6) CEO who works 10 more hours per week than average	(7) CEO who works 10 fewer hours per week than average
				Implied values for:			Implied values for:	
Share of time spent with:		(0.002)				(0.002)		
	Outsiders	0.002 (0.002)	0.38	0.36	0.40	−0.004* (0.002)	0.34	0.42
	Consultants	0.000 (0.002)	0.23	0.23	0.23	−0.004* (0.002)	0.19	0.27
Share of time spent on activities:								
	With 1–2 people	−0.003 (0.002)	0.39	0.39	0.36	−0.005* (0.003)	0.34	0.43
	Held irregularly	−0.001 (0.003)	0.50	0.51	0.49	−0.002 (0.003)	0.48	0.52
	At firm's HQ	−0.006* (0.002)	0.67	0.73	0.61	0.004 (0.003)	0.71	0.63
	Unplanned	0.002 (0.002)	0.19	0.21	0.17	0.003* (0.001)	0.22	0.16

Notes: Coefficients in columns 2 and 5 are obtained by regressing the variables in column 1 on age and weekly hours in deviation from their respective means. Robust Standard errors are reported in parenthesis. * indicates that we can reject the hypothesis that the coefficient is equal to zero at the 90% confidence level or higher. Columns 3, 4, 6, and 7 use the coefficients in columns 2 and 5 to compute the mean value for CEOs of different age cohorts and different working hours. Statistically significant differences are reported in italic. For the last set of variables in column 1, the omitted categories are: (i) with 3 or more people, (ii) held weekly, monthly, or annually, (iii) held at another site, another firm in Italy, and another firm abroad, and (iv) planned 1, 2, or 4 weeks in advance.

activities that do not take place regularly and are located at the firm's headquarters.

The analysis, however, indicates that CEOs who work longer hours tend to meet more people at any given time. The estimates indicate that a CEO who works 10 hours longer than average per week spends 34 per cent of his time in activities that involve one or two people rather than in activities that involve three or more. In comparison, a CEO who works 10 hours less than average per week spends 43 per cent of his time in activities that involve one or two people only.

The other significant difference concerns the planning horizon. Overall, CEOs spend most of their time on activities that have been planned for a week or less, but CEOs who work longer hours spend relatively more time on unplanned activities. A CEO who works 10 hours longer than average per week spends 22 per cent of his time in unplanned activities, whereas these take only 16 per cent of the time of CEOs who work 10 hours less than average per week.

8.3.4. *What firm characteristics explain time use?*

We combined the sample of 113 firms with detailed information on the time schedule of the CEO with the accounting dataset Amadeus, which provides information on employment (in Italy and worldwide), main sector of activity (3 digits US SIC codes), region of the headquarters, and definition of the global ultimate owner. We were able to find information on 108 firms in total via a name-matching procedure.

On average, the firms included in our sample were quite large (9,599 employees at the mean, 1,826 at the median), although 10 per cent of the firms in the matched sample had fewer than 100 employees. Most of the firms have their headquarters in the north-west of Italy (60 per cent). Almost all the rest of the sample firms are headquartered in central and north-eastern Italy (approximately 20 per cent each, respectively), with only 4 per cent of the sample in the south of the country. In terms of sectoral classification, most of the firms (37 per cent) are in manufacturing industries, but we also had a fair number of firms in finance and insurance activities (22 per cent), business services (14 per cent), and transportation, communication, and electrical utilities (13 per cent). The cross tabulation of the ownership classification against the main industry of activity (Table 8.6) shows an even representation of the ownership types across industry. Only 24 per cent of the firms in the sample were publicly quoted. Listed

Table 8.6 Time-use survey, ownership and industrial sectors (frequencies)

Ownership	Finance	Manufacturing	Other	Services	Transport	Wholesale	Total
Other	4	3	1	2	0	3	13
Family	2	14	0	5	1	1	23
Government	0	7	3	2	7	0	19
Private individuals	1	1	0	3	2	1	8
Dispersed shareholders	17	16	1	3	4	4	45
Total	24	41	5	15	14	9	108

Table 8.7 Time-use survey, ownership and stock-exchange listing (frequencies)

Ownership	Non-Listed	Listed	Total
Other	10	3	13
Family	19	4	23
Government	16	3	19
Private individuals	4	4	8
Dispersed shareholders	33	12	45
Total	82	26	108

companies were mostly classified under the dispersed shareholders ownership category, although 73 per cent of the dispersed shareholders firms are
actually non-listed (Table 8.7).

In what follows we use simple regression analysis to examine whether the
variation observed in the schedules of the CEOs included in our sample is
in any way related to firms' characteristics. The benchmark groups are
defined as follows: family firms for the ownership comparisons, north-
west regions in the regional comparison, manufacturing firms in the industry analysis, and non-listed firms.

Our expectation was that CEOs who operated within the performance
model would use their time differently from those within the fidelity
model. While we did not have direct survey information as in the ManagerItalia dataset, we were able to use ownership structure, geographical location, and industrial sector as proxies for the incentive structure. As we shall
see shortly, some clear patterns emerged.

Firm characteristics were correlated with the total number of weekly
hours worked by the CEO. This can be seen in Table 8.8, which reveals
that CEOs working for family firms tend to work less than others, although
the difference is significant only with respect to firms belonging to

Table 8.8 CEO hours worked and firms' characteristics

	(1)	(2)	(3)	(4)	(5)	(6)
Family	−2.774					−2.414
	(2.199)					(2.461)
Government	−2.123					−0.680
	(3.650)					(2.547)
Private individuals	5.986					6.938**
	(4.392)					(3.352)
Other	−3.234					−3.960
	(2.094)					(2.605)
Ln(Employment)		1.267**				1.295**
		(0.621)				(0.549)
Centre			4.501			0.640
			(2.993)			(2.108)
North–East			−1.637			−3.410
			(2.246)			(2.532)
South			−5.973**			−7.361*
			(2.780)			(3.827)
Finance				2.194		0.519
				(2.194)		(2.557)
Other business services				5.938		5.092
				(8.834)		(5.437)
Transport and utilities				2.846		2.233
				(2.706)		(2.459)
Retail and wholesale				−6.051**		−7.578**
				(2.988)		(3.079)
Other				2.190		2.273
				(2.880)		(2.570)
Publicly listed					4.922**	0.985
					(2.292)	(1.942)
Adjusted R-squared	0.024	0.050	0.032	0.051	0.040	0.159
Observations	108	108	108	108	108	108

Note: ** denotes significance at the 5% level; * at the 10% level.

non-family, private individuals. CEO working hours are also lower in firms classified in the 'transport and other utilities' sector (which includes several large conglomerates in the transport, electricity, and communication sectors), and in firms headquartered in the south of Italy (it is striking that the latter difference is significant even if based on only four observations). On the contrary, CEOs work longer weekly hours in larger and publicly quoted firms (note, however, that the public dummy turns insignificant when all the additional firm controls are included together).

The other aspects of the CEO time schedule for which firm characteristics matter is the share of time allocated between insiders and outsiders. This is explored in Table 8.9. CEOs working for manufacturing firms tend

Table 8.9 Activities by type of people, outsiders

	(1)	(2)	(3)	(4)	(5)	(6)
Family	−0.039					0.009
	(0.042)					(0.040)
Government	0.026					0.065
	(0.038)					(0.043)
Private individuals	0.058					0.025
	(0.071)					(0.077)
Other	0.079*					0.081*
	(0.045)					(0.046)
Ln(Employment)		0.001				−0.016*
		(0.008)				(0.009)
Centre			−0.017			−0.016
			(0.031)			(0.032)
North–East			0.047			0.038
			(0.046)			(0.047)
South			−0.132			−0.083
			(0.104)			(0.094)
Finance				0.151***		0.126***
				(0.042)		(0.044)
Other business services				0.102**		0.078*
				(0.048)		(0.041)
Transport and utilities				0.056		0.042
				(0.038)		(0.042)
Retail and wholesale				0.144***		0.121**
				(0.051)		(0.054)
Other				0.047		0.033
				(0.044)		(0.044)
Publicly listed					0.110***	0.113***
					(0.030)	(0.042)
Adjusted R-squared	0.016	−0.009	0.014	0.121	0.079	0.180
Observations	107	107	107	107	107	107

Note: *** denotes significance at the 1% level; ** at the 5% level; * at the 10% level.

to spend relatively more of their time with insiders (for example, production, finance) compared to those working for firms classified in other sectors, with CEOs working in the financial and transport industry and for publicly listed firms being the most outward oriented.

This last observation can be complemented by information on the location of meetings. CEOs of family firms are more likely to hold their meetings inside the firm rather than in other locations, even once we control for other factors.[1]

[1] Looking at the frequency of meetings and at their average size provides additional intriguing insight on the time allocation of CEOs working for publicly listed firms. First, the share of time spent in irregular/unplanned meetings is significantly larger for public-firm CEOs. Second, their meetings tend to involve fewer people compared to non-listed firms (tables omitted).

Looking at the types of outsiders in detail reveals some interesting findings, which are shown in Table 8.10. First, the share of time spent with banks is particularly high for publicly listed firms. Second, the share of time spent with politicians is particularly high for government-owned firms (as one would expect) and for firms classified in the transport and utility industry (which is less obvious). Note, however, that, when the ownership and the industry dummies are included together, the latter dominate the former (the government-owned dummy halves when the industry dummies are included). This can be interpreted as a sign that the importance assumed by politicians in the working day of a CEO is dictated by the nature of the industrial activity in which the firm is involved, rather than by the firm's ownership ties with the public sector.

In sum, our analysis shows that CEOs of certain companies (non-listed firms, firms in protected industries, southern firms) that have stronger incentives to adopt a fidelity model use their time differently, devoting more of it to insiders or to a specific class of outsiders, politicians. This finding is consistent with a fidelity model, where the manager is mainly an executor, who is expected to impose the will of the owners on the firm. The owners do not welcome excessive interaction with outside investors, who could potentially undermine the family's control. In the case of firms operating in protected industries and less-developed regions, one can hypothesize that the fidelity relation extends to politicians.

8.4. Compensation and job satisfaction

The next step of our analysis investigates whether different managerial systems are associated with different levels of pay and job satisfaction.

The average yearly fixed salary in our ManagerItalia sample was a little less than 100,000 euros. As we saw in Section 7.2.3, the average bonus amounts to about 15 per cent of the fixed salary. In Table 8.11, columns (4)–(6) show the fixed compensation that the manager receives (fixed salary but no bonus) as a function of firm-specific variables and worker-specific variables. The most interesting variable from our viewpoint is the incentive policy, which appears with a positive and significant coefficient. This means that firms that provide high-powered incentive schemes must compensate managers for the additional risk they incur. According to the regression results in column (6), a standard deviation increase in the performance index is associated with a cost of approximately 5,700 euros (5.7 per cent of the mean salary). Interestingly, the fidelity index appears

Table **8.10** Activities by type of people, banks and politicians

	(1)	(2)	(3)	(4)	(5)	(6)	(7)	(8)	(9)	(10)	(11)	(12)
	Share of time spent with banks					Share of time spent with politicians						
Family	−0.029					−0.020	−0.012					−0.010
	(0.029)					(0.025)	(0.022)					(0.025)
Government	−0.051**					−0.033	0.075**					0.032
	(0.025)					(0.032)	(0.037)					(0.041)
Private individuals	0.032					0.026	−0.006					−0.011
	(0.051)					(0.047)	(0.024)					(0.031)
Other	−0.001					−0.030	0.024					0.013
	(0.027)					(0.035)	(0.021)					(0.032)
Ln(Employment)		0.011*				0.007		0.002				0.001
		(0.006)				(0.007)		(0.005)				(0.005)
Centre			0.044			0.034			−0.002			−0.003
			(0.040)			(0.050)			(0.018)			(0.019)
North–East			0.050			0.042			0.027			0.039
			(0.031)			(0.033)			(0.029)			(0.038)
South			−0.041***			0.006			0.190			0.166*
			(0.010)			(0.035)			(0.116)			(0.098)
Finance				0.051		0.028				0.003		0.011
				(0.035)		(0.040)				(0.021)		(0.023)
Other business services				−0.027		−0.043				0.122		0.079
				(0.017)		(0.033)				(0.079)		(0.050)
				0.017		0.019				0.012		0.029

	(1)	(2)	(3)	(4)	(5)	(6)	(7)	(8)	(9)	(10)	(11)	(12)
Transport and utilities												
				(0.027)		(0.029)				(0.027)		(0.030)
Retail and wholesale				−0.014		0.004				0.072*		0.077*
				(0.025)		(0.034)				(0.039)		(0.046)
Other				0.067		0.058				−0.033*		−0.030
				(0.049)		(0.051)				(0.017)		(0.019)
Publicly listed					0.059**	0.035					−0.011	−0.003
					(0.027)	(0.034)					(0.018)	(0.019)
Adjusted R-squared	0.008	0.024	0.021	0.020	0.044	0.031	0.059	−0.009	0.081	0.086	−0.007	0.134
Observations	105	105	105	105	105	105	105	105	105	105	105	105

Note: *** denotes significance at the 1% level; **at the 5% level; *at the 10% level.

with an insignificant coefficient in the salary regression. The difference between the two indexes is statistically significant, indicating that managers who are rewarded for performance are paid more than those who are rewarded for fidelity.

Firm ownership does not have a direct effect on compensation, except for two smaller categories: other (government and cooperative firms pay less) and manager owned (which pay more). As before, this means that the type of the firm influences compensation only through the choice of the incentive scheme. Age, education, and seniority play a positive role. There does not seem to be gender discrimination.

Where are managers happiest? According to Table 8.11, column (9), only three variables are significant. Managers at a more senior level report higher job satisfaction. For example, going from middle to top management is associated with an 8.5 per cent increase in job satisfaction. Managers who are family members appear to be happier too, and this effect is very strong (a 33 per cent increase according to column (9)). Interestingly, explicit incentives appear with a positive and significant coefficient in the job-satisfaction regression (0.051 significant at the 5 per cent level), while the fidelity-index measure enters with a negative (albeit insignificant) coefficient. This may reflect excess demand for managerial jobs that provide high-powered incentives—that is, if managers with low-powered incentives were fully compensated along other dimensions (for example, with shorter working hours), we would not observe a difference in the level of reported job satisfaction.

8.5. Managerial policies and firm performance

Previous studies (e.g. Bloom and Van Reenen 2010) show that better-managed firms tend to be more productive, grow faster, and provide higher returns on capital employed. In this section, we quantify the economic relevance of the performance and fidelity indexes built using the ManagerItalia survey.

For this purpose, we analysed the conditional correlation of the performance index with a host of firm-level accounting variables.[2] The results of this exercise are summarized in Table 8.12 and Table 8.13.

---

[2] These are drawn from the Amadeus database. See Bloom, Sadun, and Van Reenen (2008) for details. We were able to match 569 (of the original 603) firms with Amadeus. The period covered by the accounting dataset goes from 2000 to 2005. All regressions are clustered at the firm level to correct for serial correlation of unknown form and include three digit SIC dummies.

Table 8.11 Manager pay and job satisfaction

Dependent variable	(1)	(2)	(3)	(4)	(5)	(6)	(7)	(8)	(9)
	Total remuneration (including bonus)			Fixed remuneration (excluding bonus)			Job satisfaction		
ln(Employment)	1,677.553	393.178	675.640	1,139.984	882.415	1,180.863	−0.005	−0.012	−0.009
	(1,039.282)	(941.978)	(1,012.917)	(800.033)	(798.982)	(859.803)	(0.014)	(0.014)	(0.016)
Area = General administration	2,622.465	−1,131.452	912.858	−1,401.542	−2,440.385	−509.091	0.122**	0.108*	0.127**
	(4,412.681)	(3,900.451)	(4,034.494)	(3,282.114)	(3,230.312)	(3,304.834)	(0.061)	(0.060)	(0.064)
Area = Sales and marketing	−2,147.701	−7,174.419*	−6,539.979*	−5,729.869*	−7,058.016**	−6,914.487**	0.068	0.053	0.055
	(4,070.240)	(3,666.288)	(3,832.124)	(3,061.625)	(3,038.286)	(3,161.684)	(0.054)	(0.053)	(0.058)
Seniority	19,456.800***	15,705.620***	15,736.888***	14,502.149***	13,579.301***	13,479.937***	0.100**	0.080*	0.084*
	(3,406.352)	(2,836.876)	(3,057.903)	(2,471.928)	(2,360.123)	(2,510.065)	(0.046)	(0.046)	(0.049)
MNE	7,336.900*	−4,476.788	−4,999.345	950.280	−2,471.101	−3,362.439	−0.009	−0.054	−0.041
	(3,779.159)	(3,543.750)	(4,094.814)	(2,835.334)	(2,932.394)	(3,376.631)	(0.053)	(0.054)	(0.061)
USA MNE	7,171.387	4,123.199	2,732.513	3,980.880	3,153.984	1,995.026	0.006	−0.001	−0.010
	(5,496.307)	(4,842.433)	(5,187.932)	(3,898.015)	(3,861.621)	(4,086.162)	(0.079)	(0.079)	(0.085)
Italian MNE	1,452.830	6,214.583	6,885.647	4,100.728	5,304.948	6,191.936*	0.051	0.076	0.067
	(4,655.711)	(4,161.428)	(4,522.406)	(3,433.923)	(3,386.358)	(3,625.106)	(0.059)	(0.059)	(0.064)
Ownership = State	−14,691.226**	−10,486.698**	−9,937.148*	−9,534.613**	−8,205.779**	−7,829.128*	−0.001	0.011	−0.001
	(5,727.036)	(4,963.653)	(5,191.117)	(4,093.013)	(4,029.171)	(4,149.371)	(0.085)	(0.085)	(0.094)
Ownership = Family	−8,560.338*	−3,446.673	−4,262.425	−4,206.103	−2,426.971	−3,536.649	−0.090	−0.071	−0.074
	(4,599.136)	(4,070.058)	(4,467.523)	(3,342.019)	(3,368.713)	(3,593.425)	(0.061)	(0.061)	(0.067)
Ownership = Founder	−6,190.688	−5,982.913	−7,767.883	−4,318.873	−4,041.466	−5,649.187	0.022	0.032	0.039
	(5,159.545)	(4,481.521)	(4,843.082)	(3,752.165)	(3,694.213)	(3,919.528)	(0.067)	(0.067)	(0.071)
Ownership = Private equity	3,060.635	2,030.497	5,200.536	1,185.079	1,139.247	3,179.799	0.080	0.077	0.039

(continued)

Table 8.11 *(Continued)*

Dependent variable	(1)	(2)	(3)	(4)	(5)	(6)	(7)	(8)	(9)
	Total remuneration (including bonus)			Fixed remuneration (excluding bonus)			Job satisfaction		
Ownership = Manager	(7,719.390) 29,627.922**	(7,329.451) 26,203.172***	(7,585.565) 24,927.414**	(5,423.821) 18,992.745***	(5,,409.332) 1,8042.179***	(5,490.960) 17,641.327**	(0.100) 0.098	(0.101) 0.069	(0.108) 0.058
Ownership = Private individuals	(11,744.327) −8,006.348	(9,938.794) −5,521.561	(11,357.678) −4,410.716	(6,950.673) −2,596.766	(6,869.775) −1,695.818	(7,945.936) −622.692	(0.151) −0.003	(0.140) 0.019	(0.158) 0.052
Family manager	(5,280.906) −7,154.389	(4,845.059) −10,631.372	(5,380.517) −12,293.978	(4,144.822) −7,933.846	(4,163.342) −10,092.311	(4,603.701) −11,520.655	(0.069) 0.190	(0.068) 0.308**	(0.073) 0.329**
Male	(11,815.280) 4,626.505	(11,610.481) 2,126.413	(12,181.738) 5,563.706	(7,519.558) −219.093	(8,169.599) −656.916	(8,517.786) 2,346.258	(0.137) 0.076	(0.135) 0.049	(0.148) 0.069
Degree	(5,133.846) 12,981.695***	(5,197.345) 10,619.234***	(5,269.523) 7,551.257**	(4,344.420) 10,951.248***	(4,387.084) 10,246.239***	(4,360.962) 7,736.184***	(0.068) −0.023	(0.068) −0.027	(0.071) −0.025
ln(Age)	(3,270.201) 31,196.044***	(2,910.695) 48,925.008***	(3,205.865) 50,286.047***	(2,375.310) 38,942.561***	(2,354.941) 42,660.361***	(2,567.270) 45,596.989***	(0.043) 0.227	(0.043) 0.321**	(0.047) 0.335**
Performance index	(10,579.254)	(9,775.393) 18,817.911***	(10,397.360) 19,089.435***	(7,695.317)	(7,917.938) 5,324.301***	(8,359.445) 5,735.695***	(0.147)	(0.148) 0.053**	(0.161) 0.051**
Fidelity index		(1,531.657) 65.816 (1,344.697)	(1,577.273) 1,108.447 (1,402.818)		(1,250.133) −562.051 (1,111.740)	(1,300.284) 359.006 (1,169.536)		(0.022) −0.028 (0.021)	(0.023) −0.029 (0.023)
N	603	603	603	603	603	603	603	603	603
Dummies regions and sectors	No	No	Yes	No	No	Yes	No	No	Yes

Note: *** denotes significance at the 1% level; ** at the 5% level; * at the 10% level

Table 8.12 Three years' sales and employment growth, 2000–2005

	(1)	(2)	(3)	(4)	(5)	(6)	(7)	(8)
	Sales growth				Employment growth			
ln(Employment)	0.023**	0.027***	0.025**	0.027***	0.084***	0.087***	0.086***	0.087***
	(0.010)	(0.010)	(0.010)	(0.010)	(0.014)	(0.014)	(0.014)	(0.014)
Area = General administration	0.018	0.016	0.013	0.015	0.035	0.033	0.028	0.032
	(0.038)	(0.041)	(0.040)	(0.041)	(0.039)	(0.040)	(0.039)	(0.040)
Area = Sales and marketing	−0.063**	−0.051	−0.059*	−0.052	−0.008	−0.003	−0.010	−0.004
	(0.029)	(0.033)	(0.032)	(0.033)	(0.035)	(0.037)	(0.036)	(0.037)
Seniority	−0.104***	−0.089***	−0.094***	−0.089***	−0.022	−0.003	−0.012	−0.003
	(0.029)	(0.029)	(0.030)	(0.030)	(0.029)	(0.030)	(0.029)	(0.030)
MNE			0.007	−0.010			0.026	0.031
			(0.034)	(0.036)			(0.035)	(0.040)
USA MNE			−0.016	−0.010			−0.031	−0.031
			(0.053)	(0.052)			(0.055)	(0.056)
Italian MNE			−0.009	−0.003			0.013	0.010
			(0.034)	(0.036)			(0.037)	(0.039)
Ownership = State		−0.006		−0.007		−0.017		−0.021
		(0.061)		(0.061)		(0.057)		(0.056)
Ownership = Family		−0.019		−0.024		−0.018		−0.016
		(0.034)		(0.037)		(0.040)		(0.045)
Ownership = Founder		−0.000		−0.005		−0.025		−0.019
		(0.037)		(0.040)		(0.041)		(0.046)
Ownership = Private equity		0.077		0.078		−0.083		−0.092
		(0.061)		(0.062)		(0.072)		(0.075)
Ownership = Manager		−0.014		−0.018		−0.023		−0.021
		(0.114)		(0.115)		(0.141)		(0.141)
		−0.016		−0.016		−0.068*		−0.066

(continued)

Table 8.12 (*Continued*)

	(1)	(2)	(3)	(4)	(5)	(6)	(7)	(8)
			Sales growth				Employment growth	
Ownership = Private individuals		(0.047)		(0.047)		(0.041)		(0.042)
Family manager		−0.174*		−0.177*		−0.127		−0.112
		(0.097)		(0.097)		(0.087)		(0.088)
Male		0.008	0.004	0.008		0.025	0.028	0.024
		(0.045)	(0.044)	(0.046)		(0.060)	(0.060)	(0.060)
Degree		−0.004	−0.005	−0.002		−0.022	−0.019	−0.026
		(0.025)	(0.025)	(0.025)		(0.028)	(0.028)	(0.029)
ln(Age)		−0.206**	−0.155*	−0.203**		−0.161	−0.135	−0.160
		(0.093)	(0.088)	(0.092)		(0.105)	(0.096)	(0.106)
Performance index	0.038***	0.030**	0.034**	0.032**	0.034**	0.029*	0.028*	0.026*
	(0.013)	(0.014)	(0.014)	(0.014)	(0.015)	(0.016)	(0.015)	(0.016)
Fidelity index	−0.006	−0.006	−0.008	−0.007	0.001	0.004	0.001	0.005
	(0.013)	(0.014)	(0.013)	(0.014)	(0.014)	(0.014)	(0.014)	(0.015)
Observations	1992	1992	1992	1992	1945	1945	1945	1945
Number of firms	415	415	415	415	445	445	445	445

Note: *** denotes significance at the 1% level; ** at the 5% level; * at the 10% level.

Table 8.13 Return on capital employed, 2004–2005

	(1)	(2)	(3)	(4)
ln(Employment)	−0.449	−0.324	−0.281	−0.310
	(0.846)	(0.852)	(0.859)	(0.862)
Area = General administration	4.287	3.714	4.242	3.777
	(2.933)	(2.946)	(2.941)	(2.965)
Area = Sales and marketing	3.757	4.476	4.719*	4.642
	(2.684)	(2.843)	(2.713)	(2.836)
Seniority	−1.975	−1.456	−1.344	−1.583
	(2.058)	(2.134)	(2.156)	(2.169)
MNE			−3.627	−3.818
			(3.114)	(3.364)
USA MNE			2.189	1.524
			(5.715)	(5.779)
Italian MNE			0.297	0.640
			(3.707)	(3.923)
Ownership = State		2.463		2.050
		(4.401)		(4.392)
Ownership = Family		−1.001		−1.864
		(3.323)		(3.353)
Ownership = Founder		3.032		1.798
		(3.457)		(3.500)
Ownership = Private equity		2.595		3.160
		(9.526)		(9.451)
Ownership = Manager		−4.059		−4.587
		(6.916)		(6.900)
Ownership = Private individuals		3.217		2.770
		(4.533)		(4.545)
Family manager		8.631		7.869
		(7.783)		(8.020)
Male		−3.702	−4.011	−3.904
		(3.493)	(3.533)	(3.567)
Degree		1.143	1.099	1.307
		(2.214)	(2.159)	(2.216)
ln(Age)		−11.400	−12.068	−11.282
		(9.011)	(9.452)	(9.013)
Performance index	2.534**	2.112*	2.587*	2.511*
	(1.162)	(1.204)	(1.341)	(1.313)
Fidelity index	0.125	−0.464	−0.489	−0.640
	(1.189)	(1.268)	(1.231)	(1.277)
Observations	832	832	832	832
Number of firms	460	460	460	460

Note: ** denotes significance at the 5% level; * at the 10% level.

We look at several outcome measures: (a) 3 years' sales growth, (b) 3 years' employment growth, (c) return on capital employed (ROCE). In these tables, errors are clustered at the firm level to account for autocorrelation patterns of unknown forms in the residuals.

The correlations between the growth measures and the incentive variable are generally positive and significant, especially when we look at the 3 years' growth rates of sales and employment. For example, in Table 8.12, column (4), a one standard deviation increase in the performance-index measure is associated with a positive increase of 0.041 percentage points in 3 years' sales growth (this corresponds to a 14 per cent increase relative to the mean). Similarly, in Table 8.12, column (8), a one standard deviation increase in the performance-index measure is associated with a positive increase of 0.045 percentage points in 3 years' employment growth (this corresponds to a 24 per cent increase relative to the mean). Incentives are also always positively associated with the return on capital measure (ROCE). For example, Table 8.13, column (4), suggests that a one standard deviation increase in the performance index is associated with an increase of 2.9 percentage points in the ROCE measure (12 per cent relative to the mean).

Interestingly, the fidelity index is typically uncorrelated with any of the variables considered in this exercise. For example, in Table 8.13, column (4), the coefficient on the fidelity index is –0.004, with a standard error of 0.013. A similar picture emerges when we look at employment growth and return on capital employed.

Finally, we did not find evidence of a positive correlation between labour productivity and any of our incentives or fidelity indexes. This may well reflect the lack of any statistical correlation between our summary measures and productivity, as well as the problematic measurement of productivity in the service sector.

9

Conclusions

According to our data, the performance model is associated to better outcomes than the fidelity model. This is true for selection: managers are more qualified and more able to bear risk. It is also true for managers' behaviour in the workplace: they are paid better, they work harder, and they are happier. And it is also true for firms: they grow faster and they have higher return on capital. If that is the case, why do not all firms move to the performance model?

There are two main lines of explanation, depending on whether one thinks that firms that are currently relying on the fidelity model are *unwilling* or *unable* to switch to the performance model. The first explanation has to do with *corporate governance*. According to it, the owners of some firms do not pursue only commercial success. They have other objectives as well, like corporate control: they are willing to sacrifice profits in order to maintain their grip on the firm. A classic case is that of the family firm, where the owners may want to reserve some of the best jobs for family members, even if they are not the most qualified applicants. In such firms, securing the fidelity of (non-family) managers is essential. Part of their informal job description is to nurture and assist family members. As this task is difficult to measure, formal assessments are eschewed and rewards are based on the long-term display of fidelity. This line of interpretation is pursued by Bandiera et al. (2009), who use the same data discussed in this book to argue that the comprehensive set of correlations that we have documented is consistent with a model where firms that attach a high value to direct control—such as family firms—attract less able and risk-tolerant managers—and because of this perform less well. Interestingly, they also discuss possible alternative interpretations, arguing that, while individual findings might indeed be consistent with other interpretations (for example, reliance on relation-driven managerial selection being the optimal response to poor enforcement), the entire set of findings cannot be.

The second explanation relates to *corporate culture*. Firms may realize that they are not offering managers the right incentive system, but be unable to switch to the performance model. Recruiting, assessing, and rewarding high-level professionals such as managers are not trivial tasks. They presuppose a corporate culture based on explicit long-term planning and focused on human capital development. It is possible that such know-how is lacking in family firms and domestic firms (although our size controls show that it is not just an issue of dimension). The cultural explanation may be particularly applicable to the difference between multinational and domestic firms. The fact that Italian firms that operate in other countries seem to be able to adopt a performance model may indicate that the kind of corporate culture that is needed for doing business in an international environment is also conducive to better incentive systems.

Our two potential explanations have different policy implications. If the governance story is predominant, one should question the ownership mode. There is already a flourishing debate (see the literature review) on the relative merits of family firms. Our results would then add to the debate by showing that on one dimension—managerial talent—family firms are at a disadvantage.

If, instead, one believes more in the cultural story, then there are two implications. First, we should welcome foreign multinationals (or at least stop making their life difficult) and we should encourage our firms to acquire an international dimension. Second, we should invest in creating the know-how that is necessary for implementing the performance model. How such knowledge can be acquired is an open question, but it is likely to be related to the role of education.

One of the striking results of our research is the low level of education of Italian managers. In other countries, especially the United States, academe has played a tremendous role in shaping the behaviour of today's managers. Top universities have invested large amounts of resources in developing business schools. For decades, there has been a feedback cycle between university and business: business-school professors research issues of interest to business, and future managers attend MBA courses.

Such a feedback loop seems to be much weaker in Italy. Universities have invested less in business programmes, and this is reflected in international rankings. According to the *Financial Times* 2008 survey, the best Italian MBA programme is ranked 48th in the world (in comparison, the best UK programme is 2nd, the best French programme is 6th, the best Spanish one is 7th). The *FT* also ranks the best forty European master programmes in management: none of them is Italian.[1]

It is unclear whether the missing link is due to the demand side (Italian firms do not hire management graduates, perhaps because of the governance reasons discussed above) or to the supply side (Italian universities are unable to create effective programmes). Certainly, it is surprising that, within the existing pool of Italian graduates, firms do not appear eager to hire managers who have earned top marks during their university career.

What future awaits the Italian managerial class? Our analysis reveals two contrasting trends. On the one hand, the fact that there is no systematic age difference between managers who are rewarded for performance and managers who are rewarded for fidelity indicates that a new generation of fidelity-oriented managers is being trained. Only time will tell whether this generation is able to tackle the challenges that the Italian productive system faces.

On the other hand, performance bonuses have become much more relevant since the 1990s, and one might expect this trend to continue, possibly matched by similar increases in other components of the performance model, such as hiring and firing practices based exclusively on individual performance. In addition, our evidence does suggest that Italian firms with global exposure tend to abandon the fidelity model. To the extent that the process of globalization will encourage more domestic firms to operate abroad, or, equivalently, will weed out domestic-only firms, we can expect the performance model to prevail.

---

[1] Things are better in executive education. Bocconi's programme is ranked 5th in Europe and 15th in the world.

References

Abowd, John M., Kramarz, Francis, and Roux, Sébastien (2006). 'Wages, Mobility, and Firm Performance: Advantages and Insights from Using Matched Worker–Firm Data', *The Economic Journal*, 116/512 (June), F245–85.

Acemoglu, Daron, Johnson, Simon, and Robinson, James A. (2001). 'The Colonial Origins of Comparative Development: An Empirical Investigation', *American Economic Review*, 91/5 (December), 1369–1401.

Acemoglu, Daron, Johnson, Simon, and Robinson, James A. (2002). 'Reversal of Fortune: Geography and Institutions in the Making of the Modern World Income Distribution', *Quarterly Journal of Economics*, 117/4 (November), 1231–94.

Ackerberg, Daniel, and Botticini, Maristella (2002). 'Endogenous Matching and the Empirical Determinants of Contract Form', *Journal of Political Economy*, 110/3 (June), 564–91.

Adams, Renée B., Almeida, Heitor, and Ferreira, Daniel (2005). 'Powerful CEOs and their Impact on Corporate Performance', *Review of Financial Studies*, 18/4 (Winter), 1403–32.

Aggarwal, Rajesh K., and Samwick, Andrew A. (1999). 'The Other Side of the Trade-off: The Impact of Risk on Executive Compensation', *Journal of Political Economy*, 107/1 (February), 65–105.

Alesina, Alberto, and Giuliano, Paola (2007). 'The Power of the Family', NBER WP 13051.

Baker, George, Gibbs, Michael, and Holmstrom, Bengt (1994a). 'The Internal Economics of the Firm: Evidence from Personnel Data', *Quarterly Journal of Economics*, 109/4 (Nov.), 881–919.

Baker, George, Gibbs, Michael, and Holmstrom, Bengt (1994b). 'The Wage Policy of a Firm', *Quarterly Journal of Economics*, 109/4 (Nov.), 921–55.

Bandiera, Oriana, Barankay, Iwan, and Rasul, Imran (2007). 'Incentives for Managers and Inequality among Workers: Evidence from a Firm Level Experiment', *Quarterly Journal of Economics*, 122/2 (May), 729–73.

Bandiera, Oriana, Guiso, Luigi, Prat, Andrea, and Sadun, Raffaella (March 2009). 'Matching Firms, Managers, and Incentives', CEPR WP 7207.

Bennedsen, Morten, Pérez-González, Francisco, and Wolfenzon, Daniel (August 2008). 'Do CEOs Matter?', working paper, Columbia University.

Bertrand, Marianne, and Schoar, Antoinette (2003). 'Managing with Style: The Effect of Managers on Firm Policies', *Quarterly Journal of Economics*, 118/4 (November), 1169–208.

Bertrand, Marianne, and Schoar, Antoinette (2006). 'The Role of Family in Family Firms', *Journal of Economic Perspectives*, 20/2 (Spring), 73–96.

Bertrand, Marianne, Johnson, Simon, Samphantharak, Krislert, and Schoar, Antoinette (2008). 'Mixing Family with Business: A Study of Thai Business Groups and the Families behind them', *Journal of Financial Economics*, 88/3 (June), 466–98.

Black, Sandra E., and Lynch, Lisa M. (2001). 'How to Compete: The Impact of Workplace Practices and Information Technology on Productivity', *Review of Economics and Statistics*, 83/3 (Aug.), 434–45.

Bloom, Nicholas, Sadun, Raffaella, and Van Reenen, John (2008). 'Measuring and Explaining Decentralization across Firms and Countries', LSE mimeo.

Bloom, Nicholas, and Van Reenen, John (2010). 'Why do Management Practices Differ across Firms and Countries?', *Journal of Economic Perspectives*, 24/1 (Winter), 203–24.

Burkart, Mike, Panunzi, Fausto, and Shleifer, Andrei (2003). 'Family Firms', *Journal of Finance*, 58/5 (Oct.), 2167–201.

Caselli, Francesco, and Gennaioli, Nicola (2005). 'Dynastic Management'. London School of Economics, working paper.

Cunat, Vicente, and Guadalupe, Maria (2005). 'How Does Product Market Competition Shape Incentive Contracts?', *Journal of the European Economic Association*, 3/5 (Sept.).

Demougin, Dominique, and Siow, Aloysius (1994). 'Careers in Ongoing Hierarchies', *American Economic Review*, 84/5 (Dec.), 1261–77.

Doeringer, Peter B., and Piore, Michael J. (1971). *Internal Labor Markets and Manpower Analysis*. Lexington, MA: Lexington Books.

Frydman, Carola (2007). 'Rising through the Ranks: The Evolution of the Market for Corporate Executives, 1936–2003', MIT, working paper.

Frydman, Carola, and Saks, Raven E. (2010). 'Executive Compensation: A New View from a Long-Term Perspective, 1936–2005', *Review of Financial Studies*, 23/5 (May), 2099–138.

Gamba, Michela, and Goldstein Andrea (2009). 'The Gender Dimension of Business Elites: Italian Women Directors since 1934', *Journal of Modern Italian Studies*, 14/2: 199–225.

Gibbons, Robert, and Waldman, Michael (1999). 'Careers in Organizations: Theory and Evidence', in O. Ashenfelter and D. Card (eds), *Handbook of Labor Economics*, pp. 2373–437, vol. 3B, Amsterdam: North Italiand.

Graham, John R., and Harvey, Campbell R. (2001). 'The Theory and Practice of Corporate Finance: Evidence from the Field', *Journal of Financial Economics*, 60/2–3 (May), 187–243.

Guiso, Luigi, Pistaferri, Luigi, and Schivardi, Fabiano (2005). 'Insurance within the Firm', *Journal of Political Economy*, 113/5 (October), 1054–87.

Guiso, Luigi, Sapienza, Paola, and Zingales, Luigi (2008). 'Long Term Persistence', NBER WP 14278 (Aug.).

Ichniowski, Casey, Shaw, Kathryn, and Prennushi, Giovanna (1997). 'The Effects of Human Resource Management Practices on Productivity: A Study of Steel

Finishing Lines', *American Economic Review*, American Economic Association, 87/3 (June), 291–313.

Kaplan, Steven N., Klebanov, Mark M., and Sorensen, Morten (2008). 'Which CEO Characteristics and Abilities Matter?', Swedish Institute for Financial Research Conference on the Economics of the Private Equity Market, DFA 2008 New orleans meetings paper. Available at SRRN:/http://ssrn.com/abstract=972446 (July 24, 2008).

La Porta, R., Lopez de Silanes, L, and Shleifer, A. (1999), 'Corporate Ownership around the World', *Journal of Finance*, 54/2 (April), 471–517.

Lazear, Edward P. (2000). 'Performance Pay and Productivity', *American Economic Review*, 90/5 (Dec.), 1346–1361.

Lazear, Edward P., and Oyer, Paul (2004). 'Internal and External Labor Markets: A Personnel Economics Approach', *Labour Economics*, 11 (Oct.), 527–54.

Lippi, Francesco, and Schivardi, Fabiano (2008). 'Barriers to Riches: Social Networks vs. Productivity', mimeo, EIEF Rome.

Lucas, Robert, Jr (1978). 'On the Size Distribution of Business Firms', *Bell Journal of Economics*, 92 (Autumn), 508–23.

Luthans, Fred (1988). 'Successful vs. Effective Real Managers', *Academy of Management Executive*, 2/2 (May), 127–32.

Murphy, Kevin J., and Zabojnik, Jan (2003). 'Managerial Capital and the Market for CEOs', mimeo (Oct.).

Pérez-González, Francisco (2008), 'Inherited Control and Firm Performance', *American Economic Review*, 96/5 (Dec.), 1559–88.

Prat, Andrea, and Sadun, Raffaella (2006). 'Una gerontocrazia solo presunta', *La Voce* (June).

Prendergast, Canice (1999). 'The Provision of Incentives in Firms', *Journal of Economic Literature*, 37/1 (March), 7–63.

Prendergast, Canice (2002). 'The Tenuous Trade-Off between Risk and Incentives', *Journal of Political Economy*, 110/5 (October), 1071–1102.

Rajan, Raghuram, and Wulf, Julie (2006). 'The Flattening Firm: Evidence on the Changing Nature of Firm Hierarchies from Panel Data', *Review of Economics and Statistics*, 88/4 (November), 759–73.

Tabellini, Guido (2008). 'Culture and Institutions: Economic Development in the Regions of Europe', *IGIER* (July).

Villalonga, Belen, and Amit, Raphael (2006). 'How Do Family Ownership, Control, and Management Affect Firm Value?', *Journal of Financial Economics*, 80/2 (May), 385–417.

Wall Street Journal (2005). 'Men Do Numbers, Women Do Strategy', 21 Sept.

Westphal, James D. (1998). 'Board Games: How CEOs Adapt to Increases in Structural Board Independence from Management', *Administrative Science Quarterly* 43/3 (Sept.), 511–37.

Westphal, James D. (1999). 'Collaboration in the Boardroom: Behavioral and Performance Consequences of CEO-Board Social Ties', *Academy of Management Journal*, 42/1 (Feb.), 7–24.

Comments

Vittorio Colao

I believe that the excellent research presented here brings to light a fundamental point: a family business rewards loyalty, insofar as the maintenance of control and the generation of extended advantages for the family (salaries, benefits, dividends, and visibility) often become primary objectives, rather than the pure generation of financial value.

This fact is not economically irrational. In fact, once you pass the threshold of 'super well-being' (homes, boats, trips, and personnel at your disposal), the marginal returns of 'value creation' are minimal, while the maintenance of *status* within society increases in value with age.

As I was once told by a simplistic but rationally lucid, well-known Italian entrepreneur, 'I prefer to have 100 million worth of assets, the power and money to enjoy myself now and people's respect when I'm the slightly senile president of my company, rather than 500 million worth of assets right now, minority stakes and rich dividends from a "know it all" who went to Harvard, manages my company and gives me lessons in board meetings.' Incidentally, he knew that I had gone to Harvard (and the exact expression wasn't 'know it all'!).

The next question is then: why does this phenomenon seem to occur less frequently abroad? With regards to this, I have three observations.

Above all, the risk associated with the 'family control loyalty' model increases exponentially with competition; this is because, if things can actually go badly, the company itself is at risk. In this case, the dividends and the 'know it all' are a better alternative. If, however, the company is less exposed to competition, much of the company's success depends on having a stable system of networks, guaranteed by managers who are loyal to the familial strategy. It is no coincidence then that Merloni, Luxottica, and Benetton, all three exposed to global competition, were opened to external management before other companies.

Secondly, I would hazard a guess: in Italy, some family businesses display a sort of managerial flexibility (with regard to recruitment, procurement policy, local, regulatory, administrative relations) that a 'perfomance' manager is not keen on, as it does not help him realize his potential or benefit his future prospects. Conversely, the 'loyal' manager is more willing to conform, as this will give him a sort of insurance policy on his managerial career (which depends entirely upon the unchallengeable judgement of the shareholder).

Finally, the histories of 'managerialization' in entrepreneurial businesses are often tied to a member of the family who is truly 'excellent'. This is an individual who is able to leverage on his excellence to be able to choose the management he sees fit, instead of having to make his cousins, nephews, brothers, and sisters happy. Inevitably, 'managerialization' conflicts with family ties, which are much stronger in some cultures than in others. In fact, sometimes the transition works and the family becomes a shareholder, while, in other cases, these 'managerialized' companies return to the loyalty model if the excellent member of the family is not able to maintain the rules for a long enough time, and family rule is re-established.

In general, I find that the loyalty model is acceptable on the whole, if limited to companies that are truly of a family nature: in the end, this is private capital, and it is only fair that the owners should be able to manage their capital as they wish and consistently with their objectives, be they economic or otherwise. The real problem arises with the imitation of this behavioural model in companies that are not 'family' companies, but replicate the same paradigms and dynamics of those that are. This occurs when corporate governance is based only on legal compliance with little substance, and the principals feel like 'owners', demanding loyalty to their own specific objectives and not those of the company. All over the world, if a state, a majority shareholder, or a foundation requests a board to behave in this way, management gets the message and quickly falls into line. As a consequence, everyone becomes more 'loyalty based' and less 'performance oriented', and the company often ends up underperforming.

A final consideration on 'performance managers'. I meet many managers from Italy when I am abroad. They are good, competent, and highly respected managers, not least because Italians have an inborn versatility that is very useful when moving around the world. Many are tempted by the challenge of 'trying to improve Italy', and all would be excellent contributors if they were inserted into the management or boards of directors of an Italian company. This does not happen often enough, and they are sought after more by overseas companies than by Italian ones.

They are happy anyway, and certainly pleased for their children to grow up with the international openness and attitudes that will be necessary in the future. But these would also be very useful for Italy today.

Luigi Zingales

'Italian Managers: Fidelity or Performance?' is an ideal report to discuss. It presents new data on a usually overlooked but extremely interesting theme: in international comparisons, Italy is among the last places in terms of the best practices in human resources. And a lack of growth seems to be attributable to this backwardness: Italian companies that make a wide use of incentives grow more and are also more profitable. The report concludes with a rather provocative thesis: the backward system of human resource management is a cause of the Italian decline. It is a pleasure to discuss this work.

My comments will be based upon four main points. The first deals with the absence of a logical passage in the reasoning that brings quality of management to lack of growth. Next, I would like to present a sceptical vision of this work, not because I do not believe in its conclusions, but because my role as a discussant is that of being the devil's advocate, casting doubt on some of the results. Thirdly, I will put on my hat of 'economist from Chicago' and try to explain the more controversial results, not as forms of inefficiency, but as optimal choices of rational agents. Finally, I will underline some interesting facts identified by this work that do not receive sufficient attention in the report.

With regards to the first point, the provocative thesis of the work is that the bad quality of managers is the cause of Italian decline. The lack of productivity growth in Italy since the year 2000 is an alarming fact. But is this really the fault of the low quality of our managers? From post-war Italy until 1995, growth was really high, superior to that of many European countries and also the United States. It is only since 1995 that this differential has inverted itself, with Italy growing much less than all the others. To demonstrate that this inversion is caused by the poor quality of management, this work must bring evidence showing that the quality of our management has worsened considerably (at least in relative terms) since 1995. Unfortunately, there is no evidence in this sense. Furthermore, it is difficult, even for a casual observer, to affirm that in the Italy of both De Gasperi and Craxi there were more meritocracy and better-quality managers. How is it possible, then, to explain that the same backward managerial methods permitted the Italian economic miracle from 1945 to 1995? What has changed in management practices or what has changed in the world? In regards to this, allow me to give a suggestion on how a theory could be developed in which the qualities required of management have changed through time. Italy has come closer to the technological frontier, and the managerial qualities that are necessary near this frontier are very different from those needed far from this frontier (Rajan and Zingales 1998). The authors can test this hypothesis with micro data, interacting the effect of the performance index with the quota of export in advanced countries. If this hypothesis is true, the performance index should have a higher effect in the companies with greater exports to more developed countries.

As a second point, I would like to be the devil's advocate. The entire report suggests that the managerial skills taught in business schools (principally in the United States) are wonderful and should be made compulsory everywhere in the world. And wherever (such as Italy) these skills are not taught, the result is disastrous. What is missing is proof that these techniques are actually better and that they generate higher profitability. It is true that the report demonstrates that the companies utilizing more bonuses and promotions are those where there are also greater profits and more growth. But this relation is easily explained in other ways. First and foremost, the relationship of cause and effect can be inverted. It could be that, in the companies where there is no growth, it is difficult to give bonuses and very difficult to give promotions, because there are no new places for career advancements. Secondly, we know that, where there are incentives, there are also incentives to manipulate indicators so as to show better performance. Finally, there will probably be a higher diffusion of systems of incentives in sectors where relationships are more formal and less 'familial', where it is more difficult to evade taxes and contributions; sectors in which profits seem better because there is less evasion and growth seems higher because more people, with regular contributions, are hired. But this does not demonstrate that incentives cause growth. I am not saying that my alternative is true, but it is necessary for the report to respond to this criticism in kind.

Another important point concerns the optimality of these systems. In the report there is an almost absolute presumption that a system based on loyalty is primitive and inferior. I agree enough with the authors on this conclusion, but, in my opinion, this must be the conclusion of the reasoning, not the assumption from which to begin. And, continuing in the spirit of devil's advocate, I would like to try and think of the motivations for which the loyalty model is, instead, a reasonable model, especially in certain countries and sectors. For example, if a serious risk of the expropriation of ideas and clients on the part of management exists because the country does not have a particularly developed system of protection for intellectual property rights, a system of promotion based on loyalty is a way of protecting the value of the company and therefore is, at least from the point of view of the owner, an optimal way of developing the company's business. Rajan and I have a company model in the *Quarterly Journal of Economics* of 2001 based exactly on these grounds (Rajan and Zingales 2001), where there is a risk of expropriation and where promotion is based on loyalty and not necessarily performance. Therefore, it is not only possible to write a model of this type, but it is also a reasonable model in a country such as Italy.

This loyalty-based organizational model is not necessarily inferior. In fact, many of the results found by the authors can be explained as optimal responses to a different environment. In family companies, monitoring is much more direct, and therefore performance can be obtained not through bonuses, but rather through the threat of being fired. This explains the scarce prevalence of bonuses. Since the owner/boss is more present, compensation is based not on input (hours worked), but rather on output. This can explain the lower number of hours worked. As the boss is more present, there is also less need to pay an informational rent to managers, and this can explain the lower salaries. Therefore all the 'evidence' of inefficiency can be explained as the optimal response to a different environment.

If the authors really consider that this is an inferior organizational model, it would be useful to specify what are the constraints pushing companies to remain anchored to the loyalty model. Is it because of the diffusion of fiscal evasion and corruption in Italy? Is it because there is greater accumulation of 'firm-specific' human capital? Or is it because there is more (intergenerational) transition of human capital?

Finally, there are some interesting results that should be emphasized. The survey of top managers' time use is fascinating and merits its own report. It is also fascinating to discover that 25 per cent of CEOs work less than 40 hours per week and the average is only 47.8: they are worse than public employees! It is also disconcerting to discover that CEOs spend the same amount of time with consultants and heads of marketing and finance, and much more time with them than with their clients. To finish, it does not seem that CEOs dedicate any time to discussions with their board members.

Other interesting facts include the extreme instability of managers: 30–40 per cent of managers between the ages of 35 and 44 disappear within about five years. Why? Do they become entrepreneurs or retirees? Is there a difference between the companies based on a system of incentives and those based on a system of loyalty?

In conclusion, this is an extremely interesting work, rich and complex, that needs to be refined and focalized. To strengthen their conclusions, the authors must consider reasonable alternatives to the explanations given, possibly finding ways to disprove these alternatives empirically. To finish, I would like to be a bit provocative: this report is a bit too Anglo-American centric. Not all that is done in the United States is correct and not all that is done in Italy is wrong.

References

Rajan, R., and Zingales, L. (1998). 'Which Capitalism? Lessons from the East Asian Crisis', *Journal of Applied Corporate Finance*, 11/3: 40–8.

Rajan, R., and Zingales, L. (2001). 'The Firm as a Dedicated Hierarchy: A Theory of the Origins and Growth of Firms', *Quarterly Journal of Economics*, 116: 805–52.

Index